THE
GREAT WAR
IN AFRICA

1914–1918

BY THE SAME AUTHOR

The Man Who Presumed: A Biography of Henry Morton Stanley
Burton: A Biography of Sir Richard Francis Burton
Prisoners of the Mahdi
Queen Victoria's Little Wars
The Great Anglo-Boer War
Mr. Kipling's Army
The Gurkhas
Eminent Victorian Soldiers: Seekers of Glory

THE
GREAT WAR
IN AFRICA

1914–1918

BYRON FARWELL

W · W · NORTON & COMPANY
New York London

Published simultaneously in Canada
by Penguin Books Canada Ltd,
2801 John Street, Markham, Ontario L3R 1B4
Printed in the United States of America.

The text of this book is composed in Aster. Composition
and manufacturing by The Maple-Vail Book Manufacturing Group.

First Edition

Library of Congress Cataloging-in-Publication Data
Farwell, Byron.
The Great War in Africa, 1914–1918.
BIbliography: p.
Includes index.
1. World War, 1914–1918—Africa.   I. Title.
D575.F37   1986   940.3'6   86-8455

ISBN 0-393-02369-9

W. W. Norton & Company, Inc.,
500 Fifth Avenue, New York, N. Y. 10110
W. W. Norton & Company Ltd.,
37 Great Russell Street, London WC1B 3NU

1 2 3 4 5 6 7 8 9 0

For my grandchildren

Cameron Farwell Lewis
and
Jenna Rae Farwell

We are too much inclined to think of war as a matter of combats, demanding above all things physical courage. It is really a matter of fasting and thirsting; of toiling and waking; of lacking and enduring; which demands above all things moral courage.

—Sir John Fortesque

Contents

Illustrations

Maps

Foreword

W hen the War of 1914–18—called the Great War until a greater erupted in 1939—broke out in Europe, all of sub-Sahara Africa, with the exception of Ethiopia and Liberia, was in European hands, parcelled out as colonies or so-called protectorates. Germany, which had a number of small possessions in the Pacific and a 400 square mile enclave on the Chinese mainland (Kia-Chow in Shantung), had her largest and most important colonies in Africa. There were four: Togoland, the Cameroons, German South-West Africa, and German East Africa. The British (Australians mostly), aided by the Japanese, captured all of the German holdings in the Far East within the first three months of the war. The conquest of the German colonies in Africa, except for Togoland, proved more difficult, in spite of assistance from the French and Belgians.

Of the four African campaigns against the Germans, that waged in Togoland was the shortest, whilst the campaign in German East Africa was the longest anywhere in the entire war, extending past the armistice. All four were campaigns carried out in exotic lands, and three of them ranged vast distances over astonishing varieties of landscapes and the most diverse climates. It was a war fought on land and sea, on great lakes and mighty rivers, in deserts, swamps, and jungles, and from the air. Germs often proved more deadly than Germans for the Allies, and tens of thousands succumbed to tropical discases.

These campaigns, fought by extraordinary men and filled

with unusual incidents, would have excited the interest of the world and been followed in detail had they occurred at any other time, but because of the clash of millions in European abattoirs, the struggles of tens of thousands in Africa were regarded as "sideshows" at the time and have been largely neglected by historians since. But interest in a war should not be gauged by the size of the butcher's bill, and, as Herbert O'Neil has said, "the conquest of Germany's colonies rank among the most stirring exploits in history."

The campaigns were the antithesis of the stagnant trench warfare on the Western Front, where the killing was steady, almost ritualistic, and progress was measured in yards of mud and the numbers killed, wounded, or captured. In Africa there were few set battles and the campaigns were marked by extreme mobility; troops marched and fought over tens of thousands of square miles, much of it unmapped and unexplored. The campaigns were replete with incidents and adventures experienced by tattered, hungry men in dust and mud, rain and broiling heat.

The history of warfare can offer few exploits more bizarre than the flight of the zeppelin Z–59 from Bulgaria to Africa, or than the longest naval engagement ever, when monitors fought a cruiser in a river, or than of troops in battle routed by bees and rhinoceruses. And surely there have been few campaigns waged by more singular leaders than Colonel Paul von Lettow-Vorbeck or Commander Geoffrey Spicer-Simson or Jan Smuts.

Many books on the First World War do not even mention the African campaigns, yet Europeans, Indians, Arabs, and Africans from dozens of tribes and more than a dozen countries took part. The British field force in East Africa probably ranks as the most polyglot in British military history.

Because so little is known, even today, of the inhospitable landscape traversed by the contending armies, many of the rivers, mountains, and towns will be unfamiliar to most readers. Indeed, some of the place names are no longer to be found on maps. Thus, many readers will find the maps used here, which are largely based on contemporary military maps, essential to an understanding of the movement of forces. It may seem ridiculous that there existed such places as Little Popo, Bongo, Dumie, and Lomie, yet men died defending or capturing them. If the siege of Mora is less familiar than Lucknow or the Alamo, its defenders were no less brave, resourceful, and enduring. If rivers such as the Rovuma and Rufiji are not as well known as the Rhine and the Mississippi, they are, nevertheless, mighty rivers—and they played important roles in the East Africa Campaign.

One reason why the African campaigns of the Great War are so little known is the exiguity of information. Most of those involved were illiterate; few of the literate participants recorded their experiences, and historians were not present. Records were badly kept, for few of the fighting units were regular regiments, and climatic conditions contributed to the destruction of many that were kept. Thus there is much that is unknown or unknowable, and there are an extraordinary number of conflicting figures for size of forces, casualties, distances, and dates. Facts contradict and some are inexplicable. I have tried to rationalize these and have chosen those which to me seem most credible.

I must acknowledge my gratitude to the many people in various countries who have been helpful to me. Among these are William D. Carey, South African Ambassador B. G. Fourie, United States Ambassador Edward Marks, Oberst Harold Mors, Colonel P.M.J. McGregor, Graham Mottran, Dr. Steven Napolitano, Gerald Rilling (who is compiling a bibliography of the East African Campaign), Commodore D. F. Sibberbauer, Peter Silk, and Angus MacClean Thuermer. As always, I owe a special debt to my wife, Ruth, for her editorial skills and sound literary advice.

Name Changes

1914 Name	Present Name
Belgian Congo	Zaire
British East Africa	Kenya
Dahomey	Benin
Elizabethville	Lumumbashi
German East Africa	Mainland Tanzania plus Rwanda and Burundi
Gold Coast	Ghana
Lake Nyasa	Lake Malawi
Moyen Congo	Congo Republic
Portuguese East Africa	Mozambique
Ruanda-Urundi (provinces)	Rwandi and Burundi
Togoland	Togo plus parts of Ghana and Benin

Both old and new names for towns have been incorporated into the text, but it is easy to become confused. The town on Lake Tanganyika that served as Commander Spicer-Simson's headquarters was successively and sometimes simultaneously known as Lukuga and Kalemie or Kalamie; during the war, after Spicer-Simson's departure, it was renamed Albertville (for the then-king of the Belgians), but since the Congo's independence it has reverted to its old name of Kalemie.

THE
GREAT WAR
IN AFRICA

CHAPTER

1

War in Togoland

Great Britain declared war on Germany on 5 August 1914, but it was not until seven o'clock on the morning of 22 August that Corporal Ernest Thomas of 'C' Squadron, 4th Royal Irish Dragoon Guards, riding with a mounted patrol near the village of Casteau, Belgium, fired the British Expeditionary Force's first shot of the war. Soon after on the same day Captain Charles B. Hornby of the same regiment plunged his sabre into the breast of a German uhlan. Today a bronze plaque in English and French memorializes these actions. Contrary to popular belief, however, Corporal Thomas's was not the first British bullet fired in anger in this war. That shot had been fired at least a week earlier a few miles north of Lomé in remote Togoland, a country larger than Ireland but unknown to most Britons. It was fired by an unidentified black African wearing a British uniform. No memorial marks the spot.

Togoland (somewhat larger than present day Togo) was then a German protectorate in West Africa sandwiched uncomfortably between the British colony of Gold Coast (Ghana) and the French colony of Dahomey (Benin). Its thirty-two miles of seaboard on the Bight of Benin in the

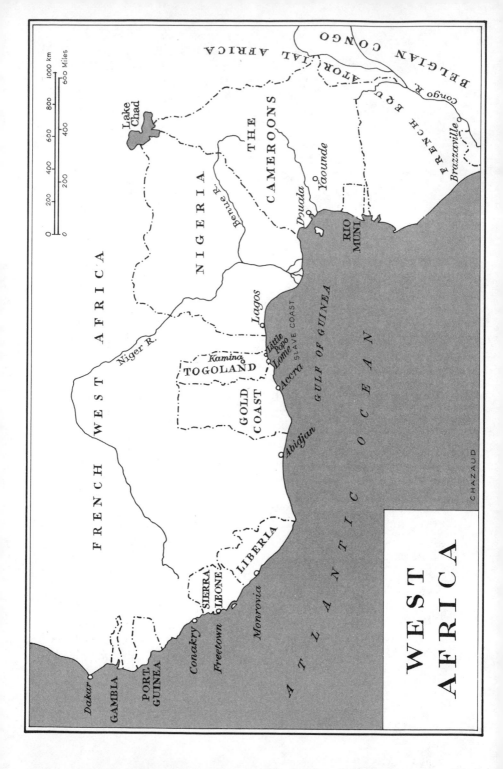

Gulf of Guinea formed part of what was often called the Slave Coast, for Togoland lay in that area which supplied most of the slaves sent to the New World between 1560 and 1860. Although only 130 miles wide on average, it extended nearly 400 miles north from the Gulf of Guinea to the plains of southern Gourma. In 1914 it had perhaps a million inhabitants.

The region was acquired by Germany in 1844, although its hinterland was largely unexplored and its frontiers were not fixed until 1899. In less than forty years the Germans managed to build a model little colony with a stable government and a reasonably prosperous economy. Agriculture—primarily the growing of yams, maize, and cotton—was fostered and a handful of efficient government officials exhibited a more careful consideration for the well-being of the inhabitants than was shown by Europeans in most African colonies. By 1914 it had become the only German colony that was financially independent of the Fatherland.

Given the bellicose nature of the Kaiser's Imperial Germany, it is curious that Togoland was the only colony on the West Coast of Africa without a standing army. There existed only a paramilitary police force, the *Polizeitruppe*, which consisted of two regular officers seconded from the German army, six German *Polizeimeisters* and 560 African non-commissioned officers and men. Most of this force was scattered about the colony in small posts; it was clearly designed for internal security and police work. It is not surprising, therefore, that the governor of this tiny colony, Duke Adolf Friedrich zu Mechlenberg, pressed closely on both sides by his country's enemies, was not eager for war. He proposed to his hostile neighbors that "in the interests of the natives and to show the unity of culture of the white race," they keep the peace in West Africa and let the big boys fight the war in Europe.

In support of this position the German diplomatists called attention to the convention signed by Britain, France, Belgium, and Germany at the Berlin Conference on African Affairs in 1885 in which a "conventional basin of the Congo" was defined as a vast area which included almost all of Central Africa in a wide belt from coast to coast. Provision was made for Powers owning territories in this area to proclaim their neutrality in time of war and for all "to refrain from carrying out hostilities in the neutralized territories and from using them as bases for warlike operations." About one third of Togoland fell within the conventional basin of the Congo, but the British and French found little difficulty in ignoring such an inconvenient agreement.

The Belgians had believed at first that they could keep the Belgian Congo (Zaire) out of the war, but when the Germans began sinking their ships on Lake Tanganyika, they soon saw that their interests would be best served by going along with their European allies, and the Belgian colonial minister declared that a Germany which regarded the treaty guaranteeing Belgian neutrality as a mere *chiffon de papier* could not blame the Allies for disregarding the international agreement on the neutrality of the Congo basin.

Even before the war British diplomatists had realized that it would not be in the best interests of the British Empire to abide by the promises made concerning African territories and that Britain should regard the neutrality clauses as facultative rather than obligatory. J. D. Chancellor, secretary of Britain's Colonial Defence Committee, bluntly declared (24 January 1911): "In a war with France or Germany observance of Articles X and XI of the Berlin Act of 1885 [the neutrality clauses] would be in the interest of France or Germany. Consequently, Britain does not intend to abide by it."

The Germans, with three of their four African colonies within the conventional basin of the Congo, persisted in their efforts to have the neutral status of their colonies recognized. On 23 August 1914 the German government approached the United States through the American ambassador in Berlin in an effort to induce the Americans to persuade the Allies to live up to their agreements and not to extend hostilities into the African colonies. Initially, the Americans refused to do anything, but finally transmitted the German message without comment. The Allies rejected the plea. By this time blood had been spilt in Togoland. It was time for the diplomatists to retire from the scene.

The French and particularly the British had good reasons for wishing to extend the war to Togoland and the other German possessions. The newly completed wireless station at Kamina (Atakpane), Togoland, was reputed to be one of the most powerful in existence, providing direct communications with Germany and by cable connections to South America. Almost as powerful were other wireless stations at Dar-es-Salaam in German East Africa, at Windhoek in German South-West Africa, and at Douala in the Cameroons. Each of these, and this was the special concern of the British Admiralty, was capable of communicating with ships in the Atlantic or Indian oceans—seas in which the Germans had or could have men-of-war, cruising barracuda in a shoal of merchant ships. The British Admiralty very much wanted these wireless stations put out of action.

Temporary Brigadier General C. M. Dobell, inspector general of the West African Frontier Force (WAFF), who was in London when war erupted, sided with the Admiralty. Called on to advise politicians and senior officers, he urged the destruction of the German wireless stations in both Togoland and the Cameroons.

Dobell was not the only official away from his post at the crucial moment. The governors of both the Gold Coast and Nigeria were absent, as was the Duke of Mecklenburg on the German side. Throughout the area junior officers and officials were minding the store.

On the Gold Coast, thirty-five-year-old Frederick Carkeet Bryant R. A., who had been left in charge of the WAFF, sprang into action. Without waiting for orders, he despatched Captain E. Barker, adjutant of the Gold Coast Regiment, under a white flag to Lomé, Togoland's capital and chief port only fifteen miles from the Gold Coast–Togoland frontier, to demand the surrender of the colony. The Germans asked for time to consider and a twenty-four hour truce was granted, but when Barker returned for an answer, he found that the police and most of the government officials had fled, leaving behind only a throw-away German official, the district commissioner, to make a curious proposal. He was authorized, he said, to surrender only the colony's coast as far inland as an imaginary line 120 kilometers north of Lomé. As Kamina and its wireless station were 170 kilometers inland, Bryant regarded this proposal as a risible absurdity.

The energetic Captain Bryant wasted no time in gathering up two companies of the Gold Coast Regiment, some machine guns, a couple field guns with their crews, and a swarm of carriers, and embarking them on the handiest ships in Accra's harbour. On 12 August he landed at Lomé without opposition.

The French had already invaded Togoland from Dahomey on 6 August, seizing Little Popo (Anecho), just across the border on the coast. This was the first occupation of German territory by any Allied army. Bryant's invasion force numbered only 57 European officers and NCOs, 535 African soldiers and some 200 carriers. The French force was even smaller: 8 Frenchmen and 150 Senegalese tirailleurs (African infantry officered by Frenchmen).

A narrow-gauge railway and a single road had been punched through the dense jungle north of Lomé and up these Bryant swiftly pushed patrols. On 12 August (or some say the fifteenth) contact with the Germans was made by a patrol of the Gold Coast Regiment and shots were exchanged—the first rifle shots to be fired by a British soldier at Germans on any front in the Great War. On 18 August Bryant's little army was joined by the French invaders from Dahomey. (Mr. W.C.F. Robertson, acting governor of the Gold Coast, had worked out satisfactory terms of cooperation with M. Charles Noufflard, the French governor of Dahomey.) Bryant was promoted to temporary lieutenant colonel and put in charge of both the French and the British troops in southern Togoland.

A Gold Coast regiment on the march, 1914

On 22 August, the same day that Corporal Thomas fired Britain's first shot in Europe, Bryant's Anglo–French force found German police and volunteers entrenched on the north bank of the Chra river just north of Nuatja. There ensued a confused battle; the fighting took place in dense bush and the attacking British and French columns lost contact with each other and they failed to dislodge the Germans. Bryant's troops dug in for the night and plans were made to renew the attack at first light, but dawn found the Germans gone. German losses had been slight, but the Allied force suffered 73 casualties, including 23 killed—a loss of 17 percent of the force engaged.

German trenches on the Chra River, 1914

The hottest fighting had taken place on the left flank of the German line, where the French had managed to work their way to within fifty yards of the German trenches before being forced back. It was in the fighting on this flank that Lieutenant G. M. Thompson of the Gold Coast Regiment (seconded from the Royal Scots), who had been given command of a company of Senegalese tirailleurs, was found dead. Around him lay thirteen African soldiers who had died in his defence. They were buried in a circle around Thompson's grave.

On the night of 24 / 25 August the Germans blew up their wireless station at Kamina and on the morning of the 25th a German officer was sent to the British lines to ask for terms. Bryant informed him that only unconditional surrender would be acceptable. Meanwhile, another British force had invaded Togoland from northern Gold Coast and another French force from Dahomey. Neither encountered serious opposition. The German position was obviously untenable, so on 26 August 1914 Major von Döring, the act-

German prisoners from Togoland arrive at Sierra Leone, February 1915

ing German governor, surrendered unconditionally, thus ending the shortest and least bloody of the African campaigns.

It was during this campaign that some of the first charges of "German beastliness" were made, the kind of charges that were to become standard fare in all theatres of the Great War. Von Döring was accused of using explosive rifle bullets and of arming natives whose behaviour he was unable to control. The first charge was unproven and the Allies themselves were guilty of the second.

It had been a smartly conducted little war from the British viewpoint, and the Admiralty was so pleased with Bryant's performance that in a rare gesture it sent a letter of appreciation to the Colonial Office. The War Office, equally pleased, promoted him substantive major. The King graciously made him a companion of the Order of St. Michael and St. George and the French awarded him the Legion of Honour. Bryant, one of Britain's first heroes of the war, took leave in England to bask in his brief glory and to marry Miss Rosamund Hope. Two years later he added a D.S.O. to his laurels.

Togoland's commercial life was only slightly disrupted by the brief campaign and in a few weeks trade was being carried on as smoothly as if there had been no interruption. No one asked the African inhabitants their reaction to the change of rulers; it would then have seemed bizarre to have suggested such a thing.

The three-week Togoland campaign was quickly forgotten—by some even before the war was over. In a London Courtroom on 19 July 1918 a witness spoke of a message that had been sent from Togoland. The judge comfortably inquired, "Where is Togoland?"

"It is one of those places we have recently acquired, my lord."

"Cheap?" asked the judge.

2

The Cameroons: A Bad Beginning

G ermany's other colony on the Slave coast, lying just 6°–10° north of the equator, was the Cameroons, or, as the Germans called it, Kamerun. It derived its name from *cameroes*, the Portuguese word for prawns, once found in large numbers near the coast. The climate, particularly in the coastal area, is hot and exceptionally humid. In 1914 it was generally regarded as one of the most unhealthy spots on the West Coast and often called the white man's grave. In a story, possibly apocryphal, a young man posted to the area who asked if his return passage would be paid, was informed that the question had never arisen.

No European power had clamoured to possess the Cameroons until the mid-nineteenth century when Britain, alarmed by France's rapid acquisition of vast tracts of Central Africa, decided to annex the coastal area east and southeast of Lagos as far as Spanish Guinea. Edward Hyde Hewett, Her Majesty's consul at Calabar, was supplied with treaty forms and sent off to negotiate with tribal chiefs.

Consul Hewett was working diligently in the Niger delta

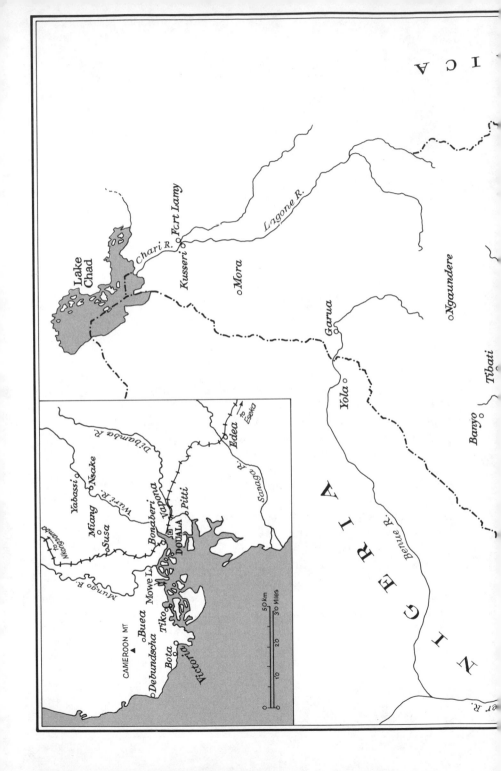

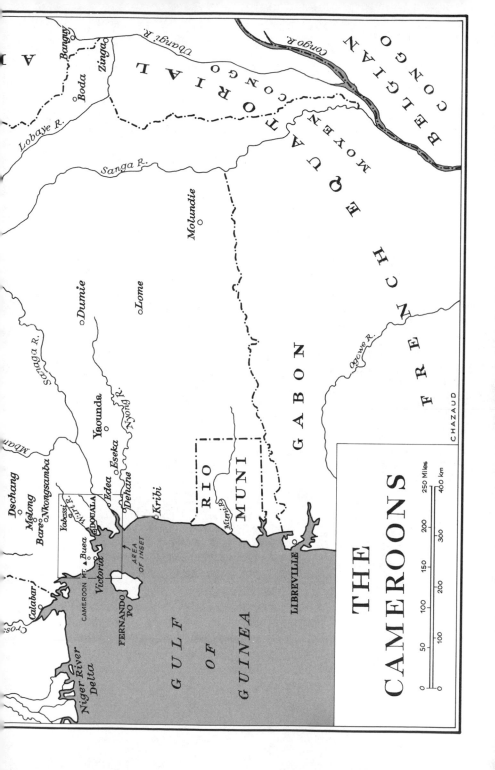

THE
CAMEROONS

when he learned that Dr. Gustav Nachtigal, scientist and explorer, now an Imperial German commissioner, had arrived in a gunboat at the mouth of the Wuri River and was busy making treaties with local tribes, including the Douala, the largest and most vigorous in the area. Hewett made what haste he could, but he arrived too late to harvest more than a few insignificant tribes. He was ever after known as "Too Late" Hewett.

Nachtigal's move took both Britain and France by surprise. Bismarck has been credited with wanting colonies to create a greater Imperial Germany, but in fact his interests and intrigues were concentrated in Europe. He did, however, appreciate the value which others placed on colonies and thus their value as bargaining chips in the game of international diplomacy.

After Britain's initial indignation cooled, she renounced all her claims and Germany staked out some 190,000 square miles of mountain, jungle, and savannah. In 1911 the Cameroons became larger than France and Germany combined when the Germans agreed to countenance French pretensions in Morocco in exchange for two sizeable chunks of land torn from French Equatorial Africa giving access to the Congo and Ubangi rivers. In spite of its size, the Cameroons had a sparse population of only about 500,000, of whom some 2,000 were Europeans.

To keep in check the Africans they were ostensibly there to protect, the Germans had in their three largest colonies raised and trained local armies—as did all of the European powers with African colonies. In 1914 the Germans had in the Cameroons a colonial force, a *Schutztruppe*, that consisted of 200 German officers and NCOs and 1,550 African soldiers. In addition, there was a gendarmerie of 40 Europeans and 1,255 African police. These forces were for internal peacekeeping; they were not designed to fight a major campaign.

It was understandable that the German Foreign Office persisted in its efforts to persuade the allies to live up to the neutrality clauses of the Berlin Act of 1885. In a note to

James W. Gerard, the American ambassador in Berlin, delivered on 15 September, Herr Arthur Zimmermann, undersecretary of state in the Foreign Office, asserted that it was Germany's aim "to prevent an aggravation of the state of war which could serve no purpose, while prejudicial to the community of culture of the white race." All this was wasted effort. The British and French invaders were already hammering at the gates of the Cameroons.

It was as well that Brigadier General Charles Dobell, the senior British officer in West Africa was in England when the war started, for there was much that needed to be done and much that needed to be discussed in London, where ultimate decisions were made. Officials and officers in West Africa wanted quick decisions, but these were not forthcoming. Colonel C.H.P. Carter, commandant of the Nigeria Regiment, who favoured an immediate invasion of the Cameroons, was told that the general policy was not to take offensive action at present. There were no plans. Neither the Allies nor the Germans were prepared for war in Africa.

Dobell was soon immersed in a seemingly endless round of meetings and conferences involving the War Office, the Colonial Office, the Admiralty, the Committee on Imperial Defence and various of its subcommittees, and in talks with officials of Allied governments, particularly the French. Orders and counterorders proliferated amidst delays and confusion.

Since the Cameroons, like Togoland, was sandwiched between British and French territories, it was obviously desirable, indeed essential, for the two allies to coordinate their efforts. But it was not until 22 August that the French agreed to put land and sea forces under Dobell's command for an attack on Douala. Eight days later Dobell and some of his staff boarded ship at Liverpool and sailed for Lagos.

Britain's available forces in West Africa were not large, but they were three times larger than any force the Germans could muster in this area. In 1914 the West African Frontier Force numbered 242 British regular officers seconded to the Colonial Office, 118 British NCOs, and 7,733 African soldiers: a grand total of 8,093—not even a World War I division. Of the Africans, 5,426 came from Nigeria, 1,553 from the Gold Coast, 617 from Sierre Leone, and 137 from Gambia.

These troops were not as well trained as the *Schutztruppe* and none was prepared to fight in a major war. Although Nigeria and the Cameroons shared a long common border and each was vulnerable to an attack by the other, Sir Frederick Lugard, governor of Nigeria, had considered manoeuvres too expensive and unnecessary. Consequently, not even units of the Nigeria Regiment (the largest) were trained above the company level. Dobell, who strongly disagreed with this policy, had only a few months earlier persuaded Lugard and the governors of the other West Coast colonies to permit training up to batallion level. Manoeuvres had therefore been scheduled to take place in January 1915. But war came five months before the war games could begin.

Until the end of 1913 northern and southern Nigeria, among the most populous regions in Africa, were administered as separate colonies and each had its own military establishment. A defence scheme based upon the new amalgamation of Nigerian forces had been sent to Lugard in early 1914 while he was on holiday in England, but Sir Frederick seems to have lost or misplaced it. It hardly mattered.

Even before the Anglo–French conference in London commenced, hostilities had already begun with the French fast off the mark. On 6 August a small French force came up from Brazzaville, capital of the Moyen Congo, and captured two small posts just inside the Cameroons in the northeastern corner of the colony. This was in the area ceded reluctantly by France to Germany three years earlier. The French were eager to reclaim it and their strategy appears to have been based more on political than military considerations, on the hopes and aspirations of France rather than any worthwhile military objective. General Aymerich, the

Nigerian troops entrained on the Northern Railway, German Cameroons

commander of the troops in French Equatorial Africa, pushed two columns into this wild and desolate area and a small force descended the Ubangi River and captured Zinga.

The British were slower. It was not until 14 August that Colonel C.H.P. Carter received permission from London to reconnoitre across the frontier. Ten days later he ordered the invasion of the Cameroons at three points: a northern column advanced on Mora, a strong German hill fort; a column from Yola on the Benue River moved on Garua; and a third column in the south started from Ikom to attack the town and fort of Nsanakang on the Cross River. All three columns came to grief.

The northern column crossed the frontier on 25 August and found the Germans in an almost impregnable position at Mora; after two days of fighting, the British, having suffered severely, retreated with a heavy load of wounded back across the border. The Yola column attacked Garua on the night of 30/31 August, and after sustaining heavy losses, it too limped home. The greatest disaster overtook the column from Ikom. On 30 August it captured Nsanakang, its objective, but the Germans launched a furious counterattack, almost annihilating the British force. Three of its officers were killed, another was mortally wounded, and four were captured; 71 African other ranks were killed, 19 were wounded, and 24 captured. The unarmed carriers also suffered 23 killed. Also lost were two 2.96-inch mountain guns, five machine guns, and much ammunition.

A doctor serving with the Nigerians described the desperate last moments of the battle when two officers led some ninety men in a bayonet charge through the German lines:

> It was only when the trenches were piled with the dead and the position was hopeless that [Lieutenant A.C.] Milne-Home gave the order to charge, and they went through the enemy into the bush. There they mostly managed to evade the Germans, and after days of starvation got back to Ikom.

A week later when the doctor and a Nigerian Marine transport officer were steaming up the river in a launch with both the white flag and the Red Cross flag flying, carrying "medical stores for the wounded and personal stores for the prisoners," they were hailed from shore by two survivors of the battle who had been six days in the bush without food:

> You never saw two such bedraggled specimens of British officers. They were dirty and torn, but they had smiles on their faces and loaded revolvers in their belts. They had evaded the enemy when they could, shot him when they could not, slept in the dense bush, cut their way at the rate of eight miles a day, swum a river, and finally brought up on British territory and saw our launch approaching. We took them on board, gave them some food, put them in a dinghy with some more and sent them down to Ikom.

The doctor appears not to have considered how the Germans would have reacted had they discovered two armed

An encampment of German troops in the Cameroons

combatant British officers on a launch flying the Red Cross
and white flags. Luckily undetected, they steamed on to
Nsanakang:

> The German officers were very good fellows, and we and they
> and the prisoners (who were on parole) sat round a big table
> and smoked cigarettes and drank sweet champagne.

These three quick victories put the Germans in a position
to threaten Calabar, then the main port in eastern Nigeria,
and the Niger delta. Colonel Carter, blamed for the defeats,
was sacked and sent home. He was replaced by the assistant commandant of the Nigeria Regiment, Lieutenant
Colonel Frederick Cunliffe.

British morale sank, and French successes made their
defeats even more bitter. With troops from Fort Lamy
(Ndjamena) they attacked Kusseri, the chief German post
on the Cameroon's frontier in the Lake Chad region. Near
the mouth of the Muni River they launched a seaborne
assault with 600 tirailleurs and after stiff fighting on land
and sea sank two German ships and on 21 September successfully established a beachhead.

The British had had bad luck in their initial efforts to
invade the Cameroons, but with the arrival of General Dobell
the character of the campaign underwent a dramatic change.

The Capture of Douala

From the beginning of hostilities the French and British eyed each other askance, each distrustful, each scornful of the methods and abilities of the other. These feelings ran high at all levels, from high-ranking officers and senior government officials to subalterns and junior diplomatists. Lieutenant Colonel Jean Ferrandi of the French Colonial Infantry noted that "les habitudes de nos Allies sont fort opposées." And Captain W. A. Ross with the Nigeria Regiment was soon complaining that "the French appear to be an idle lot and never push on a bit on their side . . . we may have to finish it off for them."

The French, who outfitted their tirailleurs with sturdy boots, scoffed at the barefooted British African troops and they complained that the British always stopped fighting at tea time. The British charged, with some reason, that the French were more interested in the division of the spoils than in getting on with the job of winning the campaign. Rivalry and petty jealousies marked every Allied joint effort in West Africa.

Given French and British attitudes, it seems remarkable that at the Anglo–French conference in London on 15 August

1914 agreement was reached on a joint attack on the Cameroons.

It seems even more extraordinary that the French agreed to a British commander, forty-five-year-old Brigadier General Charles McPherson Dobell, to lead the combined force. He was indeed remarkably qualified; he was clever and he had passed the staff college; born in Quebec, he spoke fluent French; he had seen active service in the Hazara Expedition of 1891 on the North-West Frontier and had won the D.S.O. in the Boer War. He had served in Crete, North China, and for a number of years in Nigeria. He knew the west coast of Africa and its inhabitants. The French had no one available who was as well qualified, but although they agreed to an English commander, they specifically insisted that his appointment would in no way affect the future division of the Cameroons.

There was no disagreement as to where the main attack should be made: the town of Douala was the obvious target. This meant that an amphibious force would be needed and that there would be an exceptional strain placed upon Dobell, for not only had he to maintain good relations with the French army and navy but also with his own Royal Navy and the Nigeria Marine, which was to supply a flotilla of small craft.

Indirectly, Dobell had also to consider the Belgians, who, like the Germans, at first clung to the notion that the neutrality of the conventional basin of the Congo could be preserved. Not until 28 August did the Belgians agree to provide the assistance requested by the French for the invasion of the Cameroons, and not until 30 September did askaris (African soldiers) from the Belgian Congo join the fight.

Douala was not the capital of the Cameroons; that was located in the healthier highlands, but it was the chief commercial centre and port. It boasted a powerful wireless station which the British Admiralty was keen to destroy, and its harbour, one of the best on the surf-beaten West Coast, was equipped with good quays and a floating dock. There were other attractions as well: it was known to have

a sizeable coal supply and valuable military stores that could
be looted. The quick success of the Togoland campaign led
officers to hope for another easy victory in the Cameroons.

Douala was poorly prepared to defend itself. Only a few
months before the war the German cruiser *Bremen* had visited it and her captain had written a long report on the
value of the port, including an elaborate defence scheme;
it was ignored. Still, the German authorities on the spot
did what they could. A battery was placed at Yoss Point, a
spit of land which commanded the town, and nine old ships
were sunk in the channel at Rugged Point, though six of
them were ineptly placed on the shoals clear of the channel. (One of these, the Hamburg-Amerika liner *Kamerun*,
3,660 tons, was later salvaged almost undamaged by the
British and used as an accommodation ship for prisoners
of war.)

Of the German merchant ships which had taken shelter
in the harbour at the beginning of the war, only one, the
Nachtigal, was armed. Lieutenant Phoëlig, the assistant
harbour master, hastily improvised some mines, one of
which blew up four of his countrymen when they attempted
to lay it. Some spar torpedoes—infernal machines made
out of steel gas cylinders filled with explosives and fitted
with percussion fuses—were built to be mounted on small
launches.

Douala consisted of a European settlement with perhaps
a hundred residences and several African villages fringing
it which housed some 30,000 Africans, mostly from the
Douala tribe. Brigadier General E. Howard Gorges wrote:

> The European settlement is well planned and laid out in true
> German style, containing excellent buildings and tree bor-
> dered streets, up-to-date sanitation, and a good water supply.
> Government House and offices are set in a picturesque park-
> like enclosure on a bluff overlooking the river anchorage. In
> the park were statues of Gustav Nachtigal and other German
> colonists of note. The military cantonment, consisting of offi-
> cers' mess and quarters, barracks, parade ground, etc., is neatly
> planned with Prussian precision, the parade ground worn to

the level of a billiard table from years of goose-stepping by Die Swartze Schutztruppe.

Two railway lines had their terminals here: a Midland Line that stretched 100 miles southeast to Edea on the Sanaga River and then on to Eseka and the Nyong River; and a hundred completed miles of a Northern Line (actually going northeast), destined eventually to reach Lake Chad.

To protect and support Dobell's expedition a naval squadron was at hand under a smart and efficient officer, forty-year-old Captain Cyril Thomas Moulden Fuller. The son of a cavalry officer, he had entered the Royal Navy as a cadet at the age of thirteen. By age twenty he was already a lieutenant; he had passed first class in all his examinations and had won the Goodenough Medal for gunnery. By age twenty-nine he was a commander and at thirty-five a captain—rapid promotion indeed in the Royal Navy during these years. In time he rose to be a full admiral, Second Sea Lord, and Chief of Naval Personnel.

Fuller's squadron consisted of HMS *Cumberland* (9,800 tons) and HMS *Challenger* (5,880), both cruisers; HMS *Dwarf*, a gunboat of 710 tons; and a French cruiser, later two. They were assisted by a flotilla for inshore and river work provided by the Nigeria Marine which consisted of two tugs, two motor launches, two dispatch vessels, a steam lifeboat, and the Nigerian Government yacht *Ivy*, all under Commander R.H.W. Hughes. To find a safe anchorage for this flotilla at some convenient point was one of Fuller's chief tasks, and he at once sent out exploring expeditions.

He made small raids along the Cameroon coast as well, and on one he managed to cut out a number of useful German lighters. A later expedition nearly met with disaster when on the evening of 5 September a landing party was sent to steal stocks of food stored at Bota. At daybreak, just as they had begun to stow their loot into their boats, the bush around them filled up with *Schutztruppen* who had been brought up during the night. Instead of firing on the landing party or capturing them, the German commander chose to send an ultimatum to Fuller, threatening to shoot unless he immediately evacuated his men.

Fuller was on the quarterdeck peacefully fishing for his breakfast when the ultimatum reached him. He had, in fact, just hooked a ten-pound fish. He lost both fish and rod as he leaped up to order his sailors back on board. The stores they had failed to carry away were destroyed by naval gun-fire.

After finding and destroying more than thirty of Lieutenant Phoëlig's homemade mines, the gunboat *Dwarf*, armed with four 12-pounders, passed into the estuary of the Cameroon and Dimamba (Lungasi) rivers on 9 September. It was followed the next day by *Cumberland*. A temporary base for the flotilla was established at Suellaba Point and two small boats from *Cumberland* armed with 3-pounders made their way up the Dibamba as far as Pitti, where they came under heavy fire from earthworks on the shores.

Two days later *Dwarf* was shelled by guns from the German battery at Yoss Point; the quartermaster at the wheel was killed and five sailors were wounded. Six days later *Dwarf* was rammed by the armed steamer *Nachtigal*, which then exploded. The sturdy *Dwarf*, although badly damaged, stayed afloat and was repaired within a week.

Fuller now sent boats poking into every hole and corner of the estuary and up the many creeks that emptied into it. The small boat work was arduous and dangerous in the uncharted streams and inlets. The creeks were often narrow, usually tortuous, and fringed with mangrove swamps. It was slow work and great care had to be taken, for there was the ever-present danger of encountering an armed German boat or of being ambushed from shore.

On the night of 15 September the Germans attacked *Dwarf* with one of their spar torpedoes lashed to the bow of a launch, but the sailor guiding it had been too nervous to secure the helm properly before he dived overboard and the launch crashed into the shore, where the torpedo exploded harmlessly. Four days later another try was made with a similar device. This was spotted by sailors on the Nigerian steam pinnace and sunk.

Surcharged Cameroons stamps

While Fuller and his sailors were busy preparing the way, Dobell was sailing down the West African coast, escorted by HMS *Challenger*, collecting his army as he progressed. On 10 September he picked up the Gambia detachment at Bathhurst and two days later a contingent that included carriers from Freetown in Sierra Leone.

It was at this point that a large German merchant ship, the *Professor Woërmann*, was captured in the Atlantic and brought into Freetown. It had been bound for the Cameroons and was stuffed with good things from the Fatherland, including camera accessories, perfume, soap, beer, cloth, Rhine wines, and a large number of new maps of the Cameroons, which were turned over to Dobell's delighted staff. A consignment of postage stamps was also found on board. These were soon surcharged "C.E.F." for Cameroons Expeditionary Force and used by the Allied soldiers.*

On 16 September the C.E.F. reached Accra, where it was joined by infantry, pioneers, and artillery from the Gold Coast. The following day the little fleet anchored at Lagos, Nigeria, where it remained for forty-eight hours to embark two infantry battalions, two batteries of artillery with ten 2.95-inch guns, a carrier corps, and other personnel. On 23 September *Challenger* and six transports arrived in the Cameroons estuary with Dobell and the British contingent; next day the French arrived from Dakar with 2,000 tirailleurs and six guns. The total land force under Dobell's command now comprised:

* A complete set of these stamps today is worth approximately £800 ($1,000).

	British	French
Officers	154	54
NCOs and other Europeans	81	354
Askaris	2,460	1,859
Carriers	3,356	1,000

All was ready for the troops. Captain Fuller had done his work well. His sailors and marines had reconnoitred the entire complex system of inland waterways in the Douala area and, with "trifling casualties," had surveyed all channels likely to be useful; the only armed German vessel had been destroyed; many launches and other small craft had been captured and others had been sunk; a secure base had been established for the flotilla, the transports and the men-of-war; a nineteen-foot wide channel had been swept for mines and bouyed to within 500 yards of the town; direct communication was established by cable with Lagos and London; guns had been mounted on the vessels of the Nigerian flotilla; and an appreciation of the situation had been prepared for General Dobell. No detail had been overlooked.

With some thirty British and French ships lying at anchor in the estuary and with all his land forces at hand, Dobell sent an ultimatum to the German governor: surrender unconditionally or Douala would be bombarded. In the two hours granted for a reply the waiting ships flew white flags, but when alert lookouts spotted a number of German mines floating downstream on the swift current, they were destroyed by a fusillade of rifle and machine gun fire. When the reply to the ultimatum was received, it proved to be evasive and, to the indignation of the British, was accompanied by a stiff protest against their firing while flying white flags.

Dobell did not at once shell the town, as he had threatened, but he set in motion a portion of his little Anglo–French army. The pioneer company of the Gold Coast Regiment was sent up the Dibamba River in two armed tugs and a transport to capture the town of Pitti, cut telephone lines and prevent the Germans from retreating over the railway bridge at Yapona. It accomplished none of these things. The Germans had placed a boom across the river and the boats were driven back by heavy small arms fire from the shore. Small parties that disembarked were soon floundering in the mud and slime of a mangrove swamp and none managed to reach firm ground. Further, the transport and the lighters soon found themselves stuck in the mud in an ebbing tide. The hapless force was withdrawn by Brigadier General Gorges, now in command of the British land forces in the C.E.F.

Edmund Howard Gorges, forty-seven years old, had seen considerable service in Africa since being gazetted to the Manchester Regiment at age nineteen. He had fought in Uganda (1897–99) and then in the Boer War (1900). In 1901 he earned the D.S.O. as commander of the Turkana Punitive Expedition in what is today northwest Kenya. In 1904 he was chasing the Mad Mullah in Somaliland and in 1905–06 was in charge of the camel corps and mounted infantry in the Nandi Field Force, a punitive expedition against the Nandi in the Rift Valley.

To Gorges and his chief, Dobell, it now appeared certain that Douala would have to be taken by direct assault. On the morning of 27 September Dobell and his senior commanders and staff went on board the Nigerian yacht *Ivy* to have a closer look at Yoss Point to see if it would be a suitable place to land troops. They were interrupted by a series of violent explosions. Looking toward Douala they saw the steel masts of the wireless station collapse. Soon after white flags rose over Government House and other prominent buildings and at eleven o'clock a German official hailed the *Ivy* and came aboard to surrender unconditionally the towns of Douala and Bonaberi (directly across the river). By afternoon British bluejackets had landed at Bonaberi, and Dobell with a detachment of marines had formally taken possession of Douala, ceremonially hoisting the Union Jack and the Tricolour at Government House.

The next few days were devoted to gathering in and taking possession of the considerable booty. The Germans had managed to remove into the interior most of the railway rolling stock and large quantities of stores, provisions, and arms. Still, there remained plenty for the French and British to pick up. The chief prize was 31,000 tons of merchant shipping, including nine large liners, forty or fifty smaller craft, a shallow drought stern-wheel gunboat and the German governor's beautiful steam yacht, *Hertzogin Elizabeth*. There was also a large quantity of railway and dockyard material, a battery of field guns, and the floating dock, which had been sunk but was soon raised and repaired; it proved most useful.

Dobell established his headquarters at Government House and his staff and other senior officers took over the Kaiserhoff Hotel, renaming it the George Inn. Inside they found a huge tank used to hold beer, unfortunately almost empty; only enough, said one officer, "to enable us Britishers to slake a glorious tropical thirst—a matter of a few moments only."

The object of the expedition, the destruction of a hostile naval base and its wireless station, had been accomplished. When the expedition was planned, a protracted campaign had not been anticipated. It seems to have been assumed that when Douala fell the Germans would surrender the colony, or, if they did not, that it little mattered, for almost nothing of strategic value lay in the interior. However, authorities in Paris and London now harboured dreams of greater territorial conquest and General Dobell was asked for an expression of his views on a continuation of the campaign and for a plan to complete the reduction of the colony.

4

The C.E.F. Moves Inland

The Germans retreated into the interior along three lines: up the Wuri (Wouri or Cameroons) River and along the Northern and Midland railways. Their retreat was orderly and they soon made it plain that they could make pursuit painful.

On 29 September 1914 the Yapoma railway bridge across the Dibamba River was again reconnoitred by land and by river. It was learned that two spans had been destroyed and that the Germans were entrenched on the left (east) bank. Senegalese tirailleurs sent to deal with them had to be reinforced. On 2 October a detachment of marines and engineers landed at Pitti and tried to circle behind the German positions and cut the railway in the rear, but they limped back to Douala, sodden, muddy, and unsuccessful, defeated by the swamps and dense bush.

The area was indeed forbidding. General Dobell said of it: "All the coastline and for some 150 miles inland, one meets the same monotonous, impenetrable African forest, fringed on the coast by an area of mango swamp in varying depth."

Letters written home by Dobell's soldiers reinforce his picture:

"Hundreds and hundreds of creeks, 200 to 300 yards wide: all the islands soft mud in which alligators [sic] wallow."

"We made a reconnaissance up to our knees in mud."

"The mangrove swamps are awful."

"Always wet and hot: temperature 104° F."

"Nearly every night there is a tornado, and the rain comes down in buckets."

It was in this steaming climate, at the mercy of tsetse fly and other disease-bearing insects, that most of the Cameroons campaign was conducted. From mid-March until mid-October the southern Cameroons is wet—always. Debundscha, a coastal town at the foot of Cameroon Mountain, receives the heaviest rainfall in Africa (400 inches per year) and the second heaviest in the world (after Cherrapunji in Assam, India). At Douala there are 200 rainy days a year, averaging 158 inches. (London receives about 40 inches.) It is little wonder that this was the last sector of equatorial Africa to be claimed by a European power.

On 30 September two small flotillas, each carrying 150 men of the West African Regiment, were sent up creeks to deal with German detachments located at Tiko on the Bimbia River and at the Misselle Plantation north of Lake Mowe. The Tiko party in a sharp fight drove off the Germans and killed their commander. The other party seized the plantation, took thirteen prisoners, and carried off a large stock of provisions. The Second Battalion of the Nigeria Regiment under Lieutenant Colonel Austin Hubert Wightwick Haywood first occupied Bonaberi and then advanced along the Northern Railway, encountering considerable opposition. Haywood, a thirty-seven-year-old bachelor and the son of a soldier, was an artillery officer who, although he had seen little active service, had spent almost his entire career on the West Coast of Africa. He had also achieved some degree of fame as "the only Englishman who, in recent years had crossed the Sahara."

Guns from HMS *Challenger* being set in emplacement

Other reconnaissances were made as the British and French felt their way inland. One of the most important of these was made by Commander Strong who took the captured German stern-wheel gunboat, and by 4 October had penetrated almost as far as Yabassi (or Jabassi), fifty miles above Douala. He had also explored some of the tributaries of the Wuri, destroying a telephone communications centre at Miang, twenty miles from Douala.

The situation at the Yapoma railway bridge now required a serious effort. The French were hanging on, but making no progress. On 5 October the field guns carried by the *Cumberland* and the *Challenger* were sent up to reinforce the light-calibre French artillery and 400 tirailleurs were landed at Pitti from a flotilla of small craft. A turning movement was again attempted, and again failed—for the same reasons. In spite of tremendous efforts, the troops were "unable to make headway through such appalling, impenetrable country under sustained machine-gun fire."

At last a direct assault succeeded. On 6 October, after what was considered a heavy bombardment, a passage of the Dibamba was forced by a gallant attack of the Senegalese tirailleurs, who, under a galling fire, swarmed over the broken girders of the wrecked bridge. Other troops crossed in barges and surf boats in an all-out effort. The Germans retreated and Douala was now safe from attack from the east. The way was prepared for an advance on Edea, an important inland town where the Midland Railway crossed the Sanaga River, but Dobell chose not to move in this direction just yet.

The desire for secure boundaries, and ever more secure boundaries, has led many nations and armies into difficulties. It now appeared to Dobell that the Germans who had concentrated at Yabassi and Edea must be defeated and driven further inland before the occupation of Douala could be considered secure. Dobell chose Yabassi, the easier of the two to reach, as his first objective. The rains were due to end soon, and the road to Yabassi, which passed through jungle and swamp, was still difficult, but the Wuri was high and navigation on it was relatively easy. Gorges was put in charge of this expedition with Lieutenant Commander the Hon. Bertram Thomas Carlyle Ogilvy Freeman-Mitford in charge of 100 seamen and marines with two 6-inch naval guns and one 12-pounder field gun. (Freeman-Mitford, captain of the *Challenger,* was an uncle of the famous Mitford sisters.) The soldiers, under Lieutenant Colonel Edward Vaughan of the West African Regiment, included six companies of Vaughan's own regiment, two companies of the 1st Nigerians, the Pioneer Company of the Gold Coast Regiment, and about 600 carriers; there was also a battery of four mountain guns.

The little expedition was stowed into a wonderous variety of river craft that included a dredger, six steam launches of various sizes, a steam tug, a stern wheeler, eight surf boats, eight steel lighters, two 100-foot motor launches, a motor pinnace, and the *Cumberland*'s picket boat. One of the six-inch guns was mounted on the dredger and the other on one of the steel lighters, which the sailors mockingly christened *Dreadnaught*. These two became, in effect, river monitors. The troops were embarked by the evening of 6 October and at 5.30 the next morning the flotilla set off. To Gorges it resembled "some huge sea monster moving in from the deep" with the picket boat as its pilot fish. It wound its way up the twisting Wuri, pushing its way against the swift current between the mangrove-lined banks.

For miles nothing could be seen on the river's banks but tangles of dense bush and tall elephant grass. Then, just at sundown, at a place called Nsake Hill, about ten miles below Yabassi, the flotilla was fired on. The fire was quickly silenced by the British mountain guns and a company of the West African Regiment was landed and occupied Nsake; other troops were put ashore on the opposite bank and the flotilla anchored for the night in mid-stream.

At dawn on 8 October the advance continued until, close to Yabassi, Vaughan disembarked his men and attempted a flanking movement through the bush while pushing his main force along a forest path beside the river. They soon came under a hot fire which, coming from invisible enemies, made the troops jumpy, though there were no casualties. The boats, showered with bullets, dropped downstream out of range. A tug towing the *Dreadnaught* ran aground on a small island and had to be abandoned for the time being. About two o'clock in the afternoon Gorges went forward with his staff to check on Vaughan's progress. He was not pleased:

> We found the troops suffering from the effects of the terrific heat, tactical unity completely lost in the dense elephant grass through which officers were trying to lead their men, many of whom showed signs of hanging back under the constant bursts of machine-gun fire, of which this was their first experience.

Gorges brought up reinforcements and tried to gain a foothold on the far side of a wooden bridge crossing a swamp, but this failed. He then turned to the naval detachment, on which he placed much reliance, but he found the sailors and marines "completely prostrated and incapable of further action, caused through their exertions in dragging the 12-pdr gun over the mud track and up to a hill position under a blazing sun." No sooner had he made this discovery than he received word that Vaughan's flank movement had been checked.

Although throughout the day there had been heavy firing and much noise, not a single soldier had been killed. Nevertheless it had been a hot, exhausting experience and Gorges withdrew his enervated, dirt-encrusted men and re-embarked them. It was dark before all were gathered in and the flotilla set off to work its way back to Nsake in the dark through "the strong current, some bumps, uncharted shoals, floating timber, and a tornado with a water spout." From first to last the aborted attack on Yabassi had been a nightmare for all concerned. A few days later Gorges prepared to make a second attempt, but naval advisors reported that the river was falling, and that the larger vessels would have to be moved to deeper water. Dobell came up to assess the situation for himself and ordered everyone back to Douala.

The little expeditionary force was reorganized: the West African Regiment, which had not performed well, was replaced by the First Battalion of the Nigeria Regiment and a composite battalion. A new set of naval experts determined that the river was not, in fact, falling as rapidly as had been predicted, so early on the morning of 13 October the flotilla set off again. As before, it stopped for the night at Nsake, which the Germans had not re-occupied, and the next morning everyone braced for another attack on Yabassi. This time there was no attempt at a flanking movement through the jungle. Troops moved down both sides of the Wuri with most of the force kept in reserve on the boats.

By noon the columns on both banks were hotly engaged

and the Germans were slowly falling back. By the end of the day a few *Schutztruppen* had been captured and the enemy was thought to have sustained "considerable loss." That night the British entrenched on both sides of the river with the flotilla between them. At first light the advance was resumed, and after some desultory fighting in the bush, the Germans completely withdrew, leaving the British to occupy Yabassi.

The victory had cost the life of one officer, Captain E. S. Brand. ("A dear good fellow and an officer of great promise ... he was killed leading his men through the swamps.") He was also a Chinese interpreter and was seconded from the Royal Fusiliers. Also killed were three British NCOs, "a few bluejackets, and some forty native soldiers."

For this battle Gorges had foolishly set up his headquarters in *Dreadnaught*. He found it, he said, "a fearful experience, for every time the 6-inch gun was fired, not only were we thrown off our feet, but the old lighter seemed to split in two—also our poor heads."

Dobell now designed an elaborate scheme to capture Edea. Surveys revealed that rivers little used by the Germans were navigable and could be made use of by the now considerable number of small craft available. While a diversion was created on the Sanga River by 150 men of the West African Regiment, a main force of 240 Europeans, 800 Senegalese tirailleurs with another 150 men of the West African Regiment, and 1,000 carriers, all under the command of a French colonel would proceed, first by transports to the mouth of the Nyong River and then by small craft twenty-five miles up the river to Dehane. Here the force would disembark and march twenty miles overland to attack Edea from what was hoped would be an unexpected quarter.

The operation began on 20 October. It had scarcely commenced when a surf boat capsized, drowning the superintendent of the Nigeria Marine, a naval transport officer and a French staff officer. The redoubtable Captain Fuller, who was with them, was pulled exhausted from the surf after struggling valiantly to save the others. (He was later awarded the Royal Humane Society's Silver Medal for his efforts.) Two days after this incident, having overcome what the Official History described as "every kind of navigational difficulty," the Anglo–French force finally reached Dehane.

On 26 October the French occupied Edea after stiff fighting and the Germans drew back to Yaounda, which they now made their capital. Two days later a British force, fighting its way along the railway from Yapona, also reached Edea. Meanwhile, Lieutenant Colonel Haywood with the 2nd Nigerians successfully fought his way up the Northern Railway and captured Susa. This enabled Dobell to give his attention to the Cameroon Mountain, which at 13,353 feet is the highest in West Africa, and to the former capital at Buea, a healthy resort area 4,000 feet above sea level on the southeast slope.

While Haywood continued his advance up the railway, Gorges organized two columns, one commanded by Lieutenant Colonel J. B. Cockburn and the other by Lieutenant Colonel R. A. deB. Rose. A detachment of marines was sent by sea to Victoria, Buea's port ten miles away. With only slight opposition, Buea was occupied on 16 November 1914, and while Senegalese buglers sounded their instruments, the Union Jack and the Tricolour were raised over Government House, an imposing stone structure set in a garden of tropical luxuriance. A magnificent set of elephant tusks, considered to be the largest in Africa at that time, was looted from Government House, as were two giant eland horns which for many years after adorned the reading room of the Junior Army and Navy Club in London.

The area north and east of Cameroon Mountain was then a "tuskers domain" and it was through a portion of this area that Rose's column marched and fought. A lieutenant marching with this column wrote afterwards:

> We had a rather trying time. . . . We crossed the Mungo river in canoes and then did a long and difficult march all through the night in dense forest country. . . . About five in the morning,

when it was just getting light, our advance party were on the point of stumbling on the German outpost when what should happen but an elephant suddenly walked in between and scattered both our opposing parties in all directions. I was in the rear of our little column and was left in bewilderment, all our carriers dropping their loads and everyone disappearing into the bush. After a few minutes we got our men together and our scouts went forward again to find the Germans had bolted from their outposts, but soon returned and opened fire on us.

Elephants were not the only creatures disturbed by the fighting among the humans. During one attack on a German position, a cloud of bees launched an offensive against both antagonists with such ferocity that, as one officer reported, "some of the poor fellows [were] so badly stung that they nearly died from pain and shock."

Soon after the capture of Douala the British Admiralty asked that Fuller and his cruisers be released for use elsewhere, but Dobell, alarmed at the loss of the cruisers and even more at the thought of losing the efficient Fuller, with whom he enjoyed excellent relations, vigorously protested.

If Fuller left, he might be replaced by a senior French officer. Dobell was horrified by the thought. French naval officers, he reported, were reluctant to put their men ashore for any duty and they annoyed him with "frequent complaints, which are entirely out of place in war, about the discomforts of life ashore." He also entertained doubts about French capabilities:

> Owing to the complex nature of the operations it would be a matter of grave difficulty for any British officer to act in concert with an officer of a different nationality . . . my experience of the French temperament leads me to believe that much of the methodical work that has to be performed at all hours of the day and night does not appeal to the characteristics displayed by that nationality.

Dobell also found fault with French ships, saying that their cruisers were unsuited to the work in the Cameroons.

1st Battalion, Nigeria Regiment on the march

The Admiralty reluctantly consented to allow Fuller to stay on as senior naval officer, but insisted that HMS *Cumberland* leave at the end of November.

After capturing Buea and driving the Germans out of the entire region of the Cameroon Mountain, Dobell decided to capture the whole of the Northern Railway and the region it served. Gorges was placed in command of the operation and he shifted his headquarters to Majuka (about sixty miles northeast of Douala), which had been captured recently by Haywood's Nigerians. On 3 December he began his advance: his main column followed the railway with smaller columns on each flank to clear the country of hostile parties.

Fighting daily, Gorges steadily advanced and on 8 December, after a sharp fight, the first consignment of rolling stock, which the Germans had moved with them in their retreat, fell into his hands: four coaches, four trucks, and two good trollies. The next day thirteen more carriages were taken, and several prisoners. On 10 December Gorges entered a more open undulating country intersected by wooded valleys and ravines. His advance was strenuously opposed until he reached Kilometer 150, where a German officer under a white flag was brought to him with a letter from his commander surrendering Nkongsamba (railhead) and Bare, which were just ahead.

When the British occupied the towns they found among
their spoils of war five locomotives, fifty pieces of rolling
stock, quantities of stores, tools, fuel, harnesses, and two
new airplanes, complete in every detail. There were as well
large stocks of tinned food, champagne, beer, hams, leber-
würst, and a goodly supply of sheep, pigs and poultry. Gorges
sent the prisoners, along with the women, children and
missionaries, down the line to Douala.

Of great advantage to the Allied invaders was the good-
will of the inhabitants of the regions through which they
passed. The Cameroons contains an unusual number of
tribes, each with its own language, customs, physical features, history and way of life. The British found that almost
all were willing to sell food and to act as carriers and guides.
Gorges wrote:

> The attitude of the natives was friendly and the chiefs of local
> tribes with many followers trekked in from the countryside
> bringing presents of food for the troops. One wizened white-
> haired old gentleman who came to pay his respects kept on
> muttering a curious jargon in melancholy tones . . . the inter-
> pretation thereof being that he desired eternal friendship with
> the British and offered his tribe *en masse* as labourers and car-
> riers.

Indeed, of all the chiefs of the many tribes, only one took
up arms on the German side, although the British were often
surprised by "the very warm affection that Africans had for
many German officials." In general, the tribesmen seemed
to give the Germans as much help as they did the French
and British. Most were probably indifferent as to the out-
come of the war. However, this was not true of the well-
trained *Schutztruppe*, most of whom remained loyal to the
end. As General Gorges admitted, "The manner in which
the native soldiers stuck to their German officers until the
hopelessness of the position became apparent was one of
the surprises of the campaign."

Christmas found Gorges and his men concentrated at
Melong, a village fourteen miles from railhead, which had

recently been captured by Haywood and his Nigerians. A fortnight's supplies had been dumped there, the railway to the coast had been put in working order, and the troops, said Gorges, were "getting into their stride in this new-fangled jumpy kind of ambuscade warfare." Plans were now ready for an attack on the German fort at Dschang, fifty-five miles from railhead at an important road junction near the Nigerian border.*

Throughout the Great War the Germans seemed always to attach a greater importance to Christmas than did the British or French. On the Western Front in Europe it appears to have been the Germans who initiated the informal truce that brought Tommy and Fritz out of their trenches to exchange presents in no-man's-land. In West Africa the German commander Gorges was pursuing wrote a note proposing a Christmas truce and left it in a cleft stick set upright on a jungle path where it was found by a British patrol. Gorges did not bother to reply. "We are not out for sighing and sobbing and want to get on with the business," he said. A simple dinner in the elephant grass sufficed for him and his men, but back at base there was both the time and the resources for a proper celebration.

At the Ordnance Mess in Douala some of the senior army and navy officers dined very well indeed. Christmas dinner began with caviar on toast and purée aux pois, and progressed through a fish course of mackerel to pheasant, duck and ham with potatoes, peas, and asparagus. There was plum pudding for desert, followed, should anyone still be hungry, by a savory of bologna sausage on toast. All this was washed down with four wines and polished with a choice of three liqueurs. There were, of course, toasts to The King ("God bless him!") and to Absent Friends.

On 26 December the advance of Gorges's force pressed forward to the Mhu River (a tributary of the Nkam, which is a tributary of the Mbam) and the Germans fell back, fighting bitter rearguard actions.

---

* Dschang, at 4,525 feet above sea level, is today a health resort and tourist centre. In 1949 it hosted the first International Conference on Nutrition.

A British Naval 12 pounder gun used in the bombardment of Dschang

On 27 January an officers' patrol, led by Lieutenant Fitz-hardinge Paul Butler and another subaltern, which had been sent out the previous day to round up a German detachment that had been harassing Gorges' flank, returned after successfully accomplishing its mission. Lieutenant Butler had particularly distinguished himself by swimming "the swift, unfordable Nkam River under hostile fire to reconnoitre single-handed the enemy's dispositions and numbers." For this and other remarkable acts of heroism, he was awarded the Victoria Cross, the first to be won in the Great War in Africa. He also won the Distinguished Service Order before he was killed little more than a year later (June 1916) in an action on the Ruvu River on the other side of the continent in the East Africa Campaign. Gorges called him "one of the bravest of them all."

Pushing on, subjected to continual sniper fire and intermittent bursts of machine-gun fire, harassed by clouds of mosquitoes and armies of stinging ants, Gorges's column finally passed out of the elephant grass country into a forested mountain region. By New Year's Day 1915 his troops had reached a crossroads only seven miles southwest of Dschang. Here he was joined by Haywood's column. On 2 January 1915 Dschang surrendered after an artillery bombardment and before the British could mount an infantry assault. This came as a surprise, for the Dschang fort was well built and surrounded by a stout cactus hedge. Gorges destroyed the fort and returned to railhead, thus ending the first British venture into the Cameroonian hinterland.

On 5 January the Germans launched a determined attack on Edea, but were beaten off by the French garrison. After Gorges's withdrawal the Germans also reappeared in the Bare district just north of Nkongsamba, where there was much confused fighting in January and February. On 3 March Gorges led a sizeable force up the railway into the Bare district and found the Germans entrenched astride the main road near the town of Bare. The British attacked but were met by sustained and well-directed fire from concealed machine guns. Gorges's troops, mostly from Sierra Leone, were unable to stand the strain. He wrote of their failure:

> The test was too tormenting, more than black flesh and blood could bear, and in spite of the steadfast example of their officers and British NCO's neither "Momo" nor "Bokari" would on this occasion face any more of the Maxim music. Colonel [G. P.] Newstead, in a supreme effort to sustain the fight, was mortally wounded.

The British lost eight European officers and NCOs, and 140 African other ranks. These were severe casualties given the number engaged, and Gorges beat a retreat. Unknown to him, the Germans had also lost heavily and they too had retreated. The British halted and dug in at Bare: the Germans stopped just north of Melong. And there, except for minor actions in the bush, both sides remained through the rainy season. A case, it would seem, of one side being afraid and the other glad of it.

All But Mora

By March 1915 two major Allied forces had successfully established themselves in the Cameroons. General Dobell's Allied Command, with its headquarters at Douala, had British troops holding the Northern Railway, Victoria, Buea, and the entire Cameroons Mountain region to the Nigerian frontier, and it had French troops on the Midland Railway as far as, and including, Edea, as well as a detachment of tirailleurs in the coast town of Kribi.

The other major command was that of General Aymerich, whose French troops had in the first month of the war invaded the Cameroons from the east and southeast, advancing up the Sanga River and westward from Singa up the Lobaye—all in territory France had so reluctantly ceded to Germany in 1911 and which it was now eager to reclaim. Reinforced by some light artillery and 600 tirailleurs from the Moyen Congo, Aymerich's forces had captured the important town of Molundie in October 1914 and by March 1915 were approaching Dumie and Lomie.

In April a third force took the field in the northwest corner of the Cameroons. As it was obviously impossible for Dobell to direct operations so far away, Colonel Frederick

Hugh Cunliffe was directed to prosecute an active Anglo–French campaign in this quarter.

Cunliffe was an officer with twenty-six years' service. He had seen active service on the North-West Frontier of India, where he had taken part in the Hazara Campaign and the Relief of Chitral. He had served ten years in Africa and in 1905 he had commanded the Kagoro Expedition in Northern Nigeria. So that he would be superior in rank to Colonel Brisset, the senior officer in the area, he was promoted brigadier general. He concentrated all the force he could muster at Yola, Nigeria, and at once prepared for an attack on Garua, where the Germans had a strong fort and where the British had failed so miserably eight months earlier.

As it was known that the German guns at Garua outranged the Nigerian mountain guns, Cunliffe borrowed a 12-pounder and gun crew from *Challenger* and a 95 mm gun from the French. By 18 April he was ready to open his campaign with an Allied force that included on the British side nine companies of infantry (one mounted), three guns and nine machine guns; the French contributed three companies of tirailleurs, a squadron of cavalry, two guns, and two mitrailleuses (machine guns). However, before Cunliffe could strike, the Germans sprang a surprise.

During the night of 21 / 22 April 1915 a German column of ten Europeans, 100 mounted men, and 200 infantry under Captain von Crailsheim made a sortie from Garua and, passing south and west of Cunliffe's troops, was reinforced by a detachment that marched up from Ngaundere. Cunliffe lost track of Crailsheim until one fine morning in early May he pounced on a British frontier post forty miles southwest of Garua. From there he marched across country, evading the troops sent to intercept him, and on 8 May was safely back in Garua.

Cunliffe now marched on Garua and the end of May found his Anglo–French force entrenched within 5,000 yards of the outer works of the Garua fort. He began to sap under cover of darkness and by 9 June he had a line of trenches 400 yards wide within 1,000 yards of the fort. Water was the biggest problem of the forward troops, for it had to be carried to them in pots for more than two miles.

During the night of 9/10 June the Germans made two sorties. The first was nipped in the bud by the accurate fire of the Nigerians; the second proved a disaster for the Germans. Many of their troops bolted, throwing down their weapons and plunging into the flooded Benue River. Only about fifty strong swimmers escaped; the British drew seventy bodies from the water.

On the afternoon of 10 July all was ready for the Allied assault when the Germans unexpectedly raised the white flag. "It appears that the native soldiery got completely out of hand," wrote Gorges, "the firing of our heavier guns having played such havoc that they could no longer endure the strain." The garrison surrendered 37 Europeans, 220 Africans, five guns, ten Maxim machine guns, and large quantities of ammunition, equipment, and stores.

Cunliffe determined to follow up his victory by seizing Ngaundere (Ngaoundere), an important crossroads town 140 miles due south of Garua. He ordered Colonel Brisset and his French contingent to garrison Garua and he sent a column under Lieutenant Colonel W. I. Webb-Bowen of the Nigeria Regiment to move south and take Ngaundere.

On 28 June Webb-Bowen's column, in the midst of a blinding tornado, completely surprised and routed the German outposts on the steep approaches to the northern end of the Ngaundere Plateau, and that evening an advanced guard occupied the town. The Germans counterattacked, but were repulsed and retired southwest to Tibati.

Meanwhile there occurred the most serious breach in Anglo–French relations. Brisset, a short, stocky and temperamentally prickly officer, entertained an implacable detestation of Englishmen. Disobeying the orders of his French superior, General Largeau, to place himself under Cunliffe (he maintained that he was subject only to the orders of General Aymerich), he ignored Cunliffe's orders to remain at Gurua and defiantly marched out with all his men toward Ngaundere. Apparently he hoped to capture the place before Webb-Bowen could.

This contretemps sent telegrams flying in Nigeria, Brazzaville (capital of the French Moyen Congo), London, and Paris. Governor Lugard urged the Foreign Office to protest vigorously to the French government so that this "dual or triple command subject to counter orders from Brazzaville should cease immediately." After direct intervention by politicians and senior officers in Europe, Cunliffe was confirmed as commander.

Curiously, while the bickering over command was taking place up country, Dobell had a visit from the lieutenant governor of the Moyen Congo, who suggested an immediate advance on the new German capital at Yaounda (Yaounde) in conjunction with General Aymerich's French forces. Dobell demurred. While he realized the political and strategic importance of Yaounda, he felt that the time was not yet ripe for such a move. Heavy rains were setting in and he did not believe he had enough troops for such a major advance. Nevertheless, he finally waived his objections and agreed to cooperate with all of his available force.

In the first stage of this operation Nigerians under Colonel Haywood forced the passage of the Kele River and captured Ngwe and So Dibanga, both of which were obstinately defended. Haywood then turned eastward, capturing Ndupe on 3 May and Wum Biagas the following day. These successes were not easily won; there were heavy losses among the British officers and African other ranks. The Nigerians pushed on to attack a strong German position on the left bank of the Mbila River and succeeded after an eighteen-hour battle in shaking the Germans out of their entrenchments.

Meanwhile, a French force moved on Eseka, railhead of the Midland Railway. It was a difficult advance along the railway bed against stiff opposition and over rugged terrain. The Germans had destroyed the tracks and demolished all the railway bridges. Nevertheless, the tirailleurs occupied Eseka on 11 May and then marched north to join hands with Haywood at Wum Biagas. Colonel Mayer, a

French officer, then assumed command of the combined forces.

So far, so good, but unfortunately the French force under General Aymerich could not reach its initial objective, the line Dumie-Lome, 140 miles east of Yaounda. Dobell was, understandably, unhappy. He had fulfilled his part of the agreement and had committed his troops; Aymerich had failed him. Nevertheless, he ordered Mayer not to wait but to press on east from Wum Biagas, an advance he began on 25 April with a column of 2,000 troops and a host of carriers.

From the beginning the narrow track eastward proved inadequate for an army. New paths had to be cut. Worse still, Mayer soon found himself in the grip of a primordial rain forest, a jungle through which men had to hack their way, often up to their waists in swamp water. The Germans disputed every step, sniping and ambushing from well-chosen positions. Swelling the sea of troubles was a deluge of rain so fierce that the carriers could not keep the troops supplied. Battle casualties and sickness were fast thinning the ranks. By 5 May Mayer's miserable column had progressed only twelve miles from its starting point—a rate of little more than a mile per day. Yaounda was fifty miles away.

Mayer at last reported that a further advance was impracticable. Dobell then informed the governor of French Equatorial Africa that unless Aymerich's columns could now move forward, the enterprise must be abandoned. On 7 June he ordered a retreat. The withdrawal became a nightmare. The Germans successfully attacked a food convoy while Mayer's force was so roughly handled that he lost a quarter of his column and Dobell was forced to send every available man to his rescue. The reinforcements arrived just in time to prevent a complete debacle. It was not until 29 June that opposition ended and the tattered and exhausted troops could sink to rest in their sodden bivouacs at Wum Biagas thirty-three days after they had left it.

The campaign ground to a halt. Troops on the Northern

Railway settled in; they sent for seeds, cleared land, and planted vegetables with results that amazed the Europeans. Beans ran riot, "climbing the trunks of trees and festooning the branches," radishes grew to the size of beets; "one turnip was a satisfying meal"; and a cabbage, it was said, could almost feed a platoon.

In the north, where the rainy season was shorter and the rains not quite so heavy, Cunliffe decided to make a determined effort to capture the fort at Mora, which, although completely isolated from any other German forces, refused to surrender. It was perched on the summit of a mountain that rose precipitously to 1,700 feet. All approaches were defended by strongly built sangars. The slopes were accessible only in a few places to men climbing with hands and feet up boulder-strewn terrain. From 1 September until the eighth Cunliffe tried his best, sending in attack after attack, but each failed. Finally, leaving an investing force of four companies of infantry, he withdrew the bulk of his men. Later, the French too made unsuccessful attacks. Mora proved a nut too tough to crack.

On 25 August a second Allied conference was held in Douala, the principals being Dobell, Aymerich, and the governor of French Equatorial Africa. Together they hatched the final scheme for the capture of the Cameroons. Wisely, no moves were planned until the end of the rainy season. In spite of setbacks, the Allies had, in fact, occupied strong strategic positions. Columns in varying strengths roughly surrounded the Yaounda area, which contained the new German capital and the bulk of the German forces. Both the British and French had been reinforced, the British adding the 5th Indian Light Infantry (a battalion of uncertain quality as it had recently mutinied in Singapore), and two companies of the West Indian Regiment; they also added an armoured car, twenty-five Ford vans and a 4.5-inch howitzer. The French added more Senegalese tirailleurs.

The campaign got underway in early October, just as the rains were diminishing, with Dobell advancing from the west, Cunliffe from the north, and two French columns pressing from the east. German opposition was, as always, vigorous and protracted. The *Schutztruppe* gave the invaders a particularly difficult time at Banyo, 125 miles west and south of Ngaundere, where the Germans had amply provisioned a strong position on a mountain rising steeply 1,200 feet above the surrounding country. One British officer aptly called it "grim and stupendous."

On 2 November Cunliffe had five companies of infantry on the underfeatures of the mountain and mounted infantry patrolling on the rolling grassland below. Three 2.95-inch guns were in place to support an attack. Early on the morning of 4 November the infantry under a soaking rain began to climb, struggling through thorny scrub and over boulders while the Germans subjected them to heavy rifle and machine gun fire from well-chosen positions on the slopes. One company of Nigerians, led by Captain C. G. Bowyer-Smijth, actually reached the summit in the late afternoon, but there it came under a withering fire. Bowyer-Smijth fell and his men fled to the foot of the mountain.

African carriers bravely brought up food and water under fire to the soldiers huddled on the mountainside and at dawn the sodden, sleepless, British force wearily and warily resumed its upward climb, subjected now to large stones rolled down on them and to thrown dynamite bombs. By persevering, a few stone sangers and redoubts were taken by late afternoon. By five o'clock the air was dark and soon a thunderstorm broke over the mountain. Throughout the night bombs and fireballs rained down on the attackers, but just at dawn, as the assault was about to be renewed, white flags were seen over the German positions on the crest. A British officer described the surrender site: "On the top of the hill broken furniture, bottles, and gramophones were littered about among the pigs and sheep." General Dobell spoke of this battle as "one of the most arduous ever fought by native African troops."

German morale suffered from the defeat at Banyo. British forces were now almost everywhere successful. On 3 November the important town of Tibati fell to Anglo–French forces under Brisset and Webb-Bowen, working in harmony for a change. One by one the German strongholds were toppled. The energetic Haywood with a reinforced column seized the railhead at Nkongsamba. Mangeles was occupied. Garua had surrendered to Cunliffe's forces. And on 1 January 1916 the fort at Yaounda was captured by the 4th Nigerians, who released the Allied prisoners held there: seventeen British and seven French civilians, including "some ladies," and seven British and three French soldiers.

The conquerors were disappointed by Yaounda; they had expected something better in the colony's capital. A British officer wrote home: "We found nothing in this deserted place either (sic) to eat, to drink or to play with, and by way of adding insult to injury they left it in an unsanitary condition, dangerous to the health of our troops." The "unsanitary condition" was a reference to the German practice of allowing, perhaps even encouraging, their askaris—both here and in East Africa—to defecate on furniture and floors of public and private buildings they abandoned. British officers were disgusted by this expression of "German beastliness."

All the German public officials, including Governor Ebermaier, had fled from Yaounda. Protected by the still-loyal *Schutztruppe*, they made for the border of Rio Muni (mainland Equatorial Guinea), then a Spanish possession, 125 miles away. The British and French took up the pursuit and there was a final fierce battle on the banks of the Nyong on 8 January 1916, but they were held in check until all the Germans and the remnants of the *Schutztruppe* crossed over into neutral and friendly Spanish territory, where they were warmly welcomed by Governor Angel Barrera. Later 832 Germans were transported to Spain for a not unpleasant internment.

The Anglo–French conquest of the Cameroons was now complete—except for the fort at Mora. In spite of determined attacks by British and French forces, Mora still held out, bravely defended by a Captain von Raben. In the end the British offered generous terms and, his situation being

hopeless, von Raben surrendered. Among the terms agreed
to were that German officers could retain their swords; that
all Germans would be sent to England as prisoners of war,
and that African soldiers would be given safe passage to
their homes. Captain von Raben also brazenly requested a
loan of £2,000 to pay his troops, and this was given him—
from the credits of liquidated firms in Nigeria. In all, the
survivors of Mora included 11 Europeans, 145 askaris, and
232 women and children.

The conquest of the Cameroons cost the British 4,600
casualties, including 1,668 killed, most of whom died of
diseases. The French suffered 2,567 dead, also mostly from
diseases. Casualties among the carriers were said to have
been great, but their numbers were not counted. Aside from
the British and French naval forces employed, 7,000 British and 11,000 French and Belgian troops took part in the
campaign. All the rank and file were black Africans except
for a few NCOs, the Indians in the 5th Light Infantry, and
the men in the West India Regiment, who were blacks from
British possessions in the West Indies.

On 4 March 1916 Britain and France divided the former
German colony between them, France taking the lion's share.

CHAPTER

6

A Campaign Aborted by a Revolution

Germany's second largest colony was German South-West Africa, a vast area (317,725 square miles) six times larger than England, larger than Texas and Mississippi combined. The land consists mostly of a long plateau that rises steeply from an arid coastal plain, the Namib desert, which, although only ten to thirty miles wide, follows the Atlantic seacoast for nearly 800 miles. The desert coastline is often shrouded in heavy fogs and swept by violent winds that tussle with the shifting sands. There are only two natural harbours, Walfish (or Walvis) Bay and Lüderitzbucht (formerly Angra Pequena). There are no perennial streams in this strange land, only river beds, usually dry, to carry off in a rush the water from rare rains.

At the turn of the century the land was inhabited by a variety of tribes and racial communities. Most were Bantu, such as the Hereros, Ovambos, and Damaras, but there were also diminutive Bushmen, yellow skinned Hottentots, and a people of mixed European, Hottentot, and Bantu blood who spoke Afrikaans and proudly called themselves Bas-

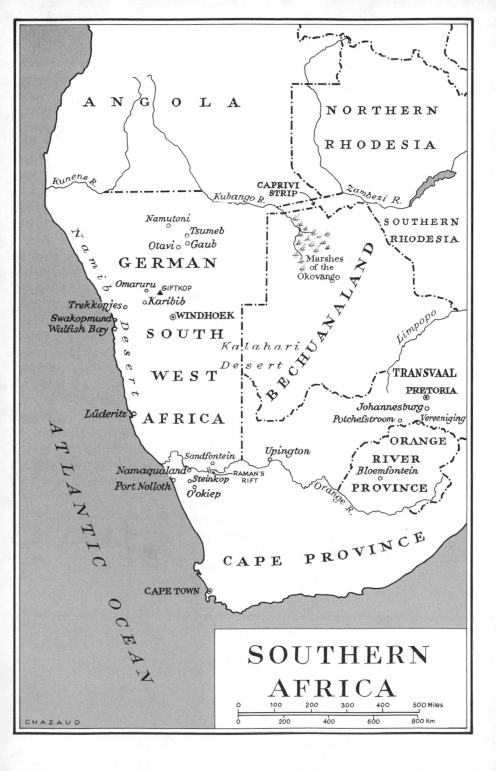

ANGOLA

NORTHERN RHODESIA

Kunene R.

Kubango R.

CAPRIVI STRIP

Zambezi R.

SOUTHERN RHODESIA

Namutoni

Tsumeb
Otavi   Gaub

GERMAN

Marshes
of the
Okovango

Omaruru   GIFTKOP
Trekkopjes   Karibib
Swakopmund   WINDHOEK
Walfish Bay

SOUTH

Kalahari

Desert

WEST

BECHUANALAND

Limpopo

TRANSVAAL
PRETORIA

AFRICA

Lüderitz

Johannesburg
Potchefstroom   Vereeniging

Namaqualand   Sandfontein   Upington
Port Nolloth   Steinkop   RAMAN'S
O'okiep   RIFT

ORANGE
RIVER
Bloemfontein
PROVINCE

Orange R.

N a m i b   D e s e r t

A T L A N T I C   O C E A N

CAPE   PROVINCE

CAPE TOWN

SOUTHERN
AFRICA

0   100   200   300   400   500 Miles
0   200   400   600   800 km

CHAZAUD

tards. Europeans, mostly Germans, numbered less than 15,000. In the nineteenth century the Hottentots were conquered by the Hereros, who were in turn ruthlessly crushed by the Germans in a series of bloody campaigns in 1904–08. The German governor at the time, Lothar von Trotha, gave orders to "kill every one of them and take no prisoners. . . . I wish to make sure that never again will there be another Herero rebellion." The tribe was almost destroyed; its scattered remnants were impoverished.

Geographically connected but politically separate from German South-West Africa was Walfish Bay, a 374-square mile enclave that was annexed by the Dutch in 1792; it became British territory in 1878, attached politically to Cape Province, and it remained British, a small red dot on the edge of German territory even after 1892 when Germany annexed the remainder of South-West Africa. It possessed the only harbour in South-West Africa suitable for a naval base.

Another geopolitical oddity of the colony was, and is, the Caprivi Zipfel (Caprivi finger, concession or strip), a narrow band of land only about forty miles wide that extends some 300 miles east of the rest of the country to the Zambezi River with Angola and present-day Zambia to the north and Botswana to the south. It was named after Count Leo von Caprivi, the German soldier and statesman who succeeded Bismarck as chancellor of Germany in 1890. He obtained agreements on boundaries between German and British possessions in Africa. The land itself is barren. Major J. J. O'Sullevan of the Northern Rhodesia Police described the area around Schuckmannsburg, capital of the Zipfel, as "not of much use to anyone," and, he said, "It breeds the largest, most vindictive and venomous mosquitoes I have seen in a long experience of tropical Africa. In the wet season it is a swamp and unhealthy; in the dry weather the heat is terrific and the sand is deep and uncomfortable to walk in." Schuckmannsburg was occupied by the Rhodesians without opposition on 21 September 1914.

Dr. Ernst Göring, father of Herman Göring, was the first

Reichskommisar (imperial commissioner) in South-West Africa and he arrived in 1885. He was noted for his over-bearing arrogance and high-handed treatment of Africans, an attitude emulated by those who succeeded him. German relations with the natives were seldom good and there were no black Africans in the *Schutztruppe.*

As in all German colonies, the colonial officials were unready for war. The official German attitude was expressed in a current shiboleth: *"Die Kolonien müssen in der Nordsee verteidigt Werden"*—the colonies must be defended in the North Sea. The *Schutztruppe* in German South-West Africa consisted of only about 140 officers and less than 3,000 other ranks, but these were all picked men. The officers all had at least three years' service, were exceptionally fit, and had to be specially recommended. The other ranks were all volunteers with at least two years' service in the regular army, of good character and exceptional physique; they engaged for three and a half years in the *Schutztruppe,* after which they passed into the reserve and incentives were offered them to remain as colonists. In German South-West Africa there were some 7,000 adult male settlers, most of whom had received some military training.

Against this tiny Germany army the South Africans were able to muster a force that eventually totaled more than 50,000 Europeans backed up by 33,000 black Africans in noncombatant roles. On the face of it the Germans did not have a chance, but they counted on the Boers in South Africa seizing the opportunity offered by the war to throw off British rule. In the expectation of aiding them, they had confidently stocked arms, ammunition, and stores of all sorts. This was not whistling in the dark. There was indeed to be a revolution in South Africa.

The Boers—people of generally Dutch, German, and French ancestry, now usually called Afrikaners—had a history of fleeing from what they regarded as British oppression, and to this day they celebrate the Great Trek, that time in the early nineteenth century when their forefathers piled their possessions onto ox wagons, left their farms in

Cape Colony, and moved into the sparsely settled interior, onto the high veld where they could establish their own republics, for they entertained a fierce love of independence. From perhaps a dozen or more small republics there finally emerged two: Orange Free State and the South African Republic, the latter usually called the Transvaal. At the turn of the century both states were crushed in a bitter war with Britain that lasted two and a half years. Although the Boers were never able to keep more than 30,000 men in the field at one time, the British were forced to employ nearly half a million men from all parts of the Empire to subdue them. That war ended in 1902, only a dozen years before the outbreak of the First World War.

In the final stages of the war the ruthless Lord Kitchener burned farmhouses and crops, killed cattle, and crowded women, children, and old men into "concentration camps." War's end found the Boers' cherished republics transformed into British colonies, their lands devastated, the people impoverished, and their institutions shattered. There were indeed many bitter Boers who viewed the war in Europe as a heaven-sent opportunity to cast off the hated British yoke, but most followed the path of Louis Botha, their most respected political leader, and remained loyal to the Crown.

The British had given the Boers good cause to reconsider their politics, for the conquerors behaved with remarkable magnanimity and generosity, pouring millions of pounds into the new colonies to rehabilitate the people and resettle them on the land; agriculture and mining were reestablished. Such an attitude towards a defeated foe was then unprecedented.

Even more remarkable, in 1907, only five years after the end of the war, free elections were permitted, first in the Transvaal and then in the Orange River Colony, as the Orange Free State had become, and the old Boer leaders again took up the reins of political power. The Boer generals and commandants, led by Botha, assumed most of the public offices. In 1910 all four South African colonies united

Louis Botha

to become the Union of South Africa with Botha as prime minister, ably backed by his former comrade in arms, Jan Smuts. The Boers now had twice the power and influence they had once enjoyed, and both Botha and Smuts with their followers were converted from the bitterest enemies of the British Empire into that Empire's staunchest adherents.

When the war broke out in Europe Botha at once cabled London to say that all the Imperial troops in South Africa could be released and that the newly formed South African Defence Force would protect South Africa. The authorities in London gratefully accepted this offer and then asked if the South Africans could do more. Botha was told that if his troops could "seize such parts of German South-West Africa as would give them command of Swakopmund, Lüderitzbucht and the wireless stations there or in the interior," it would be "a great and urgent Imperial service."

Although well aware that aggressive action against German South-West Africa would be unpopular with many of his constituents, Botha agreed to invade his country's neighbor to the west. Admiral Herbert King-Hall, the British commander on the Cape station, had already sent a man-of-war to protect Walfish Bay and to destroy the wireless station and port facilities at Swakopmund. On 19 September the South Africans landed 1,824 men commanded by Colonel P. S. Bcvcs (soon superseded by General Sir Duncan McKenzie) at Lüderitzbucht. Another little army of nearly 2,500 men under Brigadier General Henry Timson Lukin (1860–1925) landed at Port Nolloth, the only port for Namaqualand, and advanced to seize the drifts (fords) on the Orange River, which formed the boundary between South Africa and the German colony. It was in the course of this latter operation that the South Africans experienced their only serious reverse in the entire campaign.

Lukin established his base at Steinkopf on a narrow gauge railway that crossed the barren waste to O'Okiep. His force consisted mainly of mounted infantry—five battalions of the South African Mounted Rifles and two batteries of the Transvaal Horse Artillery—with one regiment of foot, the Witwatersrand Rifles. Two battalions of the Mounted Rifles seized Raman's Drift on the Orange River and then pursued a small German force for some twenty-five miles to the northeast. The main body of Lukin's force arrived at Raman's Drift on 24 September. The following day a South African patrol of 120 men under Captain E. J. Welby was attacked by Germans at Sandfontein, a group of three wells and a couple of dilapidated buildings at the foot of a 150-foot high conical-shaped kopje (hill), twenty-four miles away and inside German territory. Lieutenant Colonel R. C. Grant was sent off with a squadron of the 1st South African Mounted Rifles and two 13-pounders with a machine gun section of the Transvaal Horse Artillery to reinforce Welby.

After a long night ride Grant reached Sandfontein at 7.25 A.M. on 26 September and found Welby safe, but before his men could off-saddle, a message arrived from a lookout on a kopje that a German column was advancing from the northeast. At the same time it was discovered that the telephone line to Raman's Drift had been cut. Grant scampered to the top of the kopje and saw another German column advancing at the gallop from the east and still another from the west. Lieutenant F. B. Adler, commanding the guns, opened fire at eight o'clock from 4,000 yards. A four-gun German battery replied, and a half hour later a second battery came into action from 3,000 yards. Casualties mounted among the South Africans. Their horses also suffered, and one soldier later wrote "The poor helpless creatures stood in rows having their guts blown out, and it looked as if their riders would soon be treated in like manner."

The German forces under the command of Colonel von Heydebreck, commander of the *Schutztruppe*, were estimated to be ten times that of the South Africans. Nevertheless, there was a spirited defence, particularly by the badly outgunned Transvaal gunners, most of whom were "boys hardly out of their teens." Private P. J. Young of the Mounted Rifles later said: "The German shots were a thick rain on the hill, while their field guns struck at the two guns of the THA, around which figures were lying still. . . . The young artillerymen's courage was grand. They worked with a will till they could do no more."

At 10.30 A.M. a direct hit by a German shell destroyed one gun and killed the battery sergeant major. All of the cannoneers were killed or wounded. The remaining gun was worked by two wounded gunners.

At eleven the Germans added two more field pieces; ten new guns now pounded the South Africans. Lieutenant Adler fought his last gun until it ran out of ammunition, then he destroyed it, and took the survivors of his section to join the riflemen on the kopje.

At one o'clock there was a lull in the fighting while the Germans ate lunch and improved their positions. An hour later the battle resumed.

Lieutenant Colonel Grant was severely wounded and for a time Captain Welby assumed command. The Germans launched an infantry attack, but were thrown back. Still, by five o'clock they had worked to within 1,200 yards of the kopje and all of their artillery was focused on the South African infantry. The exploding shells flung enormous rocks into the air and sent great boulders rolling down the hill. Grant, his wounds roughly patched, resumed command, but his situation was hopeless and at six he raised a white flag.

Then a curious thing happened. The firing stopped just as the sun was setting, and thirsty men from both sides ran for the wells at the foot of the kopje. South Africans and Germans mingled, said one soldier, "as if never a shot had been fired."

The South Africans suffered 67 casualties, 22 per cent of their strength, including 16 killed or mortally wounded. The German losses were almost as great: 60 casualties, of whom 14 were killed. Among the slain was Major von Rappart, considered one of the best officers in the *Schutztruppe*. He had "found a beautiful death, that is, on the field of honour"—or so said a German account.

Thus the first attempt to establish an Allied force on South-West African soil ended with a defeat and a mortifying surrender.

General Lutkin had no idea that the Germans were present in such force in his sector. Although three days before the Sandfontein disaster the Defence Headquarters in South Africa had received word that German troop trains filled with *Schutztruppen* were rolling south, this vital information reached Lukin only ten days after the battle. Instead of being telegraphed, it had been sent by post.

The battle of Sandfontein put a period to the invasion of German South-West Africa. The entire campaign was placed on hold. There was revolution in Orange River Colony and the Transvaal.

For South Africans of British descent there was no question of where their loyalties lay; they were enthusiastic supporters of the British Empire. But Afrikaners were divided; the emotional wounds of the Boer War still suppurated. Even the Boer leaders were divided. Some, like

Louis Botha and Jan Smuts, gave their allegiance unhesitatingly to the British cause; some had doubts but cast their lot with their popular prime minister; still others, while they would not actually take up arms against the government, felt stronger cultural ties to Germany than to Britain and believed that Botha and Smuts had betrayed their people by cooperating with the British; a few did not care what side they were on but did not want to miss the excitement if there was to be a revolution. A sizcable minority raised the standard of revolt and prepared to fight, even against their own people. It was a sad time for Afrikanerdom.

In October 1914, of the three greatest leaders and heroes of the Boer War, the "Glorious Trio," Botha was committed to the British; Christiaan De Wet was preaching sedition in Orange River Colony; and the sympathies of Jacobus Hercules ("Koos") De la Rey were unknown, though it was widely believed that he would come down on the side of the rebels. Had he done so, the rebellion would undoubtedly have been more serious than it proved to be, but De la Rey was shot and killed by police when the car in which he was riding ran through a road block set up to catch some apolitical criminals.

De Wet was not the only personage to join the rebellion. Christiaan Frederik Beyers, the commandant-general (commander of the Union of South Africa's Defence Force), resigned his commission and joined the rebels. Just before the war Beyers had attended German army manoeuvres in Europe, where he had been impressed by what he had seen and flattered by the attention he received from German officers and Kaiser Wilhelm himself. He now put himself at the head of a large commando of rebel burghers.

General Jan Christoffel Greyling Kemp, in charge of the Union's training camp at Potchefstroom, was another senior officer who resigned his commission and became a rebel. The most dangerous rebel of them all, however, was Colonel Salomon Gerhardus ("Manie") Maritz, who commanded a border military district with his headquarters at Upington.

Maritz was ordered to Pretoria, but he refused to obey.

An officer sent to Upington to assess the situation there reported that "Maritz and the majority of his officers were openly saying that they would not go to German South-West Africa [to fight]. Seditious talk was rife in the camp." Smuts, as minister of defence, ordered the Imperial Light Horse and the Durban Light Infantry, two of the best units in the Union Defence Force, to Upington to operate independently of Maritz.

On 9 October 1914 Maritz declared himself for the rebels and made an emotional speech to his troops, most of whom were young soldiers, seventeen to twenty-one years old. He gave them one minute to join him or be arrested. All but about sixty did so; the stout loyalists were made prisoner and turned over to the Germans. Throughout the Transvaal and Orange River Colony there were rallies, meetings, much wild rhetoric, and some confused fighting.

The first official announcement of the rebellion was made on 26 October when Botha himself took the field against the rebels. A convoy of ships carrying Australian troops was nearing the Cape and the Imperial government in London offered them to Botha, but they were refused. In fact, to reduce intercommunity tensions, he deliberately used mostly loyalist Afrikaners to put down the rebellion. Volunteers and reserves were hastily assembled and equipped. Dr. A. Cecil Alport, a reserve captain, was given four hours to take the field, and he rushed about frantically collecting drugs, bandages, splints, dental forceps, and surgical instruments; a ramshackle laundry cart was commandeered from an Indian and given to him as an ambulance, and off he went.

Botha ordered 6,000 horsemen and several field guns to assemble at Vereeniging in the southern Transvaal and he went there to take personal charge. His aim was to capture De Wet, although no one knew where he was. As soon as he arrived at Vereeniging, he hurried to the post office to telephone Smuts, but before he could place his call, the telephone rang and a voice at the other end whispered a curious message: "Several of us were put here as prisoners at the

Mushroom Valley farmhouse by De Wet. We are locked in this room with the telephone. The general and his staff are just in front of the house. He intends camping here until tomorrow. I can say no more for fear of being discovered and shot. Please tell General Botha." Although De Wet was, in fact, leaning against a telephone pole at the time, it never occurred to him that his prisoners could simply pick up the telephone and call for help. Botha at once heliographed to two of his generals on his flank and set off with his horsemen for Mushroom Valley, about 60 miles northeast of Bloemfontein.

Most of those in the rebel camp were still sleeping when early on the morning of 12 November the shells from Botha's guns burst among them. De Wet managed with difficulty to quell the initial panic and there was a fierce fight before Botha drove home his attack and the rebels broke and fled, racing for nearby mountains. As he crossed the battlefield on his white horse, De Wet wept as he saw old Boer comrades among the dead and wounded. Perhaps he wept too for his lost cause, for the back of the rebellion was broken in Mushroom Valley. His failure had cost him dearly, most tragically in the death of his son, Danie, killed a few days earlier in a skirmish.

De Wet and a handful of his followers escaped into the Kalahari Desert, pursued by Colonel Coenraad ("Coen") Brits, one of Botha's best and most colourful senior officers, who had rounded up a fleet of motor cars, piled his troops into them, and on 1 December 1914 ran to ground De Wet and his exhausted men and horses.

Beyers and the rebels with him were also soundly thrashed, and Beyers himself was drowned while trying to escape across the Vaal River. Kemp escaped by leading his men on an extraordinarily arduous trek across the Kalahari Desert to German territory. He was later captured by General Louis Jacob ("Jaap") van Deventer and given a short prison term. After the war Kemp entered politics and in 1924 was minister of agriculture. Manie Maritz also made good his escape. When the campaign in South-West Africa ended he fled over the border into Angola and spent the rest of the war in exile in Portugal and Spain. He returned to South Africa in 1923 and during World War II led a pro-Nazi, anti-Semitic movement until killed in a motor car accident in 1940.

There were small pockets of resistance elsewhere, but these were quickly stamped out. Botha offered an amnesty to all rebels who surrendered by 15 November 1914, and this deadline was extended to 12 December, and finally to the twenty-first. As in all civil wars, neighbors and relatives were pitted against neighbors and relatives. A teen-aged loyalist scout captured his rebel father, who swore, "My lad, just wait until this business is over. I'll have a few words with you at home!"

It was often difficult to distinguish friend from foe. Botha ordered his men to wear a white handkerchief tied around their arms, but this was not a universal practice. A loyalist carrying mail to the Durban Light Infantry met a mounted man who made him prisoner, but he managed to seize a knife and turn on his captor; both were mortally wounded in the struggle and their blood stained many of the letters that were eventually delivered. Sadly, both were loyalists.

In all, about 11,500 rebels took up arms against the government; they were opposed by some 30,000 loyalists. Government casualties were 347 killed and wounded; rebel losses were 540.

The revolt was "the saddest experience of my life," said Louis Botha. "The war—our South African War—is but a thing of yesterday. You will understand my feelings, the feelings of loyal commandos when among the rebels' dead and wounded, we found from time to time men who had fought in our ranks during the dark days of the campaigns."

On 28 November Admiral King-Hall was informed that the South African government was ready to resume the campaign in German South-West Africa. Botha had saved the Union of South Africa for the British Empire and he had done it through the exercise of those qualities which made this largely uneducated man a great leader: tact, foresight, magnanimity, a deep understanding of the strengths and weaknesses of his own people, and superb organizing skills. These qualities were about to be put to use again as he personally led his men to German South-West Africa.

The Conquest of German South-West Africa

The Union of South Africa's army that set off to conquer German South-West Africa was a mixed bag of volunteers and regulars, a few Imperial troops, a regiment of Rhodesians, some foreign adventurers, and even a squadron of armoured cars supplied by the Royal Navy.

Among the foreign adventurers attracted to the fight was "Scotty Smith," whose real name was said to be George St. Leger Gordon Lennox. He was said to have campaigned on India's North-West Frontier, to have fought in the Carlist wars in Spain, and to have pioneered in Australia before coming to South Africa where, after a brief career in the Frontier Mounted Police, he turned freebooter, leading a band of outcasts on the border of Bechauanaland (Botswana). Notorious for general lawlessness, he was particularly noted for cattle rustling. Nevertheless, he regarded himself as a loyal patriot of the British Empire and he

Rhodesian troops resting in German South-West Africa

faithfully served Botha as a scout and guide.

Although never very numerous, the foreigners who joined the Union forces came from every corner of the globe. Major Toby Taylor once settled down to enjoy a cake his wife had sent him. With him were a few friends, each, as it happened, from a different part of the Empire. When a German baroness, the wife of a German officer, appeared and spoke to them in perfect English, they gallantly invited her to join them. The baroness seated herself and after introductions looked around at them and remarked, "We seem to be fighting the whole damn world."

Most of the volunteers served in what was called the Mounted Burgher Corps. These were burghers who fought much as Boers had fought for more than a century, in horse commandos of friends and neighbors. Dr. H.F.B. Walker, who served as one of their medical officers, described them: "They are all ages—some mere lads, others are grandfathers no doubt; but on the whole they are a likely-looking lot of men well above average size and inured to camp life and hardship. The oldest among them fought at Majuba [1881]

and most remember Tugela [Boer War battles, 1899–1899]."
Many of the older burghers had wounds to show; one had
eleven with two British bullets still in him, yet, said Walker,
"He is willing to extend the British Empire because General Botha is doing so."

The burghers wore nondescript clothing; often a coloured bandana was tied around the neck. Bandoliers of ammunition were draped over each shoulder and a rifle was carried in a leather bucket attached to the saddle; an overcoat, one blanket, a large water bottle, a mess tin and a haversack constituted their entire equipment. Each man supplied his own horse and saddle.

Dr. Walker, an Englishman, found his patients eccentric: "The burghers certainly like to have doctors when they go into action, but they expect nothing elaborate. Just a bandage when hit, a little something out of a flask, and the assurance that they cannot possibly recover, satisfies. But that assurance must come from a real doctor, and they shout loudly until he comes. . . . Transport of wounded, hospitals and operations are things that do not worry the average Boer general."

The mounted burghers had elan, energy and endurance; they were formidable fighters, but they lacked discipline. Brave though most of them were, they were not always dependable. One small commando sent on a sweeping movement to get behind a German force was diverted by the spoor of big game and took time out to hunt. A few found war too much for them. During a small battle at Lutzputs a burgher from Cape Province put spurs to his horse and bolted. He did not draw rein for twenty miles. When he was stopped by an officer and placed under arrest, he protested: "My God, mister, you don't understand. They tried to shoot me!"

"I understand well enough," said the officer grimly as he took out his notebook. "What is your name."

"It don't matter about my name. Just write the most terrified man on God's earth."

Not everyone, certainly, admired the burghers. Among

the volunteers in the 1st Rhodesia Regiment was twenty-two-year-old Arthur Harris, who was to win fame in World War II as Air Chief Marshall Sir Arthur ("Bomber") Harris. Later in life he expressed his opinion of those he had marched among: "I have ridden with colonial troops and shot with colonial troops and been shot at by colonial troops, and I have no hesitation whatever in saying that the dominion and colonial troops are, on average, with remarkably few exceptions, damned bad horsemen and damned bad shots."

There were other complaints. The burghers had to be kept moving, for they followed few of the rules that must govern a fixed camp. Regulars and volunteer infantry did not want to be bivouacked beside them. One soldier explained why:

> They brought with them swarms of flies. This was not simply because of their horses. They had no idea of camp sanitation and caused considerable concern to the infantry who were alongside them. Apparently war as they had known it was one of movement. They never expected to stay long in any camp and therefore were not particular about hygiene.

They certainly lacked spit and polish. They neither wore uniforms nor saluted their officers. Indeed, their officers took their ranks lightly. Coen Brits, elevated to the rank of brigadier general, ran out of liquor before the end of the campaign and discovered that the only man to have a full bottle was a private in his command. Told that he could not drink with a mere private, Brits immediately promoted him to second lieutenant. When the two had convivially finished the bottle, Brits demoted the lieutenant to the ranks.

There was, of course, some friction between the regulars and the burghers, between the English speakers and the Afrikaners, and between staff and combatant officers. In his diary for 22 April Dr. Walker wrote: "Sand has blown into the wheels of the army with resulting friction, and there has been a good deal of petty quarrelling." And five days later he added: "The fighting leaders have Afrikaner ideas and the administrative leaders have European ideas. The two at present are no more miscible than oil and water." Perhaps only Botha, the first prime minister of any country to lead his men to battle personally, was capable of keeping them all together pushing for a common goal.

When Cornelius van Wyk, chief of the Rehobeth Bastards, learned of Botha's arrival at Swakopmund, he hastened to meet with him and to offer the services of his people in the fight against the Germans. It was only with difficulty that the tactful Botha was able to persuade him that his help was not needed, for this was a "white man's war"— though Botha probably avoided that expression, for some of the Bastards had fairer complexions than his own.

From Swakopmund, one of the largest German towns on the coast, Botha intended to move inland and attack Windhoek, the capital of German South-West Africa, 175 miles away. The troops assembled here constituted Northern Force; the troops left in place in the south during the rebellion had not been strong enough to be aggressive, but Southern Force, as it was now called, had fought a few skirmishes and had pushed a railway fifty miles inland from Lüderitzbucht.

Swakopmund is today regarded as a "vacation resort," but no one would have so described it in the summer of 1914. It boasted of a number of heavy German buildings which only constant labour saved from being buried by the shifting sands. The drinking water, pumped from wells four miles away, was unpalatable. One soldier wrote:

> The flies . . . are numerous as the sea sands, and are very energetic and voracious. The days are hot and windy, the nights are cold and damp. The water is bad, and there is not much of it. . . . Our food is contaminated with dust, dirt and flies.

For the first four months the Germans enjoyed clear if ineffective air superiority. They had two airplanes, an Aviatik P–14 and an LGF Pfiel, but these could only fly in the relative cool of the early morning. Lacking aerial bombs, they simply dropped four-inch artillery shells with tails attached.

Since the South Africans merely moved out of their camps each morning, the airplanes did little damage. In March the first British aircraft arrived, two BE2c airplanes provided by the Royal Navy along with three pilots. The airframes, built of wood, stood little chance against the ravages of the climate and fell apart. By May, however, the British had six Henri Farnhams with steel airframes and nine-cylinder, water-cooled engines. Botha was delighted, but in fact they arrived too late and contributed little except for some reconnaisance.

Botha, his staff, his hundred-man bodyguard and his teenaged son, Jantje, arrived at Swakopmund on 11 February 1915. His eldest son was already serving. When a friend expostulated with Botha for bringing young Jantje on the campaign, he replied: "Look here, I am asking thousands of fathers and mothers in South Africa to send their sons to me. How could I afterwards face them and say, 'I thought my second son too young so I left him behind in safety?' "

Soon after Botha's arrival three strong commandos of mounted burghers reached Walfish Bay. They were under experienced, able leaders: Martinus Wilhelmus Myburg, Coenraad (Coen) Brits, and Manie Botha (a nephew of General Botha). The Union forces now had firm bases in both the central and southern parts of German South-West Africa. With the buildup of men and supplies almost complete Union columns began to press into the interior.

It was time for the action to begin, for the troops were becoming restless. There had been some fighting in the south when Maritz and a force of rebel Afrikaners and Germans attacked Upington and were beaten back by Colonel Louis van Deventer, but the soldiers in Northern Force were bored and impatient for the campaign to begin in their part of the colony. Some, who had enlisted for only six months, demanded their discharge. Many wanted to return to their farms, which they claimed were falling into ruin while they senselessly fought a war that was no concern of theirs.

As the Union forces moved inland across the Namib desert they encountered two German tactics which they denounced as "outrages against the rules of civilized warfare": poisoned wells and land mines. Botha sent strong protests to Colonel Viktor Francke, the new commander of the *Schutz-truppe*,* who countered that mines were perfectly legal and that he had a right to poison wells as long as they were marked as poisoned. The Germans did indeed leave notices, signs that sometimes blew down and sometimes were not heeded or noticed by thirsty soldiers. No one is known to have died, though some were made ill. In any case, the water was naturally so bad that it was difficult to know if or when the Germans had made it worse.

Dr. A. C. Alport of the 20th Mounted Rifles found a way to test water that was fast, effective and, he thought, amusing:

> I appointed my native boy, Klaas, a temporary, acting lance corporal without pay or allowances, his duty as an NCO being that of unofficial water taster to the regiment. . . . The principle of the test, of course, was that if he died we knew the water was poisoned, whereas if he continued to inflict his presence upon us there was nothing to fear, and we were thus justified in quenching our thirst at the well.

Only at the end of the campaign did Dr. Alport muse about his test. "It has sometimes occurred to me," he said later, "that I was taking an undue risk in assuming that there wasn't any substance lethal enough to cut short the picturesque career of that nigger of mine."

Some water was brought by ship from Cape Town, 800 miles away, and army engineers ("The Galloping Gasfitters") built water storage tanks, but some of this water too became contaminated before it was drunk. Botha himself fell ill. The exact nature of his disorder is not known and was perhaps unknown at the time, a stomach disorder, of some sort for which his doctor simply described a diet of eggs and fresh milk, neither of which were to be found at

---

* Colonel von Hydebreck, the previous commander, was blown up when an aerial bomb being shown to him accidently exploded.

Swakopmund. Cows, poultry, and Botha's wife and married daughter were brought in by warship. Mrs. Botha, née Annie Emett, a kinswoman of Robert Emmet, the Irish revolutionary, at once set up housekeeping in a building just north of the jetty. Dr. Walker took a picture ("a snap") of the house and described it: "The General's underclothing was drying in the yard, and his fowls were in the same place, acting up to their responsibilities, with a cow or two as well standing about."

Annie Botha not only nursed her husband but also put her hand in at the military hospital, where she was shocked by the condition of the sick and wounded, and by the laziness and incompetence of the male nurses. She set about improving matters and appears to have done so without provoking resentment. On 17 March, just before she and her daughter returned home, an Irish regiment gave them a farewell concert.

The Germans appear not to have suffered so much from the bad water; perhaps because they seldom drank it. Commander Whittall wrote:

> Every enemy camp we occupied, every place in which a German patrol had halted for an hour, had its quota of beer bottles. Where any number of them had stayed for a night, the number of empties left behind was a positive insult to people who had nothing to drink but the brakish water of the country, and too often not enough of that.

Near Swakopmund the Imperial Light Horse, a South African Regiment, put out a cossack post on a kopje, but kept it there only during the day; at night the Germans occupied the position. It was the kind of silly situation that armies sometimes arrive at. One morning the South African troopers found several bottles of beer and a note asking for cigarettes in exchange. The cigarettes were left, beginning a barter arrangement that flourished for several days until a sharp eyed ILH sergeant noticed the head of a steel pin or rod protruding just above ground that appeared to have been freshly disturbed. Wisely he sent for an engineer officer, who dug up a crude mine of a kind the South Africans were frequently to encounter.

They were made by packing dynamite into a T-piece of ordinary quarter-inch water pipe. A glass tube in the cross section held the detonating compound. A thin steel rod in the long part of the T had one end resting on the glass tube; the other end projected about a half inch above the ground when the mine was buried. When stepped on, the rod broke the glass tube and detonated the charge. These mines were not as lethal as they might have been, for the Germans counted on the blast itself to kill or maim; they did not include stones, nails, or other hardware to be spewed out when the mine exploded.

The South Africans declared such mines "a very unfair and unsportsmanlike way of fighting." On a few occasions the Union troops were so angered by their use that, according to one officer, "they were with difficulty restrained from putting Germans to death who happened to be in their hands at the moment." However, these infernal machines were, as Colonel Francke maintained, legitimate weapons of war. The Germans used them liberally, and a few South African soldiers were actually killed by them.

In mid-February Botha lauched his major drive inland. There were several stiff fights, for the Germans made a creditable resistance, but there was progress. On the Southern Front van Deventer pushed out from Upington and Lüderitzbucht. An eastern column of 2,000 men under C.A.L. Berrangé marched against the railway from Kuruman and on 14 April joined up with van Deventer.

On 11 April Jan Smuts took command of Southern Force, which by this time had formed a giant semicircle around the Germans in the south. Within three days his columns were in motion, converging on the central railway that ran down the length of the colony and which the Germans would have to use on their retreat north.

For Botha's Northern Force, crossing the Namib desert was the most trying part of the advance. Major H. F. Trew of Botha's bodyguard spoke of it as "one of the most awful scenes of desolation to be found on the face of the globe. . . . For miles and miles it stretches, a great empty expanse of grey plain; with a thin sandy surface crust covered with small pebbles." On the eighth and ninth of March a strong wind blew down tents and the temperature soared to 132° F. Under the blazing sun millions of beetles emerged from the ground, opening holes in the baked earth.

The Germans retreated slowly, stubbornly resisting the advancing Union columns and counterattacking when opportunity offered. They were, of course, operating upon interior lines and they were well supplied with artillery, machine guns, ammunition, and stores. On the night of 25 April a column of South Africans and Rhodesians under Colonel P.C.B. Skinner was sent out to reconnoitre the railway line beyond Trekkopjes and collided with a German force moving to attack the Union forces. Skinner drew back to Trekkopjes, where the Germans followed him, attacking with two batteries of artillery at first light. Skinner could not reply to the German guns for his only artillery was a home-made anti-aircraft contraption: a fifteen-pounder mounted on a wagon wheel that the soldiers named "Skinny Liz" and which could "only shoot at the sky."

Fortunately, the naval armoured car unit under Lieutenant Commander Whittall had arrived at Trekkopjes just two days before and now saw action for the first time. The cars had been spotted by German aviators but had been mistaken for field kitchens. Moving quickly to the German flank, the armoured cars' machine guns proved decisive when the Germans put in their infantry attack. After a five-hour battle the Germans drew off, having lost 14 dead, 14 wounded, and 13 taken prisoner. The Union force lost 8 killed and 34 wounded.

Botha skilfully blended Boer and British fighting methods, but the Zulu style double envelopement was his favourite. While his regular infantry advanced steadily in the centre, he sent mounted burghers in wide encircling movements to come in on the German flanks or rear. His first major objective was Karibib, the Germans' principal railway centre, and it was hoped that its fall would decide the fate of Windhoek and its all-important wireless. The Germans concentrated a large force at Karibib as though to make a stand, but as the Union forces steadily advanced, they fell back on Windhoek. On 5 May the South African Irish entered Karibib without opposition, followed the next day by the Rand Rifles and Botha himself.

Meanwhile, Southern Force under Smuts had fought a major engagement at Gibeon on 25–26 April, but, although it ended in a Union victory, it was not as complete as Smuts had hoped it would be. The South Africans failed to cut the railway line behind the Germans, who were able to make an orderly retreat by train. It scarcely mattered. The end of the campaign was near.

Instead of making a stand to defend the colonial capital, the *Schutztruppe* retreated north to Omaruru, taking most of their prisoners with them. Windhoek, the territorial objective of the campaign, was occupied without a fight. The negotiations for the surrender of the town were carried on by telephone from Karibib—it was that kind of war.

On 13 May 1915 Botha's valet wrote a note to Annie Botha: "Dear Madame and all, me and the General took Windhoek yesterday. The General keeps well."

The Victorious South Africans

O n his way to accept the formal surrender of Windhoek, Botha's great green Vauxhall sank in the sand of the dry riverbed of the Swakop. The day was hot. Botha and his staff officers, all now stranded, steadily mopped their faces as driver and passengers made futile efforts to free the car. Lieutenant Colonel Trew, who was there, wrote:

> Then sailing past us, came an old model Ford driven by a Boer commandant with a long beard. It had no bonnet, it emitted clouds of smoke and steam, and nearly every part of it was held together with green rimpies [leather thongs]. The old gentleman saluted the general as he drove steadily past. The latter looked at the old Ford, and then at his fifteen hundred pound car, and shrugged his shoulders.

Everyone was eager to see Windhoek, and indeed it was quite different from the other towns they had seen in South-West Africa. Trew was impressed:

Coming out of the sterile desert, Windhoek was to us a revelation, and a great tribute to German colonization. . . . Windhoek is situated in some low hills and is very picturesque. All of the buildings are of modern type, except one most interesting model, built high up on a hill, representing an old German castle. At the back of the town lies a rich green valley, where are situated the farms which supply the city with fruits and vegetables. Dominating everything were the great steel masts of the wireless station, at that time the biggest unit south of the line. The government buildings are most ornate, and would have done credit to any city in the world.

Grand as the town seemed to soldiers tramping out of the Namib, it probably held not more than 8,000 people and only the main street, the Kaiser Wilhelmstrasse, was paved. Nevertheless, it was not without its attractions. The retreat of the German government and the *Schutztruppe* had left stranded several thousand women and children. Dr. Walker noted that "many of the women were young, earning a living as typists, teachers, telephonists, and barmaids. Their means of livelihood suddenly cut off, and the wages due to them in many cases unpaid, their position has become desperate." A number of these unfortunates turned to prostitution, a lucrative occupation in a town filled with soldiers who had long been marching about in the desert.

Union staff officers discovered "a sort of private club for the officers of the German staff" presided over by a beautiful young Austrian woman named Regina who, while protesting her loyalty to the German cause, happily sold vintage French cognac to the South Africans. According to one officer, "Regina was easy to look at, and like all Viennese, full of the joy of life." On several evenings she invited a girl friend and the two danced with the young officers to the music of the club's gramophone.

On 11 May Theodor Seitz, governor of German South-West Africa, speaking with Botha by telephone, asked for a meeting to discuss terms. A forty-eight-hour armistice was arranged, beginning on 20 May, and Giftkop, a spot thirty miles north of Karibib was selected for the meeting. Botha and some of his staff motored there without incident in Botha's Vauxhall and met Governor Seitz and Colonel Francke under a tree.

The Germans were ready with their proposals, which *The Times* sputtered "would have been insolent if they had not had the appearance of being put forward in all serious- ness." All fighting was to stop and each side was to retain the territory it now held, with the understanding that when the war in Europe ended, South Africa would return the colony to Germany and, along with the other defeated Allies, pay suitable compensation. Until that time, the northern portion of the colony would remain in German hands with a neutral zone between the German and Union forces.

Botha listened politely and then said softly, almost casu- ally, "My terms are unconditional surrender." With each side adamant, the meeting ended. Botha collected his staff and climbed back into his motorcar.

There was now a short pause in the campaign while Botha reinforced and resupplied his army. Those who had been fighting in the south were brought round to Swakopmund and hurried northeast. By 18 June he was ready to con- tinue his advance. Two days later his troops entered Oma- ruru, from which the German government had recently beaten a hasty retreat, and on 1 July Coen Brits marched on to Otavi. Botha again paused to allow his hard-march- ing infantry to catch up. In this hot and dusty country they had marched for six days on quarter rations of water and for many more days on half rations; the last eighty miles to Otavi were covered in just four days. The Germans were ready once more to discuss terms. A second truce was arranged.

Unaware of the truce, Myburgh's burghers were engaged in a wide sweep around the German left flank, a long ride through desolate country. Botha had urged Myburgh to take a field ambulance along, but he had brushed aside such cosseting. "If I take an ambulance," he said, "the men will see it, they will be very tired and imagine themselves sick, and soon it will be full. If they know they will be left to die in the bush should they fall out, they will all ride through." And they did.

They routed a small German force at Gaub and had advanced to the outskirts of Tsumeb, the northernmost railway station and site of a large supply depot, when the advance guard was met by a flag of truce and given the news that a cease fire had been arranged. As they parlayed, some German soldiers opened fire. No one was hit but the enraged burghers leapt on their horses and dashed for the town, clattering down the streets and scattering everyone before them.

The Germans protested that the firing had been a mistake. They demanded that the South Africans leave town, but the burghers now had possession and they refused to go; there were heated arguments in the streets, but no shooting. Finally Myburgh arrived and demanded to talk with Botha. The Germans obliged by ringing him up on the telephone. Much to Myburgh's satisfaction, Botha declared that the truce applied only to the area around Otavi. Myburgh then demanded and got a formal surrender. The Germans had little choice.

At Tsumeb Myburgh captured vast quantities of arms, ammunition and equipment, for it was here that the Germans had stored all the war matériel with which they had intended to equip the South African rebels. Here, too, a prisoner of war camp had been established. Myburgh himself rode to the camp to release the prisoners. Someone brought a chair to the gate and he stood on it to address them, but the speech he had prepared left him. Percy Close, a teen-aged prisoner, said that "The general was so pleased with himself that his speech became merely a repetition of the welcome phrase: 'The gate is now open to you.' " Then one of the prisoners began the national anthem and they all joined in, singing lustily. Among the prisoners released were the young soldiers who had refused to join Maritz and the rebels at Upington.

On 6 July Coen Brits's burghers captured Namutoni and

released the Union officers who were held prisoner there. Among them was Lieutenant F. B. Adler of the Transvaal Horse Artillery, who had fought his guns so gallantly at Sandfontein. he borrowed a motorcar and jubilantly drove out to welcome a battery of his regiment that was part of Brits's column.

In spite of bitter complaints, the Union prisoners of war appear not to have been badly treated. At Tsumeb they were allowed knives and files with which to carve rings, brooches, crosses, and picture frames out of kameeldoorn wood. They staged plays, gave concerts, organized raccs, read books, and otherwise entertained themselves. They were paid for work they did and were given chits to buy clothes, food, tobacco, and other necessities and comforts. In some camps they could buy beer and liquor. At Tsumeb they were even issued a rum ration, though some complained that occasionally it was arak. Sometimes, too, they were allowed to shop in town.

All prisoners seem to have been given adequate food, although some complained of the "monotony of beef" and longed for mutton. At Tsumeb the prisoners were frequently employed at the railway yard or the warehouses, where they quickly learned to steal. One sold a pair of slippers to a guard for five shillings, a piece of chicanery that awed Percy Close. It was, he said, "a bold stroke, considering that the slippers bore military marks on the soles."

In addition to the rules laid down by the Germans, the prisoners themselves set their own, which punished those who broke them more harshly than did the Germans. One unfortunate was "court-martialed" and sentenced to be "strapped" three times on his bare back for drinking water from the water ladle. Being guarded by non-whites seems to have been the greatest indignity the prisoners endured. Young Percy Close once entered in his diary: "This afternoon we felt very depressed, but the feeling was excusable. We had never expected the Germans would descend so low as to guard white men with Hottentots."

At Tsumeb Myburgh was thirty miles behind the forti-

German prisoners of war entrain, December 1915

fied camp Francke had constructed. The end had come for
the Germans, and on 9 July 1915 they surrendered. Although
their surrender was unconditional, Botha gave them most
generous terms. Officers were allowed to retain their arms,
but not allowed ammunition. Reservists, however, could
return to their farms with both rifles and ammunition, "for
it was necessary that they should have the means of self-
protection against the natives."

Botha came under much criticism, both in South Africa
and in Britain, for his leniency. *The Times* expostulated,
"For an enemy who had fought the campaign with every
foul device that a malign ingenuity could invent, had poisoned wells, and had treated prisoners with infamous and
deliberate brutality, those terms were ... generous to a
fault."

This was not the only occasion on which Botha had been
criticized. The war was won none too soon for his career.
He had now to hurry home and mend his political fences.

In his farewell speech to his men he said: "When you
consider the hardships we met, the lack of water, the poi-

soned wells, and how wonderfully we were spared, you must realize and believe in God's hand protecting us and it was due to His intervention that we are safe today." South African and Rhodesian casualties had indeed been astonishingly low: 113 killed in action or died of wounds, 153 died of diseases and accidents, and 263 were wounded. The Germans by contrast suffered 1,331 killed.

When London asked Botha to cable a list of those whom he recommended for honours, he initially refused. "I will make no recommendations," he said. "When I think of the fighting in France and what our troops are suffering there, it seems to me that we have done nothing." But they had. They had fought the only land campaign of the war planned, executed and successfully concluded entirely on its own responsibility by a British dominion. John Ewing, when he came to write of this campaign for *The Cambridge History of the British Empire,* described it as "one of the neatest and most successful campaigns of the Great War." At small cost and with great credit to itself, the Union had rendered an immense service to the Empire." Botha's victory "increased the security of the ocean line of communication between England and the East, and it also added to the security of the Union itself."

There were enthusiastic crowds on hand to greet the returning heroes, and they were glad to be back, bringing with them the memories of their experiences and their souvenirs. The colourful Coen Brits brought back a German field gun, which the customs officials initially refused to admit, declaring that only the government could import artillery. Brits, not one to be deterred by mere regulations, flew into a passion and stormed: "You lazy hounds! I had to ride hard to capture this cannon. Now it is going to stand on my farm stoep. You say I can't land it; I have on this ship fifteen hundred burghers who say I can." The gun was landed and in due time graced the stoep of Brits's farm.

When Botha landed at Cape Town on 30 July he was met by a huge crowd and attended a reception in his honour. At Pretoria, too, when he spoke from the balcony of the

Union Building, he looked over a sea of 12,000 upturned faces. Almost all of them were white, and most belonged to English South Africans; his own Afrikaners had become suspicious of the motives of a man some sneeringly dubbed "Botha Triumphans." Botha maintained: "We took the difficult course, and that was the road of honour, truth and justice!" Was it? Many of his countrymen were unsure. Botha had become a greater hero in England than in South Africa.

9

War Comes to German East Africa

On New Year's Eve 1913 on board the S.S. *Admiral* off the east coast of Africa a middle-aged German officer brought champagne to the beautiful young Danish woman with whom he had become friendly. She was not yet a famous writer and he was not yet a famous general, though the foundations of their reputations lay in the near future. Twenty-four-year-old Karen [Isak] Dinesen was on her way to Mombasa to marry Bror Blixen, a Swedish baron who had taken up farming in British East Africa; Oberst-leutnant [Lieutenant Colonel] Paul Emil von Lettow-Vorbeck was on his way to Dar-es-Salaam to take up his appointment as commander of German East Africa's *Schutztruppe*.

"He has been such a friend to me," wrote Dinesen to her mother. Remembering him in later years, she wrote: "He belonged to the olden days, and I have never met another German who has given me so strong an impression of what Imperial Germany was and stood for."

Lettow-Vorbeck seemed indeed a perfect representative

Paul von Lettow-Vor-
beck

of all that was best in pre-war German *kultur;* he was an
officer and a gentleman. Born on 20 March 1870 at Saar-
louis in West Saar, near the French border, he was the son
of a general. After attendance at the best military schools,
he was commissioned in the artillery and served with the
German contingent that was part of the international force
sent to fight the Boxers in China (1900–01). While there he
was struck by "the clumsiness with which English troops
were moved and led in battle." It was something he did not
forget. In 1904 he served as adjutant to the egregious General von Trotha during the Herero rebellion in South-West
Africa, in which he was wounded in the eye and chest. This
was followed by service with marines at Wilhelmshaven.
Then, after serving on a mission to Norway, he was sent to
command the *Schutztruppe* in the Cameroons. Probably no
other German officer of his rank had seen as much active

service or had served in such varied posts.

Lettow-Vorbeck was a thoroughly professional soldier who took his soldiering seriously. Some thought him arrogant and overly strict. One subordinate said of him: "Life in his immediate neighborhood was a trifle oppressive." He spoke almost flawless English, and British officers who met him in China liked him. Brigadier General C. P. Fendall described him as "a tall, spare, square-shouldered man, with close-cropped grey hair, and a clear eye that looked you square in the face. He had the bearing of a Prussian guardsman, but none of the bluster usually attributed to such. His manner was just what it should have been, courteous and polite."

A medical officer thought that "understanding of human nature did not seem to be von Lettow's strong suit." But his career and campaigns in Africa would seem to indicate that he understood human nature very well indeed. Certainly he knew how to get the most out of those who served under him, and he did not do this by browbeating. He insisted on the best from his officers and men, white and black, but he recognized men's frailties, knew well that not all men can endure hardships with equal stoicism or face bullets with equal courage. Strict but fair, he inspired an exceptional loyalty in his African troops (askaris). Aaron Segal said that "one of his great abilities was to take the African precisely as he found him, without any transfer of European mores." He seems to have been unique among European officers in his conviction that "the better man will always outwit the inferior, and the colour of his skin does not matter."

At Mombasa the *Admiral* lingered long enough for Lettow-Vorbeck to dine ashore at the Mombasa Club with Miss Dineson and her fiance. He gave her an autographed photograph of himself on horseback. They expected to meet again soon; she had agreed to find ten good breeding mares for his *Schutztruppe*, but the war came too soon. More than twenty-five years were to pass before they met again: at the beginning of another war.

At Dar-es-Salaam (the name means "haven of peace")

Lettow-Vorbeck reported to the governor, Dr. Heinrich Schnee (1871–1949). The two men were almost the same age, but this was their only similarity. Schnee was born in Neuhaldesleben, a small town in Hanover. His paternal grandfather was a Lutheran minister and his father a respected member of the judicial bureaucracy. Young Schnee had a proper middle-class education and studied jurisprudence and constitutional law at Heidelberg, Kiel, and Berlin, becoming a doctor of law in 1894. He also acquired that all important social cachet, a reserve commission in the army. With all the credentials for a promising career in law or government, Schnee shocked his father by electing to make his career in the colonial service, which most regarded as a bureaucratic backwater.

After service in the south seas—Rabaul, Neu-Pommern (largest island of the Bismarck Archipelago), and Samoa—he returned to Berlin, bringing with him his British-born New Zealand wife, Ada. He wrote several books, lectured at the *Seminar für Orientalische* and rose in the ranks of the service. In 1912 he was appointed governor of German East Africa, a post formerly held only by professional soldiers or aristocrats.

He took a particular interest in education and founded nearly a thousand elementary, secondary, and vocational schools. In a speech he made in July 1914 he said:

> The natives are ignorant; they must be instructed. They are indolent; they must be taught to work. They are unclean; they must be taught cleanliness. They are ill with all manner of distempers; they must be healed. They are savage, cruel, and superstitious; they must become peaceful and enlightened. They have also the right to demand that they should be regarded as an end and not as a means. . . . We must remember that the black man is a human being.

Schnee was not the sort of person whom soldiers found engaging. General Fendall compared him to Lettow-Vorbeck:

He had not the open look, nor had he the manner, of Von Lettow. He struck me as being a small-minded man; not a man to be trusted. . . . The difference between the two men was very striking: Von Lettow gave the impression of being a regular soldier, a man of outstanding ability and a gentleman; Von Schnee [sic] of being a man of the less presentable lawyer class, full of cunning, by no means a fool, but not a gentleman.

Captain Richard Meinertzhagen, another British officer, formed a similar impression: "a nice little man, weak, no character and rather typical of all second-rate civil servants."

In the next four and a half years Schnee and Lettow-Vorbeck were fated to spend much time together, but they never learned to like each other and they seldom agreed upon anything. Nevertheless, the regulations were clear; here, as in all German colonies, the governor was the supreme commander of the military and police forces, an arrangement much resented by the officers.

There was time after Lettow-Vorbeck's arrival—eight months before the war—for him to assess the colony's military assets and to see something of this strange, wild land to which he had been posted. German East Africa had an estimated population of 7,650,000 Africans, members of more than a hundred tribes, about half of whom were crowded into the northwest corner, what is today Rwanda and Burundi. There were also 5,336 Europeans, mostly Germans with a sprinkling of other nationalities, including a number of Boers who had fled from South Africa rather than live under British rule, and about 15,000 Indians, Arabs, and Goanese.

The *Schutztruppe* contained 260 Europeans and 2,472 Africans:

      68 combatant officers
      60 warrant officers and NCOs
     132 non-combatant medical officers and officials
       2 African officers
     184 African NCOs
   2,286 askaris

The colony also had a gendarmerie of 45 Europeans and 2,154 askari police who could be added to the *Schutztruppe* in time of war. (Before the war was over Lettow-Vorbeck was to employ 3,000 Europeans and 11,000 askaris, plus uncounted thousands of carriers.)

The German askaris were comparatively well paid, receiving double the pay of an askari in the King's African Rifles (KAR), but when war began they were still armed with obsolete 1871 pattern rifles that fired cartridges using black powder. These weapons were good enough for fighting against African tribesmen equipped with spears and muskets, but they were poor weapons to carry into a war against well-armed Europeans. The *Schutztruppe* boasted 67 machine guns, but it was weak in artillery, having only 31 obsolete, small-calibre field guns.

Fourteen field companies *(Feldkompagnies)*, each made up of sixteen to eighteen Europeans and 160 to 200 Africans, formed the backbone of the *Schutztruppe*. Each company had two machine guns. The field companies were, as far as possible, self-contained units, most with their own doctor, some carrying tailors, shoemakers, and other artisans useful to a small military unit designed to live for long periods in the bush. In addition to the field companies there were rifle companies *(Schutztruppekompagnien)* and reserve companies made up of German settlers. Often, too, there were native auxiliaries, called "ruga-ruga."

The tsetse fly ruled (and still does) over much of the country. Roads were few, and fewer still were suitable for motor vehicles. Food, ammunition, and essential supplies were carried on the shoulders and heads of carriers, except along the railways that burrowed inland from the coast.

The colony's two east–west railways were marvels of German engineering. The northernmost ran from Tanga on the coast to Moshi at the foot of Kilimanjaro. This 270-mile track was known as the Usambara line. The second and longest was the Central Railway *(Mittellandbahn)*, which ran from Dar-es-Salaam on the coast to Ujiji and Kigoma on the shore of Lake Tanganyika. Each was roughly paral-

German Askaris of 21st Feldkompanie in German East Africa

lel to the Uganda Railway in British East Africa, which ran from the port of Mombasa to Lake Victoria. The railways brought western civilization inland; towns sprang up along their tracks and plantations were worked within hauling distance.

The final stretch of the Central Railway was not completed until July 1914. To celebrate its completion and German achievements in East Africa in general, a grand exposition was scheduled to open at Dar-es-Salaam on 12 August. It never took place; war was declared eight days earlier.

Although deprived of the opportunity to celebrate their accomplishments, the German did indeed have much to boast of, for they had done much within a short time for their largest colony. After an unsavoury beginning under the brutal Karl Peters, followed by nineteenth-century campaigns to subdue such warlike tribes as the Ngoni, Yao, Hehe, and Chagga, and the suppression of a serious trans-tribal insurrection (Maji-Maji Revolt) in 1905–06, German rule mellowed, grew less harsh, and turned its attention toward activities more likely to promote the prosperity and well-being of its inhabitants, black and white.

Roads and railways were built, ships were launched on Lake Tanganyika, mining was promoted, new crops were imported, and modern agricultural methods were encouraged. The slave trade was extirpated, banditry diminished, and the Arab trade monopolies eliminated. Free enterprise was encouraged; hospitals and dispensaries were built. Under Schnee a fine start was made toward providing European style education. As two American scholars* who have studied the period have affirmed: "German colonialism . . . was an engine of moderization with far-reaching effects for the future. German rule provided African people with new alternatives and a wider range of choices."

German East Africa was a vast area, 384,180 square miles, larger than France and Germany combined, and it seems remarkable that Germany was able to establish and maintain its rule with so few administrators and soldiers. It consisted of what is now mainland Tanzania and the countries of Barundi and Rwanda. It was surrounded by British East Africa (Kenya), Uganda, Northern Rhodesia (Zambia) Nyasaland (Malawi), Belgium Congo (Zaire), and, off the coast, the British protectorates of Pemba and Zanzibar—all hostile territories on the declaration of war—with only Portuguese Africa (Mozambique) to the south neutral.

It was the healthy regions of the northern part of the colony that had attracted the European settlers. Some of this land, particularly in the west, boasted spectacular scenery. Denys Reitz, a South African soldier, described it:

> The region from the Serengetti Plains on British territory, round by Kilimanjaro to Mount Meru, a hundred miles away and thence back to the Pare hills, is probably the most fascinating part of the African continent. Within this charmed circle lie game-covered plains, and swamps and jungles and impenetrable forests. There lie the snow-capped peaks of Kibu and Mawenzi with their base in the tropics and their summits wrapped

---

* L. H. Gann and Peter Duigan of the Hoover Institution.

in eternal ice and snow. There is Mount Meru like a basalt pyramid to the east, and there are lakes and craters and a network of great rivers, with strange tribes and beautiful scenery, such as no other country in the world that I know of can show within so small a compass.

The borders of the colony were not definitely fixed until 1910. The line that divided British East Africa and German East Africa made a jog at Kilimanjaro to allow Africa's tallest mountain to rest in German territory. This was done, it was said, at the whim of Kaiser Wilhelm, who expressed an interest in having it as he had no other snow-capped peak in his realm.

In his travels around the colony, Lettow-Vorbeck not only took a keen professional interest in the terrain, the flora and the climate, but he made a point of meeting with reserve officers, many of whom were important planters and some of whom would play important roles in the coming war. One of these was an old friend with a curious name for a German: Tom von Prince. He was born in Mauritius in 1866, the son of a Scots police officer and a German missionary. He was sent to school in England at an early age, but when he was orphaned soon after, his maternal relatives brought him to Germany and in due course he was enrolled at the Friederizianesche Rittcrakademie in Liegnitz, a military academy that was an excellent stepping stone to a military career. After serving for a time in the army, he went adventuring in Africa, where he served under the great explorer and soldier Hermann von Wissmann. After his marriage to a general's daughter he settled as a colonist in Africa, where he took part in numerous expeditions against recalcitrant tribes. In 1907 he was awarded the "von."

Lettow-Vorbeck found the bearded, handsome, forty-five-year-old adventurer on his farm in western Usambara about twenty miles from Lushoto, comfortably established in a large wooden house sent out from Scotland. He was frank in his assessment of Governor Schnee, whom he considered "a liberal pacifist and a weakling."

Like other German governors of colonies, Schnee hoped

that if war came German East Africa could remain neutral and he placed his hopes on the neutrality clause in the Berlin Act of 1885 that referred to the conventional basin of the Congo. Sir Charles Belfeld, governor of British East Africa, felt the same way; he, too, wanted to keep war away from this part of the world. He even regarded the gathering of intelligence about his German neighbors as something which should be resorted to only in "an extreme emergency." The threat of war was not, it seems, excuse enough. However, some unauthorized spying was being carried out.

Norman King, the British consul in Dar-es-Salaam, had begun to send out reports of military value based mostly on gossip collected on his social rounds. He frequented the clubs, including the German officers' club, and was considered a skilful bridge player. He not only passed on information, but gave his opinions of people and his own estimates of the state of affairs should war be declared. The people of Dar-es-Salaam, he reported would have "little stomach for fighting" and would be more interested in protecting their profits than their country.

King's amateur spying was sometimes too obvious. When the German cruiser *Königsberg* arrived at Dar-es-Salaam to show the flag and to be the centrepiece for the great exhibition planned for mid-August, King went aboard as a visitor and bearded the cruiser's captain, Max Loof. What, he asked casually, would be the reaction of the German navy in case of war—with Russia, of course? Loof, astonished by King's "unbelievable impudence," ordered his officers to steer clear of the British "spy consul." King skipped over to Zanzibar just before war was declared.

Belfeld had reasons as good as Schnee's for wanting to avoid war: his colony was unprepared and the single important railway and the colony's capital, Nairobi, were vulnerable to enemy attacks. Most Europeans in Africa felt that it would be unseemly for the natives to see white men fighting each other. General Fendall wrote:

There was an idea that, should war break out between England and Germany, there should be no actual fighting in Africa.

Everyone connected with the administration or colonisation believed that the tradition of inviolability of the white man must be maintained if a few hundred whites were to continue to impose their authority in governing many thousands of blacks. It was thought that it would be most dangerous to employ black troops to fight against white men. . . . It was feared that the prestige of the white man would be lowered and that the progress of civilization in Africa would be put back a hundred years.

A modern writer* has said that "Kenya settlers required armies be sent from Britain to protect them" and that "only by dint of many a massacre" were the natives subjugated. This is far from the truth. No armies, no expeditionary force, not even a battalion of regulars was ever sent out from Britain to subdue the Africans in British East Africa.

There were, of course, turbulent tribes who from time to time disturbed the peace of their neighbors. To deal with them the Colonial Office had its own little army, the King's African Rifles (KAR), made up of African soldiers (askaris) with British officers seconded from the regular army. In 1914 the KAR consisted of only 62 British officers and 2,319 askaris. These were organized into seventeen small companies, including one mounted on camels serving in the arid northern part of the colony. The KAR, more like a constabulary than an army, were dispersed over 318,941 square miles of Uganda and British East Africa—an area larger than France and Britain or Texas and Mississippi. Only three battalions were in Kenya in August 1914, and of these fewer than 150 men were in Nairobi. Most were involved in maintaining order among unruly Somalis in Jubaland, on the border of Italian Somaliland (Somalia).*

When news of the declaration of war on 4 August 1914 reached East Africa it was avidly discussed, but it seemed an event far removed from this corner of the world. It was

* Brian Lapping, *End of Empire* (1985, p. 397).
* In 1911, when one KAR battalion was disbanded, many of the discharged askaris enlisted in the *Schutztruppe*. At Neu Langenburg the garrison had so many ex-British askaris that British bugle calls and English words of command were used.

difficult to imagine that the Great War in Europe would reach so far. Nowhere were German forces within shooting distance of British or Belgian troops. On the coast the feathery palm trees waved under a hot August sky; on Lake Tanganyika there was no sudden thunder of naval gunfire; and in the interior, only the lion's roar and the busy sounds of myriads of insects broke the stillness of the nights.

10

War Comes to British East Africa

W hen word reached Nairobi that war had been declared, the town was at once beset with rumours and alarums. There were many sightings of nonexistent airplanes and zeppelins, usually at night, and hundreds of rounds were fired at bright planets and stars. It was said that the Germans had promised rewards to tribes that attacked white settlements, and so there were fears and suspicions. Certainly there was considerable excitement.

At Eldoret, on the Uasin Gishu plateau, news of the war disrupted a meeting of colonists assembled to discuss important agricultural matters. Many saddled up immediately and plunged recklessly down an ill-made road in the dark to Londiani where they could catch a train to Nairobi. Some unhitched horses or mules from wagons and set off bareback.

One of the first to volunteer was Lord Delamere—planter and breeder, "mightiest lion hunter in Africa," the man who had taken Theodore Roosevelt hunting. He was the colony's most socially prominent member and perhaps no man

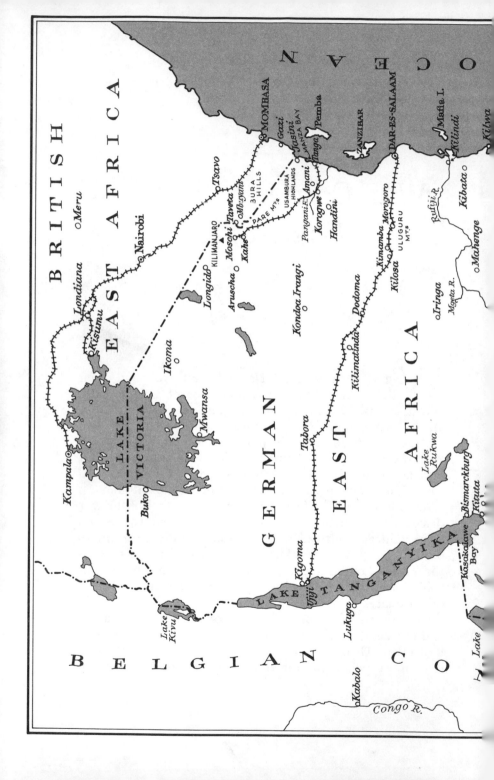

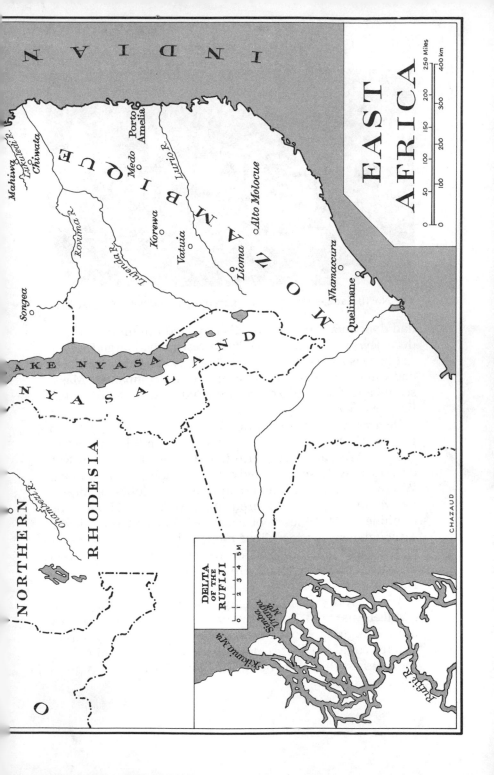

EAST
AFRICA

INDIAN

MOZAMBIQUE

NYASALAND

NORTHERN RHODESIA

LAKE NYASA

Songea

Rovuma R.

Lujenda R.

Mahiwa
Lukuledi R.
Chiwata
Medo
Porto
Amelia
Korewa
Vatuia
Lurio R.
Lioma
Alto Molocue
Nhamacura
Quelimane

Chambezi R.
Luangwa R.

CHAZAUD

DELTA
OF THE
RUFIJI

0 1 2 3 4 5 M

Simba Uranga
Kikunja Mth.

Rufiji

250 Miles
400 km

The North Lancashire Regiment arriving in Nairobi, August 1914

had done more for Kenya. His repeated attempts to introduce new crops or new breeds of livestock had largely failed,
but he was a persistent man and widely respected by blacks
and whites. He was quick to form his own company of Masai
scouts and Baron Blixen volunteered to serve as his intelligence officer.

Delamere's brother-in-law, Berkeley Cole, also hastened
to join. He had served as an officer in the 9th Lancers in
the Boer War, and later, with Lord Cranford, ran what was
described as "a small, rowdy frontier hotel" at Londiana.
When war came he was farming on the slopes of Mount
Kenya. A slight, red-haired man with fine bones, he
reminded Isak Dinesen of a cat, sensual and prejudiced.
Although he was a fastidious man, he harboured a taste for
violence and untamed natures; he quickly recruited a troop
of wild Somali irregulars. He was joined by Denys Finch-
Hatton, Isak Dinesen's lover.

All the young men were eager for war. C. J. Thornhill,
eighteen years old, had been out in the bush and it was not
until 9 August that he heard that war had been declared.
"I felt I could hardly breathe until I joined something," he
said. At first there was nothing to join. There was no regu-

lar units of white troops and the colonial government was unwilling even to add officers to the KAR. Nevertheless, eager volunteers continued to pour into Nairobi, filling the clubs and hotels. Without official support and in a helter-skelter fashion they organized themselves.

Nairobi House somehow became the centre for organizing volunteer units, and it was soon filled with bronzed men in bush shirts and broad-brimmed terai hats carrying elephant guns and fowling pieces. A plethora of volunteers, calling themselves by such names as Bowker's Horse, the Plateau South Africans, the Legion of Frontiersmen, and Wessel's Scouts, were soon formed. Many of the volunteers were former officers, or of the officer class, but had to serve in the ranks in spite of their background. Most were content to do so and a former captain of a famous regiment served as sergeant of a machine gun section.

There were, of course, non-British colonists—Canadians, Americans, Scandinavians, and other Europeans—and those from neutral countries agonized over their place in the war. The Swedes met at Baron Blixen's farm and decided they would offer their services to their adopted land provided they could be excused from duty if Sweden joined the war on Germany's side.

Almost all of the hurriedly assembled volunteer units were soon subsumed into two larger units: the East Africa Regiment and the East African Mounted Rifles (EAMR), the latter including a company of Indians. About a hundred former KAR askaris formed a company. Lieutenant A.J.B. Wavell,* special reserve, The Welsh Regiment, an adventurer who spoke fluent Arabic and had visited Mecca in disguise, raised a company of Arabs and "Wavell's Arabs" soon distinguished themselves. A railway pioneer unit was formed and two make-do "armoured trains" were hastily put together.

Governor Belfeld gave no encouragement. He still wanted no part of the war. In a speech given at Nairobi on 10 Jan-

---

* He was a cousin of Archibald Percival Wavell, who became 1st Earl Wavell, a field marshal, and one of the last viceroys of India.

A patrol of East African Mounted Rifles

uary 1915, more than five months after the start of the war, he said: "I wish to take this opportunity to make it abundantly clear that this colony has no interest in the present war except so far as its unfortunate position places it in such close proximity to German East Africa."

Across the frontier, Governor Schnee echoed these sentiments. To the fury of Lettow-Vorbeck, Schnee forbade any aggressive action, and even prevented him from concentrating troops in the Kilimanjaro area, fearing that the British might interpret this as a belligerent gesture.

On 8 August the British cruiser *Astraea* steamed within range of Dar-es-Salaam, lobbed a few shells at the wireless station and sent an armed party into the harbour. There was no opposition and two British seamen—Thomas Cann and William Smith—lounging on the jetty, idly carved their names. A curious truce was signed: the captain of the *Astraea* agreed that the Royal Navy would not attack the town and the local German authorities, with Schnee's blessings, agreed to refrain from all hostile activities for the duration of the war, and the town settled back into its peaceful ways. A similar truce was agreed upon with the German authorities at Tanga, an important coastal town 136 miles north.

Needless to say, neither the British naval officers nor the German officials possessed the authority to make such a reasonable end to the war. The British Admiralty denounced the agreements and sent a stinging rebuke to the captain of the *Astraea;* Lettow-Vorbeck, raging at Schnee, declared that he would ignore the agreements. He went into camp at Pegu, twelve miles inland from Dar-es-Salaam, and prepared to wage war. He recruited Africans, summoned reservists, and sent word to Tom von Prince to assemble his fellow planters. Lieutenant Moritz Horn, former captain of the survey ship *Möwe,* was dispatched with a small crew to Lake Tanganyika to arm a small steamer, the *Hermann von Wissmann,* and secure command of the lake.

By late September Lettow-Vorbeck was ready to mount an attack which the British saw as a major threat: 500 askaris with six machine guns marched up the coast towards Mombasa. Volunteer units rushed to stop them and the first on the scene were Wavell's Arabs. Contesting every mile and taking heavy casualties (Wavell himself was wounded in his left arm), they slowly retreated—a trying and difficult manoeuvre for undisciplined men, for, as one of Wavell's officers said, "You must remember, our troops were only hard little water carriers." Still, they gallantly fought on until at Gazi, about twenty-five miles south of Mombasa, a KAR company joined them. The Germans, forced back, made no further attempt to capture Mombasa.*

The Southern front saw small actions. On 21 September Major A. E. Capell with some South African police took Schuckmansburg, a German river port on the Zambezi in the Caprivi Zipfel, without firing a shot. That same month

---

* A few months later Wavel and his Arabs were caught in an ambush. Wavell, although wounded in both legs, continued to fire until he was shot in the chest. He and thirty of his men were killed. It was the end of them as a military unit; without Wavell's leadership the unit disintegrated.

a force from Bismarckburg (Kasanga) on Lake Tanganyika marched into Northern Rhodesia and laid siege to Abercorn, thirty-five miles away. Only local police and a few volunteers were on hand to defend the town, but aided by African villagers who, unasked, carried water for them, and prisoners in a convict camp who volunteered to carry machine guns and ammunition, they held out for four days. At three o'clock on the morning of 9 September they were reinforced by 100 men under Major H. M. Sennett, who came up by forced marches, covering 99 miles in 72 hours. They were just in time. Three hours later the Germans launched an all-out attack. Repulsed, they fell back on the Lumi River, where, on 11 September, Lieutenant J. J. McCarthy with a force of Northern Rhodesia police attacked and scattered them.

There were small actions on the lake as well. The East African Mounted Rifles saw their first action dismounted, aboard a steamer on Lake Victoria. The steamer, the *Winifred*, had anchored early in the afternoon on 15 September at Karungu Bay in the waters of German East Africa. Boats were being lowered for a landing when shots rang out from the shore. When the *Winifred* returned the fire, the Germans opened up with machine guns, pom-poms, and a six-pounder firing shrapnel.

The EAMR volunteers lay packed on the deck, not knowing what to do. A small German steamer, the *Mwanza*, put out from shore spitting one-pound pom-pom shells. The *Winifred*'s funnel was hit and on the crowded deck some men suffered minor injuries. There were no serious casualties. "We suffered mainly from fright," confessed one participant. "Over the water the pom-pom sounded like heavy stuff to our unaccustomed ears." The *Winifred* beat a hasty retreat.

There were other small actions on the southern front. By 17 November the Germans were ready to launch another attack from Bismarckburg. Two steamers carrying troops landed at Kituta at the southern end of Lake Tanganyika only fourteen miles from Abercorn where they destroyed a small steamer and burned stores of the African Lakes Corporation. Moving on to Kasakalawe, another small lake port, the little expedition captured large quantities of telegraph material, but there a combined force of Northern Rhodesia Police and Belgian askaris fell upon them. The Germans hastily re-embarked. Allied losses were two Belgian askaris killed and ten wounded; German losses are unknown.

The most important event of the war in East Africa in its first two months was Lettow-Vorbeck's initiative in sending Tom von Prince to capture Taveta, a slice of British territory at the eastern end of the gap between the southern slopes of Kilimanjaro and the northern end of the Pare Mountains in the German colony. Taveta was only twenty-five miles from the important German town of Moshi and seventy-five miles from Voi, a station on the Uganda Railway. Prince's force, except for two troops of African police, was made up of enthusiastic volunteers, planters who brought along their servants, plenty of good food, wine and beer, and all of the ingredients for a giant picnic.

Taveta was captured after a short, sharp fight. The jubilant Prince immediately sent a message by relays of Africans on bicycles to Lettow-Vorbeck: "The German flag flies on British territory." Lettow-Vorbeck promptly sent this on to Schnee, who replied by telegraph: "What is going on? I have forbidden concentration of troops in the north. All forces and all arms are needed to protect the defenceless white population from possible native uprisings. I forbid their use in unnecessary provocation of the enemy." Lettow-Vorbeck laughed. He ignored Schnee now; eventually he would dominate him.

Prince attempted to press on and capture Voi, but he lacked the strength and was beaten back. Nevertheless, the Germans continued to occupy Taveta. It was a strategic spot, certainly the gateway to German East Africa from the interior. Thus, Lettow-Vorbeck was the only German commander in the Great War actually to occupy British territory.

On 1 September an infantry brigade under Brigadier

General J. M. Stewart arrived at Mombasa. This was the first contingent of what was labeled Indian Expeditionary Force 'C.' The days of the amateur soldiers were not yet finished, but they were fast fading. The professionals were arriving. It remained to be seen whether their performance would be better than that of the volunteers.

CHAPTER
11

The Saga of the *Königsberg*

I n the months that preceded the Great War there were a number of German men-of-war on the high seas. Particularly menacing to the British were Admiral von Spee's squadron in the Pacific and the cruisers *Emden* and *Königsberg*. The captains of the cruisers had their orders: in the event of war they were to wage a *guerre de course*, the Germans called it *Kreuzerkrieg*. They were to prey upon enemy shipping and resupply themselves from captures.

It was the S.M.S. [*Sein Majistate Schriff*] *Königsberg* that was the principal worry of Admiral King-Hall on the South African station. Built in 1905 and newly refitted at Kiel, she displaced 3,400 tons and was 126 yards long.* Slimmer and longer than comparable British vessels, she was, at 24 knots, faster than most. She carried two torpedo tubes, two 88 mm guns and ten 105 mm guns—weapons that were to

---

* The *Königsberg* was a sister ship of the *Nürnberg*, which as part of von Spee's squadron at the battle of Coronel (1 November 1914) sank the HMS *Monmouth*, a ship in Sir Christopher Cradock's ill-fated squadron.

play responsible roles in the East African Campaign. Before leaving Germany she had been stocked with all that was considered needed for a two-year cruise, and she was scheduled to arrive in German East Africa in time to be a rousing addition to the great exposition planned for Dar-es-Salaam.

On 1 April 1914 Fregattenkapatän [Commander] Max Loof took command with Korvettenkapitän [Lieutenant Commander] George Koch as first officer. Loof was a slender man with a square face and ever-present steel-rimmed spectacles. Just before leaving Kiel he bought a 9 mm hunting rifle, for he looked forward to much hunting in Africa. When he took command he gave a speech to the 322 officers and ratings of his hand-picked crew that was far from pacific: "To be strong before the enemy, to be the upholder of your country, and to remain faithful through battle and all trials until death—that will always be the supreme code of this crew!"

On 25 April, a bright, sunny day, the *Königsberg* steamed majestically out of Kiel's harbour, never to return. She cruised south, turned east through the Straits of Gibraltar and into the Mediterranean, putting in at ports in Spain and Italy, then passed through the Suez canal into the Red Sea. At Aden, Loof dined with the English governor. On 6 June she anchored in Dar-es-Salaam's friendly, perfectly sheltered harbour. The *Königsberg*, although classed as a small cruiser, was the most powerful German ship ever seen at Dar-es-Salaam. She was meant to be impressive, and she was.

As August and the war drew nearer, Captain Loof was ordered to put to sea and at 4.30 on the afternoon of 31 July the *Königsberg* cleared the harbour. Anticipating this move, Admiral King-Hall had ordered her to be followed. Thus, no sooner had Loof left Dar-es-Salaam than he found himself boxed in by three British warships: *Astraea, Hyacinth,* and *Pegasus.** They were well armed, but older and slower

---

* *Hyacinth:* 5,700 tons, 20 knots. She was 16 years old and mounted eleven 152 mm guns and eight 76 mm guns, but the shells for these guns could not penetrate the armour of more modern warships.

than the *Königsberg*. It was an anxious time. War could be declared at any moment and the side that first received the word would be able to deliver the first, possibly vital shots.

The four ships sailed along at the sedate speed of twelve knots, their captains watching each other closely. Although Loof gave orders to build up enough steam to reach twenty-two knots, he held to his speed even after the engineer reported the power available. Standing on the port side of his bridge, he chain-smoked cigarettes as he watched the *Astrea* and scanned the sky, where to the southwest a monsoon threatened. When a squall struck, he was ready. He ordered his quartermaster to turn hard to starboard and his engineer to make full speed. Curving sharply 180°, Loof easily escaped his unwelcome escort, for not only were the British ships slower but, because of peacetime regulations which prohibited captains on the South Africa station from using good Welsh coal, they had taken on inferior Natal coal. By 1 August the *Königsberg*, again travelling at an easy twelve knots, her most economical speed, was off Aden and well placed in the shipping lane of freighters using the Suez Canal.

Perhaps senior naval officers had some notion of the shape of war, at least in the beginning, but for junior officers and other ranks the outbreak of hostilities only opened emotional valves. *Something* was going to happen. They did not know what or when. Most were eager for war's excitements; some were even disappointed that action was not simultaneous with its beginning.

Lieutenant Richard Wenig was a young gunnery officer aboard the *Königsberg*, plowing through increasingly heavy seas southeast of Cape Guardafui when the news arrived, somewhat late, on the evening of 5 August by the repetition over and over of the code word "enigma," signifying that Germany was now at war with France, Russia, and Britain. Wenig found it difficult to believe that his world had, in

---

Astraea: 4,400 tons, 21 years old, mounting two 6-inch and eight 4.7-inch guns.

Pegasus: 2,170 tons, 17 years old, mounting eight 4-inch guns. She was the only British ship on the Cape station with torpedo tubes.

fact, actually changed. "Strange," he wrote. "The moon shines as before, the seas roar, the rigging wails—nothing has changed! How is that possible? Doesn't the moon need to hide in the clouds, doesn't the sea have to darken? Nothing! They smile at human affairs. What does the quarrel of atoms mean to the universe?" Young Wenig's life was to change soon enough. The next few years were to hold more perils and he was to suffer more pain that he could ever have imagined.

The passenger liner *Pentakota*, on which Clement J. Charlewood was second officer, carried no wireless; it was not until she arrived at Mombasa that he learned the war had begun. His first intimation of a change in the ways of the world was when, steaming into port, he saw a fleet of Arab dhows flying American flags. Later he learned that they were carrying British, French, and Belgian refugees from German East Africa. Charlewood was a reserve sub-lieutenant in the Royal Navy. As soon as his duties on board ended, he hurried to the bazaar in search of a tailor to sew on his uniform a single gold stripe.

News of the war's beginning did not reach Dar-es-Salaam until six o'clock in the evening on 6 August—not by way of Zanzibar, where Admiral King-Hall had, over the objections of the Colonial Office, contrived to have cables to the mainland delayed, but from the wireless station in Togoland. Lieutenant Commander Georg Zimmer, senior naval officer at Dar-es-Salaam, at once readied a supply ship, the *Somalia*, 2,550 tons, for a pre-arranged rendezvous with the *Königsberg*. Working furiously, he managed to have her loaded and clear of the harbour just in time to escape the British warships that arrived on 8 August.

Aboard the *Königsberg* Captain Loof snapped into action. He ordered Lieutenant Eberhard Niemyer, his wireless officer, to send out a signal for all German merchant ships to sail with all speed to German or neutral ports. That done, he shut down his wireless except for reception.

Loof's chief worry was lack of coal. He had left Dar-es-Salaam with 830 tons and had arranged to be re-supplied later by the *Somalia*, but he was down to 200 tons by 6 August. However, on this active day he encountered two German merchantmen, from whom he took 80 tons. He also, by accident or design, intercepted the Norddeutcher Lloyd S.S. *Zieten*, which had left Colombo, Ceylon (Sri Lanka), on 29 July bound for Germany. On board were a number of sailors and marines (including two divers) who had just finished a long tour of duty on the China station and had been looking forward to again seeing friends and relations in the Fatherland. Few ever did so, and those who did came home with bizarre tales of adventures in little-known lands, for they were taken off the *Zeiten* and put aboard the *Königsberg*.

On this same day Loof captured the 6,600 ton *The City of Winchester*, the first British merchant ship taken in the war. Loaded with choice Ceylon tea, she carried only a single gun. Loof's prize carried only inferior Bombay coal, which he decided not to use, although re-supply was uncertain at best. When he was at last able to rendezvous with the *Somalia* off the coast of Italian Somaliland (Somalia) near Guardafui, he was down to a mere fourteen tons and he had been forced to ration drinking water to one-third litre.

With 850 tons of good coal in the bunkers, full tanks of fresh water, mail from home, and plenty of supplies, the spirits of the crew from captain to stoker were high. News that the *Königsberg* was prowling the Indian Ocean shipping lanes near Aden caused merchant ships to flee to safe ports and remain there, so Loof took his ship to Madagascar, hoping to pick up French freighters, but in this part of the world Allied ships had taken shelter in the harbour of Diego Suarez under the protection of the large caliber coastal guns there.

Disappointed by a lack of prizes and again low on coal, Loof rendezvoused with *Somalia* on 23 August at the Isles of Aldabra northwest of Madagascar. This time the *Somalia* had only 250 tons to give and rough seas made the transfer difficult. The *Königsberg* took on a four-day supply and then arranged for another meeting in the delta of the Rufiji river, where the transfer of coal and supplies could be easily effected and where some much needed work could be done on her engines.

The German survey ship *Möwe* had, before she was scuttled in the Dar-es-Salaam harbour, charted the complex maze of waterways that make up the delta of the Rufiji, about 100 miles south of Dar-es-Salaam, and had found four channels deep enough to float the *Königsberg*. As this was unknown to the British, the delta of the Rufiji was probably the safest haven in Africa. On 3 September the *Königsberg* passed over the bar of the Simba Ouranga branch of the delta in five meters of water—just enough. German officials ashore provided Loof with the latest maps, fresh fruit, facilities for repairs, and a resupply of coal. Lieutenant Niemyer rigged up field telephones and telegraph lines; a coastwatching service was established and all possible measures were taken to protect the cruiser during a period when she would be vulnerable.

The *Königsberg* was almost completely ready for sea again when on 19 September Loof received word that a British warship had entered the harbour at Zanzibar. It was HMS *Pegasus*, Captain J. A. Inglis. Although undersized and undergunned, she had been left alone and unprotected to undergo repairs to her engines and boilers when it was known that the *Königsberg*, three times her size, was lurking somewhere nearby. Loof at once ordered steam up and on the afternoon tide swiftly glided out of the delta into the sea and sped north. The distance was only about a hundred miles and shortly after five o'clock the following morning the *Königsberg* arrived under full steam in Zanzibar's harbour and found *Pegasus* anchored broadside to and 200 yards from the shore.

Loof ran up battle flags and while still four miles away fired ranging shots from the 105 mm guns on his port side. At the third shell *Pegasus* replied, but without effect. The *Königsberg* swept into the harbour, turned smartly, and fired a salvo from her starboard guns. Within twenty minutes *Pegasus* was afire and obscured by smoke, her forward turret smashed. Her replies grew feeble and her guns were soon completely silenced. In all, *Pegasus* took more than 200 hits; 31 of her crew, including two officers, were dead or dying, and 55 were badly wounded. Not a single German sailor was scratched.

The only precaution the British had taken was to post a picket ship, the *Helmut*, commanded by Sub-Lieutenant Clement J. Charlewood, outside the harbour. The *Helmut* had failed to detect the arrival of the *Königsberg*, but as the triumphant German cruiser sped out of the harbour, Loof spotted the *Helmut* and pumped three shells into her in passing. It was enough. The *Helmut* exploded and the *Königsberg* sailed on, leaving the survivors to fend for themselves in the shark-infested waters.

Loof was now eager to go raiding in the waters off the Cape of Good Hope, but within hours of his victory complex boiler problems forced him to change his plans. Repairs could not be made at sea; the needed work could only be done in the well-equipped workshops of Dar-es-Salaam. As this was hardly a safe port, Loof again made for the delta of the Rufiji, this time steaming well inland to a place called Salale.

The ship was camouflaged as much as possible by attaching trees to masts and funnels, and the damaged machinery was quickly dismantled. A safari of thousands of Africans was organized to manhandle the tons of parts over more than a hundred miles of dirt roads and narrow paths to Dar-es-Salaam. Loof sent out landing parties with machine guns and positioned field guns at the mouths of the Rufiji; signalling stations were set up between posts ashore and the cruiser; a corps of coastwatchers peered out to sea from perches in palm trees and through mangrove swamps, watching for British warships. The *Somalia* brought in supplies. New parts, ingeniously made at Dar-es-Salaam, were carried back within ten days, a most remarkable achievement in every way, but before they could be installed the British discovered the *Königsberg*'s hiding place.

The brazen sinking of *Pegasus* in Zanzibar's harbour set off lights and bells in the British Admiralty. The highest priority was assigned to the task of finding and destroying the *Königsberg*. No effort was to be spared, and, indeed some ingenious methods were employed.

There were, of course, many guesses as to where the *Königsberg* could be, and there were many false reports of her whereabouts, but the most educated guess was that she was lurking somewhere in the watery maze of the vast Rufiji delta. No one was sure, and even if true, no one would venture to say where.

Captain Sidney R. Drury-Lowe in *Chatham* began an intensive search of the harbours, bays, and inlets along 1,700 miles of coastline. He met with some important small successes. The German tug *Adjutant*, 250 tons and drawing only eleven feet of water, was captured when she was on her way to Loof with supplies. Nine days later *Chatham* arrived at Lindi at the mouth of the Lukuledi River and sent a boat prowling upstream. It found the German liner *Präesident*, whose documents showed that she had dispatched coal in lighters to Salale on the Rufiji about six weeks earlier. The British were now drawing close and they pulled out all the stops.

Somehow the Royal Navy learned of a famous elephant hunter, the forty-one-year-old Afrikaner named Peter J. Pretorius, who knew well the Rufiji area. Jan Smuts, who was asked to locate him, described him as "so lost to the 'civilized' world" that he did not hear of the Boer War until it was over. He was, said Smuts, "thin, lithe, and coloured brown from continued bouts of malaria." Smuts, who later employed him as a scout, spoke of his "courage, coolness in facing danger, extreme resourcefulness in emergencies" and of his "singular combination of dash and caution, acute observation, and a sense of realities which . . . amounts to instinct or genius." Pretorius described himself as having been born with a "divine unrest."

He had just made his way back from German East Africa where he had been jailed for murdering forty-seven natives—

in self-defence, he claimed. He was ambushed by German askaris and wounded in both legs, but had managed to escape. Safely back in South Africa, he tried to enlist but his wounds were not yet healed and he was rejected. When Smuts gave orders to find him, it was quickly done; he was under surveillance. Having just come from enemy territory, he was regarded as a suspicious character, possibly a German agent. Hustled aboard a warship, he was carried to the delta of the Rufiji. Pretorius enjoyed the novel experience and he found Admiral King-Hall "a charming man."

Also found in South Africa was a young man with a seaplane. He was H. Dennis Cutler, holder of Royal Aero Club Certificate No. 189. He was giving demonstration flights at Durban in his aircraft (called a hydroplane) when King-Hall discovered him, bought his seaplane, and commissioned him a sub-lieutenant in the Royal Naval Reserves. Plane and pilot were put aboard a cruiser and they too were sent to the delta of the Rufiji.

Cutler's aircraft was a fragile contraption with silk-covered wings held in place by a dozen braces and a network of wire struts. The pilot sat on a chair fixed to the lower wing in front of the engine and a pusher propeller. Two large pontoons were attached in place of wheels. Cutler asked for a mechanic, but none could be found. On his first flight— the first aerial reconnaissance ever made over East Africa— he lost his way and his radiator gave out. He was found sitting on the sea near an island calmly waiting to be rescued. Captain Drury-Lowe of the *Chatham* described Cutler as "an entire novice at observation work, but a good pilot and absolutely without fear." The radiator could not be repaired as there were no spare parts, but someone remembered seeing a Model T Ford at Mombasa and a warship, HMS *Fox*, was dispatched 200 miles north to fetch it.

Both Pretorius and Cutler were to play valuable bit roles in the coming drama, but it was an unknown sailor from *Chatham* who on 30 October 1914, from the top of a tall palm tree, spied the mast of either the *Königsberg* or the *Somalia*, both of which were in the river. The *Chatham* fired a few shells in the general direction, but all fell short. The guns of the Royal Navy had to move closer and they had to be directed by someone who could see their effect. For the moment all that could be done was to collect a naval force large enough to guard all the mouths of the Rufiji, repair Cutler's seaplane, and land Pretorius to spy out the delta.

The *Dartmouth* and *Weymouth** soon joined the *Chatham* on the scene, and an old collier, *Newbridge*, 3,800 tons, was sunk to block the Simba Uranga channel—at a cost of three sailors' lives. With the Ford radiator from Mombasa in place, Lieutenant Cutler managed to fly over the *Königsberg*, which he discovered had moved two miles further upstream. There were no more successes for young Cutler. On 10 December he crashed his aircraft in the Rufiji and was made a prisoner.*

On board the *Königsberg* life was cramped and dull; there were few diversions. One day Loof went ashore with his new 9 mm rifle and shot a hippopotamus, but his enthusiasm was dampened when he found that his kill was a mother. Her infant was caught and brought aboard the cruiser, where a wooden hut was built for it on deck. In spite of careful nursing, it died two weeks later.

Christmas provided a welcome break in the wearisome routine. The sailors took pains to make it cheery. A mangrove tree was hauled on board and decorated. A service was held on Christmas Eve. German colonists ashore sent gifts, mess tables were decorated, toasts were drunk in pineapple juice, cigarettes were issued. More cigarettes were distributed on New Year's Eve and the last made-in-Germany beer was drunk. On New Year's Day HMS *Fox* sent a wireless message: "A Happy New Year. Expect to have the

---

* The *Chatham*, 5,400 tons, built in 1912, was one of the Royal Navy's finest warships and could make 26 knots. It carried eight 152 mm guns and four 47 mm guns. *Weymouth*, built in 1910, and *Dartmouth*, built a year later, were in the same class.

* Cutler was seen in a prison camp, but his subsequent history, like his prior history, is unknown. He was one of those people who sometimes appear from no-one-knows-where, play their bit parts in a momentous event, and then return to obscurity.

pleasure of seeing you soon. British cruiser." To this the Germans replied: "Many thanks. Same to you. If you want to see us we are always at home. *Königsberg.*"

Soon the ever-present mosquitoes and the polluted water began to take their toll. By 10 January there were fifty cases of malaria. A week later two sailors died of typhoid. More deaths followed. The *Königsberg* became a floating pest-house. For Loof there were other losses. Lettow-Vorbeck, aware of the disciplined men sitting idly on board the cruiser, asked that the crew be given to him. Loof protested but was finally forced to turn over to the *Schutztruppe* a hundred sailors and marines under Lieutenant T. Angel.

The British pressed ever tighter against the delta doors. The Germans, with twelve Europeans and forty askaris, held Mafia Island (170 square miles) just 22 miles from the mainland. It was a useful outpost for observing British naval activities until the British brought in troops from Zanzibar and on 12 January 1915 successfully landed them under covering fire from *Fox.* The blockading squadron was reinforced by HMS *Pyramus,* a light cruiser from New Zealand, and a small fleet of whalers pressed into service.

The Germans, too, could celebrate small successes. The German tug *Adjutant* was recaptured when it ran aground in the delta. The British shelled it heavily, but it was reloaded, re-armed, and again served the Fatherland.

The loss of his aviator by no means diminished King-Hall's fascination with the possibilities of aviation. He wanted a squadron of airplanes and he persuaded the Air Department of the Admiralty to provide one. On 20 February two marine officers, Flight Lieutenant John Tullock Cull and Lieutenant H. E. Watkins, together with sixteen men* and two Sopwith seaplanes powered by 100 h.p. Gnome engines arrived off the delta of the Rufiji.

When the Sopwiths were assembled and ready to fly, Cull attempted to take off with an observer, extra gas, and four

---

* Twenty-year-old Sutcliffe, one of the mechanics, was still alive, age 91 and living in Weymouth, Dorset, in 1985.

bombs. The plane would not leave the water. When he finally did get aloft, he was alone, without bombs and with only an hour's fuel supply. Even then he could not get above 500 feet and found himself a slow-moving target for German riflemen. There was another problem in this steaming corner of Africa: the wooden propellers warped and the glue would not hold them together.

In April more seaplanes arrived, but they were not new and their engines had to be overhauled; still, they flew better than the Sopwiths. On 25 April Cull managed to get aloft with an observer and to climb to 1,200 feet. He set out to find the *Königsberg*, encountering heavy rifle fire all the way. He sighted the newly painted German cruiser and reported on her condition: "Her side screens and awnings were spread, smoke was issuing from her funnels and in general she was looking very spic-and-span." Cull managed to take a picture of her with an ordinary box camera.

Watkins and a mechanic/observer were shot down on 5 May and landed in a "nasty sea" at the Simba Uranga mouth. Cull came to their rescue. He snatched them from their sinking aircraft and then, as he could not take off with the extra weight, taxied to one of the British whalers. The *Königsberg* now appeared to be trapped, although the British were unable to reach her. Thus began the most protracted naval engagement in history. Captain Drury-Lowe, a fine seaman, tried without success to work in close enough to shell the *Königsberg;* on 23 December he sent two shallow draft ships into the delta and they managed to score a single hit on the *Somalia,* before being driven back by artillery and machine gun fire from the shores.

On board the *Königsberg* supplies of all sorts were now exceedingly low. However, Loof had not been forgotten by the German Admiralty, which sanctioned a daring scheme to succor its stranded cruiser. The plan was to send a cargo ship laden with supplies through the North Sea, around Scotland, down through the North and South Atlantic, around the Cape of Good Hope and up into the Indian Ocean, where it was to make contact with the *Königsberg.*

The beginning of the war had found the British steamer *Rubens*, 3,600 tons, in Hamburg's port. She was confiscated and in early 1915 was put to a clandestine use. Officially she became *Sperrbrecher* A (Blockade Runner "A"), but the name on her bow and on her papers was *Kronborg* and she was fitted out as a Danish freighter. Her skipper was Lieutenant Carl Christiansen, who spoke fluent Danish. His handpicked crew also spoke Danish and looked Danish.

Deep in the hold were the important stores—1,000 shells in watertight cases for *Königsberg*'s 105 mm guns, thousands of rounds of 47 mm ammunition for Lettow-Vorbeck's small field pieces, 1,800 modern rifles with three million rounds of ammunition, two new 60 mm guns, six machine guns, tons of dynamite, medicines, tinned food, clothing, machine tools, and other valuable goods. On top were 1,600 tons of good Westphalian coal for the *Königsberg* plus 1,200 tons for her own use, and the decks were piled with lumber.

The *Kronborg* set sail on 18 February 1915 and cleared the Skaw on the northern extremity of the Jutland Peninsula the following day. Christiansen chose the shorter but riskier route south of the Shetland Islands, then headed south through the length of the Atlantic. In early March, off Cape Verde, he exchanged greetings by wireless with two British freighters from Mombasa. He swung wide around the Cape of Good Hope and then steamed north between Madagascar and the mainland. On 9 April the *Kronborg* anchored in the clear water of the lagoon at Aldabra Island.

Meanwhile, Loof manoeuvred the *Königsberg* downriver and prepared to make a dash for the open sea. The ship's company was drilled frequently in "Clear for Action" and a sense of excitement replaced the lethergy which had for so long pervaded the ship.

Christiansen was now forced to break radio silence to contact Loof, and on the night of April 10/11 he raised anchor and steamed off to the rendezvous Loof had selected in the open sea 400 miles northeast of the Rufiji delta (Lat. 6S, Long. 45E). The meeting never took place. Signalman Ritter on the *Königsberg* wrote in his diary:

13 Apr. Today was the day on which we were to have run out. But the English were waiting for us, and put a thick line through all our calculations. They lay outside the mouth with three cruisers and two auxiliaries.* This overwhelming strength was too much for us. Everything points to the fact that the English knew our Morse Code, and have caught our exchange of telegrams with the ship.

This was indeed the case. Loof's message had been intercepted by a French cruiser at Madagascar and relayed to Admiral King-Hall. The German naval code had long ago been broken.

Loof signalled that he could not get out and ordered Christiansen to Manza Bay, a sheltered anchorage near Tanga. This message, too, was intercepted and King-Hall himself in *Hyacinth* found the *Kronborg* there at dawn on 14 April waiting for a pilot to board. The pilot boat was in sight when *Hyacinth* came into view. Without waiting for the pilot, Christiansen steamed further into the bay. *Hyacinth* came on at full speed until the starboard engine stopped. The connection between the piston and the connecting rod had "collapsed," reported the engineer. Nevertheless, steaming on at reduced speed, her guns began to pummel the *Kronborg* and she was soon ablaze.

Christiansen ran his ship into the shore, let go both anchors, and opened the sea cocks. Two boats were lowered, the crew tumbled into them, and they rowed with a will for the mangrove-lined shore, pursued by British bullets and shells. The first boat to reach shore was blown to bits moments after the last sailor had leapt out. In the second boat, Christiansen felt a sharp pain in his right leg as a shell exploded nearby. He watched his pantleg turn red

---

* In fact, two cruisers, an armed merchant ship, an armed auxiliary, and four armed whalers.

with blood and then lost consciousness. When he came to he found himself on shore with four of his sailors sitting quietly around him. They had bandaged his leg and they now helped him to his feet, but he was too weak to walk. Working quickly, they made a litter of their belts and palm fronds and set off, carrying him towards a beach where they had seen huts.

The sailors were soon overtaken by a detachment of askaris under Lieutenant Kemper, who had been a government official on Governor's Schnee's staff before the war. He was now part of Captain Baumstark's Tanga Defence Force stationed in this area to oppose any British landing. Kemper had also found the sailors from the first boat; not a man was lost.

In the meantime *Hyacinth* had sent boarding parties to complete the destruction of the *Kronborg*, but they were driven back by machine gun fire from the shore which *Hyacinth*'s guns were unable to silence. About midday the attempt was abandoned and the *Hyacinth* shipped her boats and steamed away.

Nis Kock, one of the *Kronborg*'s officers, wrote: "All of us who could stood up and stared at the ship which had carried us so long and so well, and which lay there with her one gunwale barely a yard above the water, and her whole superstructure gutted." Christiansen was taken to Dr. Ludwig Deppe's hospital just outside Tanga, and from here he directed salvage operations. The ship itself was a total loss, but an astonishing amount of its cargo proved capable of being saved. The two trained divers Loof had taken off the *Zieten* were dispatched north to Manza Bay, and they, together with soldiers, sailors, and some 2,500 Arabs and Africans laboured to bring everything salvageable ashore. Ships' boats and Arab dhows plied back and forth between wreck and shore. In just one day 293 rifles, 375 rounds of rifle ammunition, a field gun, 4 machine guns, 100 rounds of 105 mm ammunition, 40 officers' tents, a boat repair kit, and other valuable supplies were landed.

The rifle cartridges were badly affected by the salt water,

but every askari and carrier that could be spared was put to work on them. Each round was opened, brass was cleaned, and the powder was dried. It took months, but it was patiently and thoroughly done. It was, said Nis Kock, "a salvage job Africa talked of for years."

Lettow-Vorbeck wrote that the arrival of the *Kronborg* "aroused tremendous enthusiasm, since it proved that communication between ourselves and home still existed ... Many who had been despondent now took courage once more, since they learned that what appears impossible can be achieved if effort is sustained by determination."

Most of the crew of the *Kronborg* was absorbed into the *Schutztruppe*, but Christiansen refused to fight on land. Carrying reports from Lettow-Vorbeck, Loof, and Schnee, he made his way to Mozambique, where he boarded a neutral ship and returned to Germany.

As the Royal Navy and the British army rarely communicated with each other, it was some time before the soldiers learned that King-Hall and his sailors had botched their work at Manza Bay. It was not until they discovered that their foes were using ammunition manufactured in 1915 and possessed modern Mauser rifles that inquiries were made and the story of the great salvage operation became known. Not surprisingly, the soldiers were angry. Lettow-Vorbeck later said that the failure of the British to destroy the cargo of the *Kronborg* was the greatest mistake of the entire campaign.

Admiral King-Hall, making excuses after the war, said:

> It was, of course, impossible to do anything towards preventing the enemy from salving the arms as soon as the fire was extinguished, for, short of an occupying force of troops to hold the surrounding district, it was out of the question for a man-of-war to remain in an enemy's harbour day and night for weeks, even had a ship been available. . . .
>
> Shortly after this occurance I proposed returning to Manza Bay to disturb any operations of salvage that might be in the making, but on learning of my intention the Admiralty prohibited

the proceeding, on the grounds that the approaches to the bay were mined.

It is difficult to resist the conclusion that the admirals were not nearly as concerned about the *Kronborg* as they were about the *Königsberg* because the former was a threat only to the soldiers while the latter posed a threat to their ships.

The Royal Navy's fear of mines bordered on paranoia. There were no mines in Manza Bay. The Germans had none. They did, however, float a few oil drums, and this simple ruse was sufficient to discourage the admirals. Even had the oil drums been mines, the destruction of the cargo of the *Kronborg* ought to have been worth considerable risk and to have ranked with the sinking of the *Königsberg* as a priority mission. It is difficult to conceive of a more important task to which men-of-war on the South African station could have been put.

[The *Rubens*, alias *Kronborg*, remained half submerged in Manza Bay for more than forty years. A salvage company raised her in 1957 and cut her up for scrap—but not before several tons of that good Westphalian coal had been removed and, still being good, were sold.]

Meanwhile, the beseiged *Königsberg* was serving her country well, for her very existence was costly to the Royal Navy, a fact of which the British Admiralty was acutely aware. One evening radio officer Niemyer intercepted a message and took it to Loof. It was from the Admiralty in London ordering that the *Königsberg* be destroyed at any cost. Niemyer thought that this was "*Königsberg*'s death warrant."

However, it was all very well for the Admiralty to order the destruction of the *Königsberg*, and the power of the mightiest navy in the world ought to have been able to perform this task, but the Royal Navy floated in deep blue water and its dreadnoughts could not enter the sinuous, shallow Rufiji, whose muddy mouths were uncharted (by the British) and whose mangrove-lined banks concealed riflemen, machine guns, and artillery. Before the *Königsberg* could be destroyed, a way had to be found to reach her with heavy guns.

It is convenient at this point to ignore for a bit the chronology of the East African campaign in order to tell how the Royal Navy solved its unique problem in a unique way.

CHAPTER

12

The *Severn* and the *Mersey*

Before the war the Brazilian navy had ordered the construction in British shipyards of three shallow-draft gunboats for use on South American rivers. Armoured and turreted, they were, in effect, little more than floating gun platforms and were called "monitors" because of their resemblance to the first ironclad man-of-war used by the United States Navy in the American Civil War. They had just been completed and had been christened *Solomos*, *Medeira*, and *Javery* when the war broke out. Before they could be delivered, the British government intervened, confiscated them, and renamed them *Humber*, *Severn* and *Mersey*.

Three regular Royal Navy officers were appointed to command the monitors: Commander J. A. Fullerton (the senior of the three and the captain of the *Severn*), Commander A. L. Snagge (captain of the *Humber*), and Lieutenant Commander R. Amcotts Wilson (captain of the *Mersey*). When they arrived at Barrow-in-Furness to inspect their new commands, they were astonished by the peculiar con-

Captain J. A. Fullerton
D.S.O. on the quarter-
deck of the *Severn*

figuration of their ships, and even more by their lavish fittings: gleaming brasswork, beautiful oak panelling, chairs
with interchangeable seats to suit the weather, Turkish
carpets, expensive curtains, and fine blue tablecloths orna-
mented with little blue anchors. Soon enough the white
hulls were repainted grey, the brass was blackened, and
the superfluous articles were sent ashore.

Each monitor was 265 feet long and 49 feet wide. Forward and aft there was only three feet, three inches of free-
board, but even when fully loaded they drew no more than
six and a half feet. Each had a single funnel and an 80-foot
mast amidship. Tonnage was 1,260 and top speed was supposed to be 12 knots, though even this modest speed was
never reached. Each was capable of carrying only 187 tons
of coal and 90 tons of shale oil, so they could not be long
away from a coaling station. Very much on the plus side
were the guns. Each ship mounted two 6-inch and two 4.7-
inch guns, all larger than the *Königsberg*'s.

The ship's officers were mostly from the Royal Naval

Reserve or the Royal Naval Volunteer Reserve. One was an actor; another a schoolmaster who had taught German and came on as an interpreter. Most of the ratings were men from the reserves who had not been to sea for many years; only a few were from the merchant service.

The "acceptance trials" quickly uncovered the deficiencies of the monitors. They were ridiculously slow, and in the open sea almost uncontrollable when the wind was at right angles to the hull. In almost any circumstance they were a danger to themselves and a cause of anxiety to any other vessel near them. There were also problems with the guns; the ammunition provided did not fit the 4.7-inch guns and a half inch had to be filed off each brass cartridge cylinder.

In spite of these defects, the three seemed ideal for inshore work because of their six-and-a-half-foot draught, and there arose a need for such work on the Belgian coast. In the so-called "race to the sea" the line of battle on the Western Front extended to the English Channel, where warships could lend the support of their big guns. The monitors were sent to do this, and they worked so close inshore that they came under fire from German field artillery, sustaining damage and casualties. They were credited with saving the Belgian army and preventing the fall of Calais, Dunkirk, and Boulogne. This may be giving them too much credit, but Mr. Winston Churchill, then First Lord of the Admiralty, sent them a glowing signal: "The Inshore Flotilla and Squadron have played an appreciable part in the great battle now proceeding. You have shown the Germans that in this case there is a flank they cannot turn." In the New Year's promotion list Eric Fullerton was made captain, and a pint of beer was issued to every man aboard the *Severn* to drink his health.

In March 1915 the monitors were sent to dockyards where they were substantially strengthened. All boats were removed, portable fittings were dismantled, topmasts were stowed, and the hulls were made watertight. The crews were perplexed to find that no room had been left for them. It was rumoured that the monitors and their crews were to be sent to the Dardanelles in support of the Gallipoli campaign, which had opened in mid-February 1915, and this was indeed the case.

The monitors went to sea with each pulled by two tugs. Captain Fullerton's officers and men were put aboard another ship, the *Trent*, and carried as passengers. This curious flotilla moved at a stately six and a half knots down the European coast, through the straits of Gibraltar to Malta. Here it became evident that they would be too late for Admiral John de Robeck's schemes in the Dardanelles, but it occurred to someone that they would be just the thing for Admiral King-Hall's use in the Rufiji delta, for these shallow draught ships could carry their big guns up the Rufiji to within range of the *Königsberg*. Consequently, on 28 April 1915 two of the monitors, *Severn* and *Mersey*, "unseaworthy steel boxes," they were called, left Malta and were hauled by tugs 5,000 miles through the Suez Canal, into the Red Sea, and south along the African coast to where the muddy waters of the Rufiji empty through its many mouths into the Indian Ocean. At 7 P.M. on 3 June 1915 they reached Mafia Island.

It had taken a curious sequence of events and a never-before-attempted naval operation to bring these curious crafts to this remote corner of the world to do what they, and they alone, could do. Even so, the results could not be accurately predicted.

Shipwrights and seamen from other ships helped the crews of the *Severn* and *Mersey* prepare the monitors. Boat decks were built up with sand bags; half-inch steel plates (some salvaged from *Pegasus*) were laid on decks as protection against plunging fire; compass and hand-steering-wheel were protected with sand bags and mattresses, and the bridge was screened with hammocks. Both ships were painted a kind of mangrove green, and they were loaded with 10,000 empty kerosene tins, tightly packed below deck to sustain buoyancy if they were struck below the water line. Guns were mounted and ammunition put aboard. In

Fore 6″ gun of the British Monitor *Severn*, July 1915

addition to the two 6-inch guns (one forward and one aft) and the two 4.7-inch howitzers, each monitor carried five semi-automatic 3-pounders (one with a high-angle mounting) and eight machine guns. The crew of each consisted of 10 officers and 150 ratings.

On 10 June the officers of the monitors joined Admiral King-Hall in the *Weymouth* and steamed down the delta's coast as close inshore as they dared to see the entrances and familiarize themselves with the landmarks of the route through the river maze recommended by Pretorius the elephant hunter. Two days later the crew of the *Severn* moved out of the *Trent* into their own ship and started the engines, which had not turned over for more than three months. Soon after, the *Mersey*, too, was ready for duty.

Not until both monitors were prepared for battle did King-Hall and his officers give serious consideration to fire direction, for the *Königsberg*, screened by the intervening jungle, would be invisible to the monitors. Airplanes would have to act as spotters, and they, someone remembered, would need an airfield. By chance, Wilson of the *Mersey* (recently promoted commander) had had some experience with aircraft, and he recollected that a Maurice Farman biplane would require a 200-yard landing strip. On 18 June three more pilots arrived with two Henri Farhams and two Caudrons; soon after came other aircraft, including some Short seaplanes. Not until 22 June was a rough airfield— with a swamp at one end—staked out on Mafia Island.

When the aircraft were assembled and a field cleared, the first airplanes took to the air. It was then discovered that the monitors were unable to hear the wireless messages they sent. A conference between Squadron Leader Robert Gordon of the newly formed Royal Flying Corps and the naval officers settled on a system of coloured lights and an arc lamp. The latter proved a failure, but luckily the wireless was finally made to work and at last all was ready for battle.

Tuesday, 6 July, when there would be high tide in the delta at 10.55 A.M., was selected as the date for the monitors to enter the mouth of the Rufiji at the Kikunja entrance, which was the widest. On the day before, Admiral King-Hall signalled some words of encouragement:

> The Commander-in-Chief desires to wish the captains, officers and crews of the monitors every success for tomorrow. He is confident that all ranks will uphold the honour of the British flag for King and Country.

King-Hall was not Nelson and he did not plan to share the dangers to be encountered in the sweltering Rufiji delta, but his message was heartening.

On 5 July everything not needed was removed from the monitors: mess tables, doors, beds, and chairs. All shale oil and all but 60 tons of coal were taken off. Even the crew's spare clothing was put aboard the *Trent*. Then, on the day of battle, galley fires were extinguished and each man was issued four large meat sandwiches—thirst slaker baskets of oranges, bottles of fresh water, and buckets of oatmeal and water—were placed about the ship.

The other warships took up positions to give such sup-

port as they could, ready to open fire on German shore batteries and machine gun posts. *Trent* was left at Tirene Bay,
Mafia Island, and made ready for use as a hospital ship. At
4 A.M. the monitors began to make their way in the dark
toward the delta, *Severn* in the lead, each towing a motorboat amidship.

In spite of British attempts to keep the monitors and their
mission secret, German intelligence knew about them. Just
how and when Captain Loof learned of their approach it is
impossible to say, but he most certainly knew it at least six
days before their arrival at Mafia Island. Early on the
morning of 6 July Lieutenant Commander Paul M. Koohl,
one of the *Königsberg*'s officers, was leading a routine beach
patrol when he saw through the morning mists the approach
of the monitors. A week later he described in a letter his
surprise at seeing the "shadowy-looking ships coming rapidly up the middle of the channel. . . . The monitors advanced
gaily up the stream 6,000 to 7,000 yards, as if they were at
home."

The monitors were soon under fire, running a gauntlet of
bullets and shells from both shores. Loof had put ashore
his 47 mm guns, which were under Reserve Commander
Werner Schönfeld, commander of the Delta Defence Force,
but in spite of Schönfeld's pleas, he had refused to yield
any of his 105 mm guns. It was a fatal mistake. Had a battery of the *Königsberg*'s 105 mm guns been on the shores as
the monitors approached, they could not have survived. As
it was, *Severn* and *Mersey* were able to protect themselves
by rapid employment of their quick-firers and machine guns
at close range. The Germans launched a torpedo, but it was
blown up by one of *Severn*'s 4.7-inch guns. At 6.23 A.M. the
monitors ended their two-hour trip up the sinuous river
and let go their anchors at a point safe from shore batteries
and which Fullerton estimated to be 10,800 yards from their
target. Koohl estimated the distance at 14,000 yards.

More than an hour earlier Flight Lieutenant H. E. Watkins had taken off from the Mafia airfield for the thirty-
minute flight to the *Königsberg* carrying six bombs. He found

the German cruiser and dropped his bombs, but failed to hit anything but mangroves. Ten minutes later Flight Lieutenant J. T. Cull (pilot) and Flight Sub-Lieutenant F.S.L. Arnold (observer) rose up to act as spotters. At 6.17 A.M. Cull and Arnold signalled to the *Severn* that they were ready to report on the firing. But not until 6.48 did the *Severn* open fire with her 6-inch guns.

Signalman Ritter aboard the *Königsberg* recorded the opening of the battle as he witnessed it:

> We were sitting, all of us, at the breakfast tables. The middle watch were still lying in their hammocks, when suddenly the cry rang out: "Clear ship for action!" The alarm gongs sounded, and in a second all were at their battle stations. I was signaller at the central in 1st Div. . . . Hardly were we at our stations when our guns opened fire on—as I later learned—two airmen who were approaching the *Königsberg*. Shortly afterwards the signal arrived that the monitors *Mersey* and *Severn* had run up the mouth . . . keeping both banks under sharp machine gun and rifle fire.

Just as the battle opened, Reserve Lieutenant Jaeger on the *Königsberg*, who before the war had served on a liner of the German East Africa Company, chose to shoot himself. He did not die instantly, but lingered until the day's battle ended. This event did nothing to improve German morale. Still, most seemed to welcome the end of the monotony, and an end to their dying by inches of fevers.

Severn's opening shots fell short by 200 yards. The German ranging shots were also short, but Loof's gunners quickly found the range and both monitors were soon straddled by German shells, one of which splashed only fifteen yards away. Yeoman-of-signals Greenshields, who served in *Severn*'s fighting top, later recalled that the *Königsberg* was "firing four salvoes to our one, and they were whistling over us, falling just short into the banks, throwing up mud and bushes into the air."

Mersey, anchored 400 yards astern of *Severn*, got the worst of the duel at first. By 7.40 she had been struck twice. One German shell had penetrated the two-inch hardened steel shield of the fore 6-inch gun and knocked it out of action, killing four men and wounding four others. Another shot sank her motorboat and holed her below the waterline. Fullerton ordered Commander Wilson to weigh anchor and shift the position of his ship, the better to use her stern gun. No sooner had Wilson made the manoeuvre than a salvo landed exactly where the *Mersey* had been sitting.

At 7.51 A.M. a shell from *Severn* struck the *Königsberg* for the first time. It penetrated the officers' galley and killed a sailor. Then a second shell crashed into the upper deck, killing two seamen, one of whom had been taken off the *Zieten;* a shell fragment tore open Lieutenant Richard Wenig's left foot from ball to heel. A third shell struck the signal bridge, killing another seaman.

The *Königsberg* was taking a pounding, but her own shells were persistently straddling the *Severn* and it seemed only a matter of time, perhaps minutes, before she was hit. Fullerton wisely decided to shift his position in the river. As he did so, one of his officers noticed a German spotting position on a platform in a tree on an islet in midstream. It was wiped out with 3-pounder and 6-inch lyddite shells.

Loof's gunners had depended primarily upon the spotting of a lieutenant equipped with the best available binoculars who reported from a rise called Pemba Hill. This arrangement collapsed when the monitors shifted their positions and were no longer visible from Pemba Hill. Thus, the loss of the observers in the tree was a serious one, for the *Königsberg's* firing was now almost blind.

Throughout the battle the British airmen cooly circled and made their reports. Signalman Ritter wrote: "They were fired on with shrapnel on various occasions, but without success." When Cull returned to base at 8.40 A.M. to refuel, a bullet hole was found in a wing. Fresh pilots and observers took turns in the sky, including Squadron Leader Gordon with an assistant paymaster as his observer.

The *Severn* changed position once more, and in doing so

ran aground. It was an unpleasant time for Fullerton and his crew—stranded in an unhandy ship opposite enemy lookouts in an almost unknown river on a falling tide—but with reversed engines and the aid of the stern anchor Fullerton worked her free and she was soon again firing.

By mid-afternoon the monitors had fired 635 shells, four of which had struck the *Königsberg*, but Fullerton could not be sure of the extent of the damage. He was still receiving fire; the Germans had not given up the fight. But his men were hot and weary, his guns had overheated, the tide was falling; it was time to return to the safety of the sea and the protection of the cruisers of the Royal Navy. At 3.45 P.M. *Severn* and *Mersey* made for the river's mouth, again running the gauntlet of German machine guns and field artillery. Shells fell perilously close; a sounding boom on *Mersey's* starboard side was carried away, but there were no further casualties. By 4.30 both monitors were safely in the hands of tugs, their crews heartened by the cheers of seamen manning the rails and rigging of the larger ships.

The crews of the monitors were given ample suppers and allowed to turn in for a well-deserved rest, but there could be no rest for the crew of the *Königsberg*. One of the monitors' shots had pierced her hull below the waterline. The fore and aft bunkers of the stokehold were filling with water. All hands were put to work. The four dead were buried; thirty-five wounded were loaded on a river paddleboat and carried five miles upstream to a field hospital at Neu Streten Plantation on the Mbuni River. In the next few days all combustible material, including paint, was removed; important papers and spare parts were put ashore; a telephone system to new spotter positions and to Pemba Hill was installed; aiming stakes were erected to improve gunnery. Captain Loof knew that the monitors would return.

The day after the battle an airplane made a reconnaissance flight over the *Königsberg* and the airmen reported that although the German cruiser was obviously damaged, she was still very much a fighting ship. Such was indeed the case. King-Hall and Fullerton knew that the monitors would have to return to the river and finish the job.

On Sunday morning, 11 July, tugs pulled the *Severn* and *Mersey* to the Kikunja mouth of the Rufiji, and at 10.30 A.M. hawsers were slipped and the monitors moved inland under their own steam. Again they had to run the gauntlet and again *Mersey* was hit on the starboard side; two sailors were wounded. Aided by fire from the cruisers offshore, the monitors fought back and pounded the German batteries and machine gun nests. Lieutenant Commander Paul Koohl later wrote:

> It is a wonder that today, after the two bombardments, I am still alive. The first on 6th July was very sharp and damaging, but child's play compared with the second on 11th July. . . . The dispiriting effect is so great as to make one ill to think of it, trying with two or three men and rifles to stand up against such a bombardment, knowing one can do nothing.

Koohl exaggerated somewhat, but undoubtedly the British fire was effective.

Mersey assumed her former position in the river while *Severn* continued another 1,000 yards upstream. *Mersey* was soon hit again, this time by two shells, one of which struck the captain's cabin and wounded two ratings. *Severn* also came under fire and was straddled before she even anchored, but the *Severn* was a lucky ship. By 12.25 she was ready for action and three minutes later Cull and Arnold in their flimsy flying machine arrived over the target, ready to call the shots. The *Severn* opened fire, but the aviators were unable to see where the shot fell. In spite of this unpromising beginning, the eighth salvo found the *Königsberg* and in the next ten minutes seven more hits were made. Still the *Königsberg*'s guns fought on, continuing to straddle the *Severn*, one shell passing only three yards from the quarter-deck. None hit home.

At 12.49 P.M. the airplane signalled "We are hit. Send a boat." Cull later wrote: "I started to glide toward the *Mersey* as, though *Severn* was nearest, I did not want to interfere with her fire. . . . On our way down my observer [Arnold], with great coolness, gave a correction by wireless to the *Severn*, bringing her hits from forward on the *Königsberg* to amidships." Cull made what Fullerton called "a magnificent landing" in the crocodile-infested water within 150 yards of the *Mersey*. The landing was not quite perfect—the aircraft somersaulted and capsized. Arnold was thrown clear, flying over the head of Cull, who, as he explained, was less fortunate:

> I, however, had foolishly forgotten to unstrap my belt and I went down with the machine. My feet were also entangled, and I had great difficulty freeing myself, tearing off my boots and the legs of my trousers in so doing. When I came to the surface, my observer was hunting through the wreckage for me, and we both started swimming for the *Mersey*, whose motor boat picked us up.

At 1.16 P.M. there was a series of violent explosions on board the *Königsberg*. The British could see a mushroom cloud of smoke rising 200 feet above the trees. The *Königsberg*'s guns fell silent. The *Mersey* was ordered to move upstream and was about 7,000 yards from the *Königsberg* with a second airplane overhead to direct her fire. Twenty-eight more directed salvoes were fired, and a hit was scored with the first one. Fullerton climbed to the topmast-head of *Severn* and through his glasses saw the German cruiser burning fiercely from bow to stern. He climbed down and reported by wireless to King-Hall that the *Königsberg* was destroyed at last.

At 2.30 P.M. the monitors again ran down the river with the tide, blazing away at the shores but receiving little fire in return. However, the unfortunate *Mersey* took still another hit, this time on her quarterdeck. By four o'clock the victorious monitors were out of the delta and were greeted by *Weymouth*, carrying Admiral King-Hall and flying flags reading WELL DONE MONITORS.

There had been courage enough and skill enough on both

The Rufiji River, 11 July 1915. British Monitor *Mersey* passing the *Severn*

sides in this curious battle; it was largely a matter of luck that the monitors escaped with so few casualties and so little damage. They had actually been more fortunate than they knew, for Loof had equipped a steam launch, *Wami*, and a steam pinnace with torpedo gear. On the monitors' approach, he had sent the *Wami* and the pinnace by circuitous routes to torpedo them, but bad luck dogged the Germans. The *Wami* ran aground and the pinnace was delayed and arrived fifteen minutes after the monitors had left the river.

Signalman Ritter recorded the final hour of hell aboard the *Königsberg* when "the monitors shot with bewildering accuracy" and "salvo after salvo crashed into the ship." He himself was slightly wounded and before he could be bandaged he heard the cry, "All hands abandon ship!" There was, understandably, a certain amount of panic, but Ritter was shocked to see an officer who "behaved abominably, as he pushed any of the crew into the water who stood in his way." He saw many who "only worried about their own safety and paid no heed to the wounded." In spite of his own wound, he was able to leap overboard and swim to shore.

German casualties were heavy. Lieutenant Eberhard Niemeyer, the red-haired radio officer, was killed while manning a gun firing the last shots. Captain Loof was wounded in several places, including a serious wound in his abdomen. George Koch, the first officer, went with a seaman into the torpedo room, put detonators under three torpedoes and blew up the *Königsberg*—while there were still wounded on board, according to Ritter.

On shore after the final fight, Surgeon Karl Eyerich could do little more than bandage wounds and give morphine. Many of those unwounded had lost clothing, and as they stood disconsolately and half naked around camp fires that evening, they were bitten by malaria-carrying anopheles mosquitoes. Richard Wenig was raving in an onslaught of malarial fever when a few days later they amputated his leg near the knee.

Loof and the other wounded were sent upriver to the field hospital (where Loof was to make a remarkable recovery in sixty days). The surviving sailors marched inland several miles to Kilindi, where they made camp. Some returned that same evening to begin salvage operations. The cruiser itself was beyond repair, but none of her 105 mm guns was seriously damaged. All were eventually salvaged and each was pulled by 400 Africans to Dar-es-Salaam, where wheels and mountings were built in the railway and naval workshops. Lettow-Vorbeck soon had ten guns of heavier metal than any British artillery on the ground, and he distributed them around the colony, giving British soldiers another cause for complaint against their navy.

The blockade and battle in the Rufiji lasted 255 days: from 30 October 1914 until 11 July 1915. It had tied down twenty-seven British ships which had consumed 38,000 tons of coal. In his final report Loof wrote that "SMS *Königsberg* is destroyed but not conquered." Captain Christiansen carried the report back to Berlin. Loof was decorated with the Iron Cross, first class, and promoted Käpitan sur See (captain), which raised him one rank higher than Lettow-Vorbeck. He was also permitted to decorate nearly half of his

The destroyed *Königsberg*

crew with Iron Crosses, second class. The medals themselves did not arrive until a year later, when a second supply ship, *Marie von Stettin*, arrived in East Africa.

Captain Fullerton, Commander Wilson, and the two most
intrepid fliers, Cull and Arnold, were awarded the Distinguished Service Order. Nearly two years later a prize court
(formed on 4 September 1914 under Sir Samuel Evans and
said to have been the first of its kind since the Crimean
War) awarded £1,920 to be distributed among the officers
and ships' companies of the *Severn* and the *Mersey*—and
the crews of the airplanes as well. It was the first time in
history that naval prize money was shared with the crews
of aircraft.

On 12 July, the day after the battle, the officers of the
Royal Naval Air Service gave a victory luncheon on Mafia
Island to which they invited a number of other naval officers. It must have been a jolly affair. After eating they went
out and "solemnly burned" three Short seaplanes that were
"no longer required and no longer cherished." It occurred
to no one that they might have been useful on one of the
great African lakes.

Other aircraft which had been assembled at Mafia Island received kinder treatment. Squadron Commander Gordon transported crews and airplanes to Mesopotamia; Cull took crews and two Caudrons inland to help the army's land campaign in East Africa.

King-Hall, perhaps stung by criticism of his attempt to destroy the *Kronborg*, sent out on 5 August 1915 a Caudron to make a reconnaissance up the Rufiji. The pilot reported that the *Königsberg* was listing fifteen degrees to starboard; it was rusting and obviously destroyed. He also noted "a sharply defined road across the sand" as well as a large lighter, several dhows, and a supply ship with an awning. It was obvious that salvage operations had been taking place and probably still were. Still, nothing more was done.

For nearly half a century the wreck of the *Königsberg* could be seen in the Rufiji. In 1962 it was finally completely demolished to improve river navigation.

CHAPTER
13

Longido and Tanga

The British conquest of German East Africa began with a two-pronged attack: on the important port town of Tanga and on Longido, just across the frontier on the slopes of Kilimanjaro. The strategy was fine; the execution execrable.

The lesser part of the plan was the thrust at Longido. On 3 November 1914 an Anglo-Indian force of 1,500, including colonial volunteers of the East African Rifles, with four field guns and six machine guns assembled at Namanga and then moved in three columns about twenty miles across a waterless waste toward the German positions, the exact location of which they were only vaguely aware. One hundred mules carried their water supply.

They arrived in the early morning when a heavy mist lay over the entire mountain, obscuring their route and their objective. The Germans, who knew the terrain, were well aware of the British advance. Major Georg Kraut, a professional, highly competent officer with high cheek bones and habitually narrowed eyes, commanded at Longido with a force of 80 Germans and 600 askaris. He launched his men in ferocious, well-aimed attacks on the British columns and sent them reeling back, inflicting 52 casualties and stampeding the water mules. Kraut was to earn a reputation as the cleverest bush fighter in the *Schutztruppe*. Back at Namanga one of the colonial officers neatly summed up the battle in the best light possible: "We marched all night, attacked at dawn, fought all day, and then, having failed to turn the Germans out, came back here as we had no water."

The defeat of the British invaders by a force half their size composed of German-led askaris dampened morale, particularly that of the colonial volunteers, whose enthusiasm for the war was considerably cooled. Ironically, Lettow-Vorbeck, who considered the Longido position too exposed, had sent orders to Kraut to move back to Moshi, but the orders failed to reach him before the battle. Two weeks later the Germans pulled out and General James Stewart was able to occupy Longido without opposition.

The British attack on Longido had been intended as little more than a diversion. The main effort was an ambitious amphibian assault on the port of Tanga.

The Battle of Tanga was neither the biggest nor the bloodiest of East African battles, yet it has been the most written about and it remains the best documented of the entire campaign. It is certainly worth examining for its psychological effect upon both British and Germans and its bearing on later strategy. In its details it illustrates many of the aspects of bush fighting in East Africa.

Tanga was the ocean terminus of the northern, or Usambura, railway, which ran to Moshi. Before the war it exported twice as much as Dar-es-Salaam (the chief port of mainland Tanzania today). It is located at the southern end of the Usambura highlands, where most of the European colonists settled. The town is built on a plateau above an almost landlocked harbour, and in 1914 it was a pretty place with well laid-out streets and, in the European section, tidy white houses set among mango trees and coconut palms. It was surrounded by plantations enclosed by hedges, beyond which were the ever-present mangroves. Tanga is 136 miles north of Dar-es-Salaam and 80 miles south of Mombasa.

Being just over five degrees south of the equator, it is ener-
vatingly hot for much of the year, and in November it is
uncomfortably humid.

Arthur Edward Aitken, a burly man with a heavy, Kitch-
ener-style moustache, was an Indian Army officer with
nearly thirty-five years service whose only African experience had been as a subaltern in the Sudan campaign of
1885. He was serving as a brigadier general (not a substantive rank) in command of the Poona Infantry Brigade when
the war began, but on 17 August 1914 he was raised to the
rank of temporary major general and given command of
Indian Expeditionary Force 'B' with orders which stated
simply: "The object of the expedition under your command is to bring the whole of German East Africa under
British authority." It was a tall order, but Aitken was
supremely confident: "The Indian Army will make short
work of a lot of niggers," he said.

The expedition was treated as though it was a "Foreign
Office war," the sort of small colonial war which Britain
had been fighting for more than a century, and as though
it were unrelated to the Great War in Europe. Aitken was
responsible to the Secretary of State for India; Lord Kitchener and the War Office were merely to be kept informed.

Aitken's force was divided into two brigades: Brigadier
General Richard Wapshare, a cavalryman of thirty-four
years service ("A blimpish but respected officer"), was to
command the 27th, or Bangalore, Brigade with Major Henry
de Courcy O'Grady as his brigade major. His troops consisted of one British and three Indian battalions; Brigadier
General Michael J. Tighe ("leather-faced . . . tough as old
boots and known as a scrapper") commanded the Imperial
Service Brigade, which consisted of two battalions and two
half battalions contributed by the princely states of India
and called Imperial Service troops. Brigadier General Sey-
mour Hulbert Sheppard, D.S.O., was Aitken's chief of staff.

In all there were some 8,000 troops, but except for the
2nd Battalion, Loyal North Lancashire Regiment, in the
Bangalore Brigade, they were generally poorly trained and

ill-equipped. A number had just exchanged their obsolete rifles for the short Lee-Enfields, whose mechanism and sightings were quite strange to them. They had been hastily assembled from all parts of India. They were of different castes, spoke a variety of languages, worshiped different gods, and were accustomed to eating different foods. A few had seen service on India's North-West Frontier or in Somaliland, but most were unacquainted with war. Some of the officers were newly posted and almost unknown to their men, many of whom were drafts shipped in to bring units up to strength.

When Captain Richard Meinertzhagen, Aitken's intelligence officer, first saw some of these troops in Bombay, he wrote in his diary: "They constitute the worst in India, and I tremble to think what may happen if we meet with serious opposition. The senior officers are nearer to fossils than active energetic leaders." The Official History was later to refer to the troops of Expeditionary Force 'B' as being of "doubtful fighting quality."

For fear of the *Königsberg*, the troop transports waited in Bombay harbour to be convoyed to Mombasa. Foolishly, troops were put aboard long before they were to leave. One battalion was kept on shipboard for sixteen days before sailing.

At last, at five o'clock on the afternoon of 16 October 1914 a convoy of forty-five ships, fourteen of which were troop transports, left Bombay Harbour. Most of the sepoys were soon seasick. The transports were badly overcrowded and any physical exercise was difficult; this was particularly true on board the small *Assouan*, 1,900 tons, which carried the 63rd Palamcottah Light Infantry. Many of the Indian units were not provided with their accustomed food; their digestions were upset and their religious scruples outraged. One officer declared the slow two-week voyage to Mombasa to be "a hell on crowded ships in tropical heat." Not surprisingly, the troops were dispirited and discouraged.

Aitken and his staff travelled in the S.S. *Karmala*, a converted P&O liner, and were somewhat more comfortable. In the course of the voyage the personalities and peculiarities of the leaders emerged and they became better known to each other and to their staffs. The results were not entirely satisfactory. Meinertzhagen wrote in his diary:

> Ever since we left Bombay it has been remarked how cold and even rude Aitken has been to Wapshare. He clearly has no confidence in him and makes no effort to conceal it. Wapshare is no great soldier, perhaps not so sound as Aitken—which does not say much—but he deserves better than this. Tighe is a thruster, much beloved by us all and clearly a fighting man.

The *Kermala* docked at Mombasa on 31 October, several days ahead of the transports, and Aitken and his staff met with the military people ashore. Later Aitken was to complain that "The meagreness of our information as regards not only Tanga itself, but the interior of German East Africa was very marked." Yet when Lieutenant Colonel B. R. Graham, commanding the 3rd KAR, offered Aitken some of his British-led askaris who were familiar with the area, Aitken declined their assistance. Captain Meinertzhagen, the only officer in the expeditionary force who had served in East Africa (in the KAR), had warned that the German askaris were well-trained, disciplined soldiers, but Aitken ignored him, insisting that the *Schutztruppen* were badly trained and that "bush or no bush, I mean to thrash the Germans before Christmas." Another staff officer, Major Frederick Keen, who tried to persuade Aitken to put his troops ashore for a few days after their miserable voyage and long confinement aboard ship, was told that he was making an unnecessary fuss. Failure to allow his troops time to recondition was one of Aitken's worst mistakes.

Aitken's plan for the attack on Tanga was simple, as all good military plans should be, but he neglected the details, an oversight usually fatal to any enterprise. He ignored local advice and failed to learn all that he could about his enemies and about the terrain where he proposed to land. He also neglected security. Secrecy was almost nonexistent. Crates in Bombay were marked "Indian Expeditionary Force 'B,' Mombasa, East Africa." Newspapers in British East Africa wrote of the intended attack and Germans in Mombasa wrote about the preparations to friends and relations in German East Africa. Lettow-Vorbeck was kept well informed. After the war he wrote:

> I had from general considerations considered a hostile attack on a large scale in the neighborhopod of Tanga. I went there at the end of October, drove all over the country in a car I had brought with me, and discussed the matter on the spot with Captain Adler, commanding the 17th Company.

However, while he was there Lettow-Vorbeck received a telegraphed order from Governor Schnee:

> You are forbidden to subject Tanga and the defenceless subjects of the town to the rigours of war. Even should the enemy land in force, there must be no resistance. Tanga must be saved from bombardment.

Lettow-Vorbeck wired back: "To gain all, we must risk all." He assured Captain Adler he would take full responsibility for the defence of Tanga, and he ordered up additional field companies, including those of Major Kraut at Longido.

While the troop transports were still making their way down the coast, a curious scene was enacted just outside Tanga's harbour. Captain F. W. Cauldfield, RN, in HMS *Fox* had steamed ahead of the convoy and on 2 November arrived off Tanga at 7:05 A.M. With his crew at action stations and his guns pointed toward the town, he lowered a boat and sent it in with the demand to see the district commissioner. Because of the 17 August agreement between the captain of the *Astraea* and Governor Schnee guaranteeing the neutrality of Dar-es-Salaam and Tanga, Cauldfield thought it only fair to warn the Germans that the deal was off.

Herr Auracher, the commissioner, hurried aboard, stopping only long enough to send a message to Lettow-Vorbeck. Cauldfield greeted him with the demand that he surrender the town, which he threatened to bombard if it was not given up. Naively, he asked if the harbour was mined. He was afraid of mines. Auracher assured him that the harbour was filled with mines and asked for an hour's grace to confer with his superiors. Back on shore he donned his uniform of reserve lieutenant, placed himself at the head of the local police force, and with fifteen volunteers joined Captain Adler in the town's defences.

While Cauldfield waited, Lettow-Vorbeck with a trainload of askaris rocketed down the tracks at top speed. He needed all the time the British would give him, for there were only eight locomotives on the narrow-gauge line and they could transport only one field company with its baggage or two companies without baggage in one haul. The askaris boarded the train in high spirits, for they seldom rode and the train ride was a thrill.

Cauldfield lingered for ten minutes after the hour before he decided that Auracher was not going to return and that Tanga was not going to surrender. Even then he did not fire a shot. He wired for a minesweeper and rejoined the convoy.

British inefficiency and sheer stupidity gave the Germans even more vital time. The *Helmuth* arrived to sweep the mines: there were none and never had been. The *Helmuth* collected only floating logs and empty tins. Captain Meinertzhagen wrote in his diary of Cauldfield: "He seems nervous, yet pompous, shifty-eyed, and not at all inclined to help. It strikes me that he is definitely afraid and is always referring to the safety of his blasted ship, ignoring the fact that it is his business to protect us even if he loses his ship."

There was further delay while Cauldfield and Aitkens tried to decide where the troops should be landed. Eventually they settled on the south side of Ras Kasone, a headland about two miles from the town that guards Manza Bay from the sea and the only part of the shore free from mangroves. The transports anchored off the landing site and *Fox* at last fired its six-inch guns—at some unoccupied entrench-ments.

It was intended that the troops disembark that after-noon, but it was almost ten o'clock that night before the first troops of Tighe's brigade, the 13th Rajputs (the Shek-hawat Regiment) and the 61st King George's Own Pioneers, landed on a hostile, unreconnoitred shore, and it was past midnight before both battalions were landed. None of the senior officers expected serious opposition. When a patrol reported that it had been fired on by two machine guns on the edge of town, the report was "received with consider-able scepticism."

It is not surprising that raw troops who had been con-fined for more than two weeks—and some for more than a month—aboard steamy, stinking transports, who had been fed bad food, been overcrowded, been seasick, and who were now kept sleepless all night, were not eager at first light to engage a fresh enemy in unknown strength on a strange shore. That they failed is not to be wondered at; that they failed so miserably was cause for dismay.

Tighe and many of the staff disembarked at four o'clock the following afternoon and set up shop in a building they identified as the White House. A building with a red roof, called the Red House, was converted into a hospital, although bandages, medicines, and other medical supplies were not landed until some time after the battle started. Mienertzhagen made himself a bed on the lawn of the White House using women's underclothing taken from the house for a mattress ("nice soft bits of lingerie"), a Union Jack and a German flag for blankets, and a corset stuffed with palm leaves for a pillow.

By eight o'clock that night (3 November) the invading force was at last ashore. As expected, the landing was unopposed. Few patrols had been sent out and no one seemed sure of where the enemy was. The sepoys were ner-vous, and when someone accidently fired a rifle, the 13th Rajputs and the 61st Pioneers panicked, rising up and rushing for the shore. It was only with difficulty that their officers could persuade them to return to their bivouac. A British soldier who witnessed their flight remarked: "These are jolly fellows to go fighting Germans with!"

Not until the following day, 4 November, after giving the Germans fifty-four hours to prepare for the battle, did Aitken feel ready to advance on Tanga. The advance was begun with the Loyal North Lancs and the Kashmiris on the right and most of the Imperial Service battalions on the left. A jaunty sergeant of the North Lancs went into action with a pet green parrot on his shoulder. (Both sergeant and parrot survived.) Cauldfield, instead of bringing *Fox* in to support the advance, anchored too far offshore to be effective.

Lettow-Vorbeck had arrived in Tanga at three o'clock that morning with the first reinforcements and received a report from Major Paul Baumstark, who said that he did not think that Tanga could be held if the British pushed home their attack. He had therefore withdrawn most of the troops about four miles from the town, leaving only patrols in Tanga and its environs. At this point the town could have been captured almost without a shot, but since the British had failed to send out proper patrols, they knew nothing of their opportunity.

To assess the situation for himself, as he always did, Lettow-Vorbeck set off with his adjutant, Captain Alexander von Hammerstein, and another officer on bicycles. They came upon an advanced post of a field company, but the men there could tell them nothing. They pedaled on until they entered the streets of the town. "It was completely deserted," said Lettow-Vorbeck, "and the white houses of the Europeans reflected the brilliant rays of the moon into the streets down which we rode. We finally reached the harbour at the furthest edge of the town." They could see the transports a quarter mile out, "a blaze of lights and full of noise" as they continued to disembark troops and offload supplies. The trio then rode towards Ras Kasone. Tanga's hospital stood just northeast of the town and they left their bicycles there and walked to the beach. Directly in front of them lay *Fox*, which had finally moved close into shore.

They watched the bustle in silence for a time and then collected their bicycles and started back for camp. On their
way they were challenged by an Indian sentry who did not
bother to fire when they ignored him and rode on.

Lettow-Vorbeck, having appraised the situation, believed
that some circumstances favoured him:

> For one thing, from experiences in East Asia, I knew the clum-
> siness with which English troops were moved and led in battle,
> and it was certain that in the very close and completely unknown
> country in which the enemy would find himself directly he
> landed, these difficulties would would grow infinitely larger.
> The simplest disorder was bound to have far-reaching conse-
> quences.

Such was indeed the case. With only the shore on the
right as their guideline, the British troops bunched on the
right of their line, creating gaps on their left. When the
sepoys on the left came within 600 yards of the town, the
Germans opened fire with machine guns. Half of the 13th
Rajputs bolted at once, carrying most of the 61st Pioneers
with them. This left a gap temporarily between the North
Lancs and the Kashmiri Rifles. The Gwalior infantry also
panicked. "It was a ghastly sight," said one officer.

Meinertzhagen tried to stop the flight of the Rajputs. When
an Indian officer drew his sword on him, Meinertz-
tzhagen shot him. He killed another frightened Rajput for
refusing his order to go forward. ("I shot the brute," he
said, "as he lay half-crazed with fear.") He was stopped
from further carnage when a shell from one of *Fox*'s six-
inch guns, firing apparently without benefit of spotters
ashore, landed near enough to blow him against a palm
tree. He was dazed but not seriously hurt. *Fox*'s shells not
only fell among British troops, but one hit the German hospital.

It is not entirely clear what Meinertzhagen was doing on
the firing line. He clearly had no business there. His explanation is that he did not know what he was supposed to do
and "could not imagine what an intelligence officer's duties

are in a fight like this." It seems not to have occurred to him that he ought to have been at headquarters sending out scouts, interviewing returning wounded, interrogating prisoners, and trying to give his commanding general some notion of the course of the action.

The picture was not uniformly black for the British. On the right of their line the North Lancs and the Kashmiri battalion (composed mostly of Gurkhas) made headway and drove back the German askaris. They cut the railway line and actually entered the town. One group reached the Kaiserhoff Hotel and tore down the German flag there. German officers tried to stem the rout of their men. Captain Alexander von Hammerstein threw a wine bottle at the head of one fleeing askari. At this crucial point, Tom von Prince arrived with two companies. He halted the advance of the North Lancs and drove the Kashmiri Rifles out of houses they were occupying by the beach.

There was much confused fighting in the plantations outside of town. A British battalion commander, with his adjutant and another officer, climbed to the top of a mound to get some idea of where they were. He and his adjutant were shot dead and the third officer was severely wounded. There were acts of great bravery. Captain B.E.A. Mausen, and his company of 61st Pioneers held fast and fought until they were annihilated.

The Battle of Tanga has been called "The Battle of the Bees," for at one point swarms of angry bees joined the fighting with an elan that Aitken and Lettow-Vorbeck would have admired. Local Africans habitually made hives of hollow logs and hung them in trees. When rifle and machine gun bullets battered their hives, the bees swarmed out in force. Some men were driven almost insane by their stings. A signaller of the Royal Engineers who tried to remain at his post suffered 300 stings on his head. A North Lancashire officer, knocked unconscious by a bullet in his face, was stung back to life and staggered to the beach. *The Times* later reported that the hives were devilish devices which the Germans had deliberately incorporated into their

German troops fighting at the battle of Tanga

defences, and this was widely believed for many years, but in fact the German askaris were also forced to flee. In parts of the battlefield the shooting ceased while both sides fled from the fury of the angry bees.* This was the first but not the last time in this campaign that combatants were routed by bees.

* During World War II a weekly Air Ministry bulletin ridiculed an old lady's suggestion that strategically placed bee hives be incorporated into Britain's coastal defences, but Sir Arthur ("Bomber") Harris took the editor to task, reminding him of the Battle of Tanga. Giving the bees somewhat more credit than was their due, he wrote: "The intervention of those bees cost us £150,000, 250,000 casualties and three years of war in East Africa [sic]. So now apologize to the lady who made the suggestion at which you so sneeringly mock. Have her posted to the Air Staff against the apprehended invasion. Meanwhile, we are collecting bees; and not in our bonnets."

An even more bizarre incident of the battle was the excursion of a few sailors (civilian crewmen of a transport apparently) who seemed to think that the soldiers' war did not much concern them. In the midst of the fighting they rowed a ship's dinghy into Tanga's harbour. Their intention, they said, was "to buy food in the town." The details are blurred, but they were fired on and at least one was wounded. Three managed to rejoin their ship by swimming and pushing the dinghy.

Lettow-Vorbeck was outnumbered eight to one, but he was eager to counterattack and anxiously awaited the arrival by train of the 4th Field Company. The moment they arrived, they were pushed forward. Lettow-Vorbeck said that

> no witness will forget the moment when the machine guns of the 13th Company opened a continuous fire. . . . The whole front jumped up and dashed forward with enthusiastic cheers. . . . In wild disorder the enemy fled in dense masses, and our machine guns, converging on their front and flanks, mowed down whole companies to the last man. Several askaris came in beaming with delight with several captured English rifles on their backs and an Indian prisoner in each hand.

Aitken's general reserve, which had been foolishly positioned only 200 yards behind the firing line, fled without firing a shot. Soon the last remnant of the firing line consisted of a few British soldiers, each fighting his own little battle. By nightfall the bush, mangrove swamps, and sisal and rubber plantations were full of clusters of disoriented sepoys trying to retreat to the beach where they had landed. Their flight had panicked the carriers, adding to the chaos. One officer said:

> It is too piteous to see the state of the men. Many were jibbering idiots, muttering prayers to their heathen gods, hiding behind bushes and palm trees and laying down face to earth in folds of the ground with their rifles lying useless beside them. I would never have believed that grown-up men of any race could have been reduced to such shamelessness.

Aitken and his chief of staff, Sheppard, both of whom should have been ashore, stood on the bridge of the *Karamala* listening to the firing. When it drew closer, Sheppard exclaimed, "They're falling back!"

"It looks like it," agreed a staff officer.

"What do you think they are doing that for?"

"Can't imagine, sir."

"You don't suppose they're being driven back?"

"I shouldn't be surprised, sir."

"That's extraordinary."

Sheppard turned to Aitken. "It'll be all right, sir," he said with as much conviction as he could muster.

Aitken nodded vigorously. "Of course it'll be all right," he said, and he began to pace the deck looking thoughtful.

Casualties were heavy among those engaged. One battalion lost five out of twelve officers, including the only officer with an intimate knowledge of Tanga. Some of the losses were from sepoys shooting wildly into the bush, sometimes into the backs of their comrades. During the fight one North Lanc complained. "We don't mind the German fire, but with most of our officers and NCOs down and a bloody crowd of niggers firing into our backs and bees stinging our backsides, things are a bit 'ard."

Just as it grew dark, Meinertzhagen, with two volunteers from the North Lancashires, went forward to make a reconnaissance. On the outskirts of the town they heard German being spoken and saw two or three figures. Meinertzhagen fired and missed; the Germans returned the fire and missed. [After the war, Lettow-Vorbeck and Meinertzhagen became friends, and they liked to believe it was they who had shot at each other on this evening. Lettow-Vorbeck joked that "This was my first social contact with my friend Meinertzhagen."]

Lettow-Vorbeck was eager to push forward and drive the British into the sea, but it was dark, his men were weary and scattered; he had to pull back and regroup. Aitken, too, had thoughts of gathering his forces and renewing the attack by moonlight, but as dismal reports of the day's disasters came in, he gave up the idea. Meinertzhagen said that Aitken was "tired out and seemed disgusted with the whole business. His ambition seemed to be to get away."

Fearing the guns of *Fox*, Lettow-Vorbeck pulled his troops out of the town. All night long Tanga lay deserted. The British had only to walk in. But they could not. They were beaten.

The next morning (5 November) Meinertzhagen, carrying a white sheet on a pole, was sent to the German lines with bandages, chloroform, and other medical supplies for the wounded prisoners. He also carried a letter of apology from General Aitken for the shell from *Fox* that had struck the German hospital. On the way he passed the body of an officer who had been a close friend and a row of dead sepoys lying face down in a plough furrow, each with his own bayonet stuck in his back.

Meinertzhagen was courteously, even warmly received by the Germans. He turned over his medical supplies to Dr. Deppe and then breakfasted with a group of German officers with whom he "discussed the fight freely, as though it had been a football match." Meinertzhagen gave the Germans their first indication that the British were going to abandon the fight. In this case, said the Germans, they would agree to allow the British to evacuate their wounded on the beach.

After breakfast, Captain von Hammerstein arrived and conducted him through the German outposts. As he approached the British lines, still with his flag of truce, an Indian sentry, probably ignorant of the meaning of the white flag, fired at him, the bullet passing through his helmet and grazing his head. Meinertzhagen, enraged, jammed his flagstaff into the sepoy's stomach, wrenched his rifle from him, and stabbed him with his own bayonet.

Aitken had already begun to put his troops back on the transports. The North Lanc and the Kashmiri Rifles covered the embarkation. The Germans made no attempt to stop the British departure and all was progressing smoothly until the covering party fired a few shots at a German patrol.

The nervous and frightened sepoys standing on the shore waiting to be taken off panicked. Rifles were dropped and men rushed into the sea. Some tried to swim, but hundreds merely stood up to their necks in water.

In addition to the wounded who had been gathered in by the British to the beach, there were wounded lying as yet uncollected in the streets and in the plantations and in the bush. Lettow-Vorbeck later wrote: "In unknown tongues they begged for help which, with the best will in the world, could not always be accorded at once." There were also, of course, British wounded at the German hospital just outside Tanga and Meinertzhagen with his white flag was sent back a second time to try to persuade the Germans to release them. Again he met Hammerstein and was courteously received. At the hospital the situation of the wounded was discussed with Dr. Deppe and the German officers over a bottle of brandy.

The Germans agreed that British wounded able to leave the hospital could do so if they gave their word never again to fight against Germany. Meinertzhagen walked about the hospital and talked with some of the wounded there. An unguarded, lightly wounded Indian Army major, under no parole, asked if it was permissible to escape. Try, said Meinertzhagen, who then watched him walk out of the hospital. The major found a small boat and persuaded an African to row him to *Fox*. "I saw him go off, and no one stopped him," said Meinertzhagen. "It makes one wonder if this is really war."

For reasons unknown, Aitken ordered that all arms, ammunition, and supplies be left ashore. Meinertzhagen had the unpleasant task of turning over this matérial to the Germans. As he and Hammerstein approached the supply dump, a British colonel, unprotected by a white flag, was seen making an inventory. Meinertzhagen shooed him off and mumbled an apology, "Mistake." Hammerstein shrugged, "All right, let him go, but by rights he should be a prisoner. You English are really quite incomprehensible. You regard war as a game."

No sooner had the colonel left than a lighter pulled onto the beach and disgorged a score of naked North Lancashires who began to bathe. Hammerstein threw up his hands: "Really, I must protest this. If they do not go back at once, I shall have to order my men to fire on them." They were ordered off, but then "to my intense disgust," said Meinertzhagen, "I found that 200 armed men of the North Lancashires had been left ashore as a hospital guard. Hammerstein allowed them to rejoin their unit. It was all very embarrassing." It was difficult to teach the British how to behave in defeat.

Their work on the shore completed, Meinertzhagen and Hammerstein returned to the hospital for breakfast with Dr. Deppe: "good beer, ice, plenty of eggs and cream and asparagus." Meinertzhagen, a knowledgeable ornithologist, had a long talk with a German officer who was a keen bird enthusiast. Before they parted, Hammerstein gave Meinertzhagen an autographed photograph of himself. The two men promised that if either was captured the other would do what he could to make prison life more comfortable. Hammerstein also passed on a friendly message from Lettow-Vorbeck: He was expecting two field guns to arrive shortly, and while he disliked the notion of firing on unarmed transports, he would do so if the British did not quickly depart.

Sub-Lieutenant C. J. Charlewood of *Helmuth* was busy all day supervising the removal of wounded from the shore. That evening the German officers invited him to supper and he accepted. There was soup, fish and steak, all "well cooked", and he found the conversation "astonishingly bright." One German reserve officer who had been an executive of the firm that had owned the *Helmuth*, asked, "How is my little man-of-war getting on? I fired at you the other night."

"I know you did," Charlewood replied, "and it may satisfy you to know that you have ruined my greatcoat."

The evacuation continued into the night, but at last the survivors of Indian Expeditionary Force 'B' were embarked

English officers taken prisoner at the Battle of Tanga

and steamed away to Mombasa. The Germans were left with an enormous quantity of war matériel. Lettow-Vorbeck was able to re-arm three companies with modern rifles, for which he now had 600,000 rounds of ammunition. He also had sixteen more machine guns, some valuable telephone equipment, and large numbers of coats and blankets.

British casualties were 817 out of a total force of 7,972, including 20 officers and 340 other ranks killed or mortally wounded. Tighe's brigade lost 50 percent of its officers. Total German casualties were said to be 148, of whom 16 Europeans, 35 askaris, and 16 carriers were killed. Among the German dead was Tom von Prince, who had been a lynchpin in the defences. He was struck in the head by a stray bullet at the end of the fight. Meinertzhagen thought perhaps the bullet was his.

So ended what the British *Official History of the War* described as "one of the most notable failures in British military history."

14

Tanga's Aftermath

"The brilliant victory at Tanga has pleased me greatly," wrote Kaiser Wilhelm to Dr. Wilhelm Solf, the colonial secretary. "I heartily congratulate you upon this glorious deed of our colonial troops. . . . The Fatherland is proud of its sons." German newspapers were ecstatic, and for the moment the African victory overshadowed the news from the Western Front. C. W. Kiesslich painted a picture of the battle so popular that it was reproduced on postal cards that were sold to benefit a war charity.

Before Tanga there had been little interest in supporting the remote German colonies. The loss of Togo and the Pacific possessions aroused little concern, the general feeling being that all would be returned after Germany won the war. But with Lettow-Vorbeck's brilliant victory a new feeling was created, a notion that colonial resistance ought to be supported. In the Reichstag a member rose to say:

A German David is fighting alone against the British Goliath in Africa and it behoves the Fatherland to ensure that his gallant struggle shall not be lost for lack of the encouragement to sustain him. If we cannot fight by his side, at least we must make sure that he is well supplied with shot for his sling.

This was easier said than done, but it was at this time that the German Admiralty converted the *Ruben* into the *Kronborg* and prepared her for the momentous and daring voyage of Captain Christiansen to East Africa.

The battle had an even greater impact upon those in East Africa. Before Tanga there had been a party among the German businessmen and planters who urged the government to make terms with the British and normalize trade. After Tanga there was no more of such talk. "The success at Tanga called forth and revived the determination to resist all over the colony," said Lettow-Vorbeck, for whom the victory brought not only the material rewards of the enormous booty, but also hundreds of volunteers, white and black, who thought they had found a winner and were eager to enlist. In the *Schutztruppe* "Tanga was the birthday of the soldierly spirit of our troops," he said. Equally important, the Tanga victory undermined the authority of Governor Schnee and raised to an unassailable pinnacle the prestige of Lieutenant Colonel Paul von Lettow-Vorbeck.

The heightened morale of the German forces was apparent to all, including the British. Christopher Thornhill, a British intelligence officer, later wrote:

> Von Lettow's men, especially his black troops, were full of themselves at having slaughtered so many white men like sheep. The askaris' tails were now well up, and the black man always fights best under these conditions, and it was a long time before we made him forget Tanga and get his tail down again.

Dr. C. J. Wilson, serving in the EAMR, said: "Before the battles of Tanga and Longido our troops were full of confidence. . . . it might have been supposed that the Germans were 'windy.' Tanga and Longido changed all that: thereafter any windiness was all on the other side."

On the night of 5 November General Aitken cabled his after action report on the Tanga fiasco to London. The news was not published. The government had no desire to add to the stream of bad news flowing over the British public—Admiral Maximilian von Spee had soundly defeated a British squadron near Coronel, off the coast of Chile; Turkey had entered the war on the side of the Central Powers; Austria had again invaded Serbia, capturing Belgrade; and there was desperate fighting at Ypres in Flanders. Not until several months later was the story of Tanga released.

Among those in the know in London there was dismay. Kitchener was furious and the focal point of his wrath was Aitken, who was relieved of his command and ordered home. Before he sailed from East Africa forever, one of his officers described him as being "cheery, calm, and courteous." When he reached London, Kitchener refused to see him, and, unable to produce a plausible explanation for 8,000 British and Indian troops being so soundly whipped by 1,000 Germans and African askaris, Aitken soon found himself reduced to the rank of colonel and retired on half pay. He took his rebuke in a manly fashion, expressing great concern that the officers who had served him should not suffer for his mistakes. It was lack of brains and imagination, not deficiency of character, that brought about his downfall. His place was taken by Wapshare.

There was no welcome for the remnants of Indian Expeditionary Force 'B' when they returned to Mombasa. The customs officials there at first refused to permit the Expeditionary Force even to land its equipment and stores unless it paid a 5 percent *ad valorem* tax. It took an officer and a squad of armed North Lancashires to convince them that perhaps they had erred.

The defeated troops were jeered. A song, "Steaming Down to Tanga," written by a civil servant in Nairobi, became popular:

> Steaming down to Tanga
> Over the briny main,
> See our major general
> And his brilliant train.
> Three brigade commanders,
> Colonels, staff galore,
> Majors count for little,
> Captains they ignore.

Armoured trains and sleepers,
Guns of different bores,
Telephones and mess plate,
Hospitals and stores,
Medicoes in thousands
Anxious to avoid
Work outside the units
Where they are employed.

Earnestly they study
Each little book
Which, compiled in Simla,
Tells them where to look.
Local knowledge needed?
Native scouts of use?
For so quaint a notion
There is small excuse.

See them shortly landing
At the chosen spot,
Find the local climate
Just a trifle hot.
Foes unsympathetic
Maxims on them train,
Careful first to signal
Range to ascertain.

Ping, ping go the bullets,
Crash, explode the shells,
Major General's worried,
Thinks it just as well
Not to move too rashly
While he's in the dark.
What's the strength opposing?
Orders to re-embark.

Back to old Mombasa
Steams 'B' Force again.
Are these generals ruffled?
Not the smallest grain.
Martial regulations
Inform us day by day,
They may have foozled Tanga
But they've taken B.E.A.

Wapshare (nicknamed "Wappy"), now a temporary major general, was said to have turned apoplectic when a daring young woman sang the song after dinner one evening when he was present.

While the soldiers damned the colonials as unpatriotic, the colonials resented them, especially the Indian Army officers, who frequented Nairobi (where Wapshare set up his headquarters) and filled up the clubs and hotels. One settler complained that "they groused at the absence of pukka sahibs, pukka golf, pukka polo, pukka bearers, pukka clubs, and all the other pukkas they had left behind in India."

The Colonial Service, the Government of India, and the War Office each managed separate armies. Each had its own ways, it own forms, pay scales, customs, and attitudes. When British regulars, Indian Army units, colonial volunteers, and the King's African Rifles tried to work together there was more than a little confusion and frustration. On 22 November 1914 the War Office assumed responsibility for the war in East Africa, but as General Wapshare was an Indian Army officer and Governor Sir Henry Belfield was in the Colonial Service, matters were not greatly improved. Lieutenant Colonel H. Moyse-Bartlett, who wrote a history of the KAR, said: "British, Colonial, Indian and African troops were all so differently administered, rationed, and supplied, and this gave rise to so many difficulties that even at the end of the war some of them were still unsolved."

As the sepoys had generally behaved badly at Tanga, there was an inclination to allow the Indian Army to soak up the blame. Governor Belfield in congratulating the North Lancashires told them: "You set an example of steadiness and pluck to some other units of the force which would appear to have been in need of it." All knew who was meant by "some other units." Such remarks did nothing to heal wounds and make the British military presence in East Africa more cohesive.

The settlers, who regarded the sepoys as little better than coolies, added to their humiliation. Indians had been imported to build the Uganda Railway, and although most of those who stayed on had prospered as artisans or as shopkeepers and other commercial middlemen, they were generally dispised by blacks and whites. For the sepoys to be regarded in the same light was not flattering.

Even later in the war, when trained, disciplined Indian Army regulars came to East Africa, the feeling against them remained. One British soldier wrote, with some exaggeration, "From end to end of Africa all races had a great contempt and strong dislike for natives of India." When a deserter from the 129th Baluchis was captured and sentenced to be shot, the 2nd Rhodesia Regiment was ordered to find the firing squad. There was some concern at headquarters that the Rhodesians, not being regulars, might baulk at this unpleasant assignment, but every man volunteered. For their part, the Indians and their officers despised the KAR, regarding them as little better than irregulars. Such rampant snobbery made needlessly difficult the task of creating a workable British army in East Africa.

In addition to the battles of Longido and Tanga, there was one more important action in November 1914. The Royal Navy had at last located the *Königsberg* and Admiral King-Hall now began to worry about the German liners bottled up in the harbour of Dar-es-Salaam, which, if they escaped, could be used as supply ships. He therefore sailed round with a small squadron to render them useless. Early on the morning of 28 November the cruiser *Fox*, the battleship *Goliath*, the tug *Helmuth*, and a former cable ship, *Duplex*, anchored off Dar-es-Salaam—three miles offshore, for the sailors still feared the nonexistent mines.

In response to a signal, the governor of the town came out in a motorboat and was told that men would be sent in to inspect the ships in the harbour and that the town would be bombarded if there was any resistance. The Germans themselves had sunk the survey ship *Möwe* in the harbour entrance, much to the disgust of both Loof and Lettow-Vorbeck. Trapped inside were three liners—*Tabora, König,* and *Feldmarschal*—and a small coastal steamer. The *Tabora* was said to be a hospital ship and carried the Red Cross flag and large red crosses on her hull, but the British wanted to confirm this.

At eleven o'clock in the morning the *Helmuth* and a steam pinnace from *Goliath* left the squadron for the harbour. They carried Commander Henry Peel Ritchie, first officer of the *Goliath;* Lieutenant Commander J.C.S. Patterson, an explosives expert; and Surgeon E. C. Holtom, *Goliath*'s doctor, who was to inspect the *Tabora*. It was a beautiful day, bright and sunny. Holtom thought "the town of Dar-es-Salaam looked very pretty that morning." Looking at it from the sea, he noted that "its well-built, two storied stone houses, painted white with tiled and slate roofs, are set among trees and flowering shrubs, and some of them have deep shady verandahs which looked cool and inviting. . . . But there was no sign of a human being. The town looked absolutely deserted."

The *Tabora* lay closest to the harbour entrance and Dr. Holtom was dropped off there. On board he found a doctor, a nursing sister, and one bed patient who, when the sheet was pulled back, was found to be wearing trousers. "This looked very suspicious," thought Holtom. He was about to express his incredulity when he heard the loud chatter of a machine gun.

Running out on deck, he saw the *Helmuth* with two boats in tow steaming as fast as possible for the harbour's mouth and the safety of the open sea. Around her the water was lashed by bullets and from the bushes on shore he could see spurts of smoke drifting up in the still air. Beside him on the deck was the old captain of the *Tabora*, wringing his hands and crying: "Mein Gott! Mein Gott! Mein Gott!"

Holtom watched anxiously as the *Helmuth* sped away and he gave a sigh of relief when it was clear that she had escaped. Beside him the captain exclaimed, "Oh, Doctor, what fools! Oh why did they fire? Your ships will shoot now, won't they?"

Holtom nodded grimly: "Yes, I expect so."

Holtom, the captain, and the German doctor stood on the deck watching and waiting. Soon they heard a dull boom from out to sea and a moment later the first shell crashed onto the beach' then others, tearing down great palm trees, throwing up fountains of sand or water. Occasionally a shell hit a building or one of the liners. A shell fragment struck the forecastle of the *Tabora*, but no one was injured.

The bombardment lasted only about fifteen minutes. When it was over the captain asked Holtom and the ship's engineer to join him for a drink. "After two whiskies and a cigar, I felt much better," said Holtom. He knew that the pinnace had not yet emerged and he wondered if she had been captured.

About an hour later he saw through glasses the pinnace coming down with a lighter lashed to each side. He asked if he could borrow a boat and the captain offered him the ship's skiff if he promised to send it back. Four Africans rowed him out to meet the pinnace and he "hugged the idea that [his] troubles were over." Commander Richie, standing by the coxswain, waved that he saw him and would pick him up. Holtom had just positioned his skiff so that the pinnace could run alongside when a hail of bullets whizzed past his ear and splashed in the water. The African rowers gave a wild howl, dropped their oars and fell to the bottom of the boat.

Holtom grabbed the oars as they floated by, kicked the nearest African, and swore at the others until they returned to their seats. But the German fire became more accurate and one of the rowers was struck a mortal blow in the chest. The rest took refuge on the bottom of the skiff and refused to budge. The pinnace was still fifty yards away, so Holtom crouched down and waited, hoping it would come between him and the shore and that he would be able to scramble aboard. He listened for the sound of the pinnace's engines, but they seemed to be growing fainter. When he cautiously raised his head, he discovered to his horror that the pinnace had passed him by. He lay on his back in the bottom of the skiff and cursed.

When all was quiet, he tried raising his topee and pro-
voked a hail of bullets, one of which hit the gunwale just
above his head. Eventually, by working the tiller back and
forth and with the help of the ebb tide, he made his way
back to the *Tabora*. The pinnace managed to escape, but
not without losses. Commander Ritchie was wounded in
eight places. He was recommended for and eventually
received the Victoria Cross, the first naval award of the
medal in the Great War and the first earned in the East
Africa campaign. [Ritchie died in Edinburgh in 1958 at the
age of eighty-two.]

Two white flags still flew at the harbour entrance; the
town's governor had agreed, under threat, to the operation.
What had gone wrong? The British believed it was an act
of deliberate treachery.

One of Lettow-Vorbeck's ablest officers was not a member of the *Schutztruppe* and was, in fact, technically a superior officer. Major General Kurt Whale was a retired German
officer who had come to East Africa just before the war to
visit his son, a young colonist, and he had decided to stay
on to see the exhibition scheduled to open in August at Dares-
Salaam. Caught up in the war, he had generously offered
his services. Only two days before the arrival of the British
squadron, he had persuaded Governor Schnee, then at
Morogoro, to consent to the defence of Dar-es-Salaam should
it be attacked. Either the decision had reached the officers
of the *Schutztruppe* but not the governor of Dar-es-Salaam
or the civil and military authorities disagreed as to whether
the British "inspection" was or was not an attack upon the
town.

Whatever the source of the confusion, the result was the
civil authorities compliance with British demands and the
white flags as well as the rifle and machine gun fire of the
Schutztruppen.

Surgeon Holtom was not the only Englishman left behind.
Patterson and his party had placed charges on the *König* to
disable its engines while Ritchie had gone on to the *Feldmarschal.* When the firing started, Patterson naturally

expected Richie to pick him up, but Ritchie, seeing no one on board and perhaps assuming that the *Helmuth* had taken off Patterson and his party, steamed away, and left them to become prisoners of war.

Holtom could not at first take in the fact that suddenly his situation in life had radically changed for the worse. He was glad to have reached the safety of the *Tabora*, where he was still treated courteously. The captain invited him to dine and, said Holtom, he "provided a very nice meal." When they had eaten, he was shown to a cabin and left with a new toothbrush and a tin of Three Castles cigarettes.

Because he was a doctor, he fully expected to be returned to the *Goliath*, but next morning he was greeted with the news: "Your ship sailed away in the direction of Zanzibar just before dawn this morning." He had just time to drink a cup of coffee supplied by the friendly captain when an armed guard came aboard and escorted him ashore, where people on their way to church stared at him with undisguised curiosity. He was given a good lunch, complete with whisky and soda, but he "missed the bread and pudding, neither of which is here considered essential to the midday repast."

In the afternoon he was passed from office to office and there appeared to be some uncertainty as to what should be done with him, but that night he was taken to a prison:

> Crossing a courtyard in which several native soldiers were standing, we entered an echoing stone-flagged corridor with small but solid doors on either side. Here we were met by a WARDER! ... unmistakably ... a warder! ... armed with a revolver, and having a heavy bunch of keys at his belt. I was ushered through one of the doors into a cell.

A man who spoke English was brought in to convey the commander's apology for the accommodation and to explain the necessity for locking him up. Holtom was furious.

The following morning he was able to meet and talk with Patterson and other captured British officers. They were given a breakfast of coffee, blood sausage, and bread; an African barber arrived to shave them. Holtom's hopes of being repatriated were dashed when he was told that he was to be taken with the others to the prisoner of war camp at Kilimatinda. There he was sent and there he endured two years of captivity.

The first bombardment by the Royal Navy had done little damage to the ships or the town, but two days later the British returned for a more serious and prolonged bombardment, which smashed the governor's house, a soda water plant, the brewery, a bank, and the casino. British soldiers were later to curse the navy for the destruction of the brewery.

The bombardment of Dar-es-Salaam seemed a brutal and unnecessary act to the Germans, and hatred of the British, which had not been strong, now became virulent. Even Governor Schnee became almost hawkish. Altering his tone and adjusting his philosophy to the current circumstances, he girded for the fight.

chapter 15

1915: The Lull Before
the Storm

The early months of 1915, when neither side possessed the strength to launch a serious offensive against the other, provided time for reorganization, preparing plans, and building up resources for the struggle ahead. In all these activities the Germans were more successful than the British. Two factors accounted for this: the British lacked a brilliant, resourceful leader of the stature of Lettow-Vorbeck and they lacked a clear perception of what they ought to be doing.

Quite early in the war it became clear both to Lettow-Vorbeck and to Schnee that, outnumbered, cut off from the Fatherland, and surrounded by enemies, there was no way that the *Schutztruppe* could win a military campaign in the conventional sense in East Africa, for no matter how many battles were won, the British, were they so minded, could summon countless battalions and draw on unlimited quantities of arms and stores.

Given the inevitability of defeat, Schnee's instinct was to do all that he could to see that the colony's inhabitants, particularly the German colonists, suffered as little as possible in their persons and property. Germany would, of course, win the war in Europe and all would then be put right again.

Lettow-Vorbeck took a quite different view of the same fact. As a soldier he had sworn to defend the Fatherland and the Kaiser; he saw that the best way to do this was to encourage the British to attack German East Africa with as many men as possible, thus taking away Allied soldiers who could otherwise be used on the Western Front. His duty, as he saw it, was to delay the inevitable, to prolong the conflict as long as possible. And he set about to do just that.

He divided the *Schutztruppe* into three main parts: a northern force under Major Georg Kraut, a southwestern force under Count Falkenstein, and a western force under Major General Kurt Wahle. The ten 105 mm guns off the *Krönigsberg* were divided among them. In addition to these main forces, he formed units from groups of volunteers at Lindi, Bismarckburg, Mwanza, Langeburg, and elsewhere. Thousands of carriers were employed, 8,000 being used to supplement the railways. Headquarters for the western part of the colony was established at Tabora, the largest town in the interior and the colony's principal recruiting and training depot. Schnee moved the government there from Dar-es-Salaam to protect it from the guns of British warships.

Contrary to the popular stereotype of rigid, nonthinking Prussians, the officers were extremely flexible in their duties and were given much independence in their operations. The niceties of rank and seniority were often ignored. Major General Wahle willingly served under Lettow-Vorbeck; captains often commanded forces of brigade size. Max Loof was one rank higher than Lettow-Vorbeck, but he did not assume command. In fact, in spite of his objections, his crew was split up and a full company of *Schutztruppen* was formed from sailors under Georg Koch, the *Königsberg's* first officer. They were drilled, sent on route marches, given rifle practice, taught bushcraft, and made to study Swahili.

Loof did not accept his inferior position gracefully, and he generally sided with Schnee in rows with Lettow-Vorbeck. On 25 October 1915, when Lettow-Vorbeck ordered the 20th Field Company to move from Lindi in the southeast corner of the colony to the northern front, Schnee cancelled the order, saying that the troops were needed in Lindi to preserve order among the natives in the district. Lettow-Vorbeck, enraged, sent Schnee a scathing telegram, which said in part:

> In no circumstances must the 20th Company remain in Lindi for protection against dangers which exist only in the district commissioner's imagination. I therefore reiterate my urgent request. . . . Should your Excellency be unable to share my opinion, I request a formal order stating the explicit refusal . . . because I am unable to supply His Majesty with solid reasons for such a grave mistake.

Schnee refused to back down, so on 31 December 1915 Lettow-Vorbeck wrote to the Kaiser, listing all of the instances in which Schnee had interfered with his conduct of the war. Schnee wrote his own view of their differences, saying that Lettow-Vorbeck did not have "a balanced judgment of the natives." He ended his letter by saying: "I should also like to point out that my views regarding the present situation are fully shared by the *senior* officer of the East African Corps, Naval Captain Loof. . . ."

It was late August 1916, before these letters reached Berlin, and they were never shown to the Kaiser, but the Colonial Secretary rapped Schnee's knuckles, telling him he "should not have issued orders which hampered the conduct of the war," adding that "the playing off of a naval captain against the commander of the *Schutztruppe* appears inappropriate."

Lettow-Vorbeck cared no more about race differences than differences in rank when it came to finding the best men for the work at hand. He put Africans in companies of white *Schutztruppen* and whites in the field companies of blacks until they became identical, thus creating the first racially integrated modern army.

The British in the early stages of the war imagined him to be a tyrant, feared by both his officers and his men. *The Times* reported: "It is known that through fear of Colonel von Lettow-Vorbeck at least two German officers committed suicide." This was a persistent story, but evidence to substantiate it is nonexistent. Lettow-Vorbeck appears to have enjoyed good relationships with his officers, and he shared with them the hardships of the long campaign.

Recruits, black and white, poured in after Tanga and new recruiting and training depots were established in the most populous districts. By the end of 1915 the *Schutztruppe* contained 2,998 Europeans (including sailors, administrators, hospital staff, and those in the field postal service) and 11,300 askaris. Lettow-Vorbeck struggled with Schnee and the civil administration to keep his growing army equipped and supplied. He complained bitterly that his men were not getting enough food, boot leather, or "even the necessities to make life tolerable," and he demanded that "frivolous waste by civilians be severely punished." Schnee, however, insisted that nothing be done "to upset the social equilibrium," and he frequently stated his fear of a native revolt.

German fears and British hopes that local tribes would rise in revolt against their German masters were largely groundless. Most Africans appeared eager and willing to serve the *Schutztruppe* as soldiers or carriers. Within the *Schutztruppe* there was a growing comaraderie between whites and blacks. Serving side by side in battles and raids created mutual respect. Lieutenant Von Ruckteschell, after scrambling about all night on a mountain covered with rocks and thorn bushes, was seen to be bleeding from a bad scratch on his face. One of his askaris took off his sock, which Ruckteschell was uneasily sure had not been changed in a week, and gently wiped the wound with it, explaining that "this is a custom of war; one only does it for one's friends."

Thanks to Lettow-Vorbeck's prodding, the colony was

eventually on a wartime footing and the Germans proved ingenious in providing for their needs. Even Schnee got into the spirit of the thing and in a speech delivered on the Kaiser's birthday (27 January 1916) he said:

> The enemy cannot crush us economically. We get all we require from the country. We find all our food supplies and materials in our German East Africa. The value of our colony shines forth in this war. . . . There is . . . an unexpected wealth in this country such as we had never imagined in the past, and we find we have an adequate supply, even of such things as previously we thought it necessary to import.

This was not entirely whistling in the dark. The Germans managed remarkably well without imports. The British blockade did not bring the colony to its knees.

On the farms in the northern highlands the production of dairy products, vegetables, and livestock increased dramatically. Looms were built and put to work; spinning and weaving became a major occupation in missions and in the homes of blacks and whites. Candles were made from beeswax and coconut oil; rubber was vulcanized with sulphur and tires were manufactured for bicycles and motorcars. At Morogoro a motor fuel called trebol was made from cocos. Missions that in peacetime tanned hides and made good boots now expanded their activities and found that they could tan hides with mangrove bark. Wine and a fiery brandy were also produced.

The Amani Biological Institute in the Usambara district was a tremendous help in discovering substitute products, but one of the most important developments was due to the genius of Staff Surgeon Moritz Taute, who found a large quantity of cinchona that had been stored and discovered a way to make a vile-tasting but effective quinine water from it that came to be called "Lettow schnapps."

One way or another, the Germans managed to provide themselves with almost everything needful, though there seemed never to be enough boots for the hard-marching

Schutztruppen. When Lettow-Vorbeck visited Major Kraut in the Kilimanjaro area and asked him what he needed, Kraut replied, "Boots, beer, and whisky."

For the British in East Africa, 1915 was the most depressing period of the war. Even fire-eaters such as Meinertzhagen grew tired of this East African backwater. He wrote despondently in his diary, "I have a burning desire to get home and fight in the trenches where all my friends are falling fast." The initial enthusiasm of the settler volunteers had evaporated; most had received permission to return to their farms on indefinite leave. Those who stayed on worried about their farms, although many of their wives were managing them efficiently. One woman managed six farms, including those of her neighbors who had gone off to fight, riding great distances every week to superintend them.

The ill feeling between soldiers and settlers persisted. *The Leader,* a Nairobi newspaper, demanded that those of foreign extraction be thrown out of the army, and it pointed its editorial finger at Meinertzhagen: "Even the head of our intelligence section boasts a German name." Meinertzhagen was incensed. He railed at the editor, had him thrown in gaol, and shut down his newspaper. Such highhandedness did nothing to ease civil–military relations.

Baroness Blixen (as "Isak Dinesen" now was) seethed with contempt at British arrogance and racial prejudices. In a letter to her sister, Ellen, she confessed that she found the German spirit more congenial than the British. Many Englishmen considered her a spy. Meinertzhagen thought it scandalous that German and Austrian nationals who, if not actual spies, were unsympathetic to the Allied cause, still lived unhindered in British East Africa. But when he persuaded his commanding officer to recommend that enemy aliens be rounded up and interned, Governor Belfield replied by telegraph: "I am awaiting your reasons for recommendations. I consider nothing less than extreme urgency would warrant course proposed." The war obviously was not an urgent enough matter.

In the absence of facts about the Germans across the frontier, there were rumours aplenty. It was said that the widow of Tom von Prince, embittered by the death of her husband, led patrols that took no prisoners, and many believed that the widow of Major von Sturm, another officer who had been killed at Tanga, had vowed to castrate seven British soldiers and that she went out on patrols for this purpose. A protest was sent to the Germans. Major Kraut, who received it, was highly amused. The only white woman he had seen was the one who brought up sausages for the Europeans at Moshi. Lettow-Vorbeck took a wider view. Such beliefs, he said, "merely served to show the degree of nerves with which the enemy authorities have become afflicted." When the British finally occupied Tanga, they found Frau von Sturm to be a gentle, dignified lady who was devoting her widowhood to charitable activities on behalf of German soldiers.

More accurate information regarding the activities of the Germans was provided British commanders by the energetic and resourceful Captain Meinertzhagen, who had a talent for intelligence work. He learned so much from captured mail that he found it "difficult to understand how intelligent people can intrust to the post important matters." He claimed to have used 2,500 African scouts and hundreds of agents. One of his more imaginative schemes he called his DPM or "dirty paper method," which required his African agents to extract used papers from German officers' latrines. Orders, messages, private letters, notes, and coded material were all used as toilet tissue. From such "dirty paper" he acquired much valuable information—and the signatures of every senior German officer.

He also developed a counterespionage unit. Two African spies were caught and shot. The cleverest German spy, an Arab operating out of Mwanza, he put out of business by sending his most inept agent, a man he was sure would be caught, with a considerable sum of money for the Arab along with a note thanking him for his help. Both the Arab spy and the British agent were shot.

Meinertzhagen was the sort of man often characterized as being too clever by half. In East Africa he was a male Cassandra, and he later complained: "Throughout my service in East Africa, information I gave commanders about the army was ignored. . . . commanders disregarded it because it did not suit them or they listened to unreliable gossip."

In Uganda Governor Frederick Jackson placed all the resources of the colony at the disposal of the military and a small band of local forces operated successfully in the area northwest of Lake Victoria, but in British East Africa nothing stirred Governor Belfield into enthusiasm for the war. Unperturbed, he spent much of his time pleasantly fishing in the sea near Mombasa and civil servants continued to take their usual generous leave. A bitter Meinertzhagen said, "It is sometimes difficult to believe that the Governor and his administration are British."

A proposal was made to raise two more battalions of the King's African Rifles, but the governor and the civil servants considered it unwise to arm Africans on a large scale. Colonel Henry Elliot Chevallier Kitchener, was sent out to report on local resources and the proposal was submitted to him. Colonel Kitchener was a blimpish character whose only active service had been as a transport officer in campaigns in Manipur and Burma in 1891. He had been placed on half pay as a colonel in 1898—at the time when his younger brother, Horatio Herbert, was winning a peerage in the Sudan. As a "dug out" colonel he was packed off to East Africa, where he proved his worth by concluding that "the value to be derived from African troops would not justify the increased expenditure." Before the campaign ended this view was to be proven decidedly false, but at the time it coincided with the views of Governor Belfield and was accepted. No new KAR battalions were raised in 1915.

Not all the colonists were apathetic. Ewart Grogan, a fierce chauvinist noted for having once walked from Cape Town to Cairo, called a mass meeting in Nairobi where a resolu-

tion was passed that the government be put on a war footing and that compulsory military service be instituted. The
resolution was passed on to the governor, who ignored it.
[More than a year later, in 1916, the colony became the
first government in the British Empire ever to use con-
scription.]

War in this part of the world continued for the most part
to be conducted in a courtly manner. Admiral King-Hall
several times sent the *Hyacinth*, flying a flag of truce, to
Dar-es-Salaam, where it would anchor just outside the harbour and wait for the Germans to send out a steam launch
to see what was wanted. A subject of discussion on more
than one occasion was the welfare of the British ladies of
the Church Mission in German East Africa. On one occasion the British women on Zanzibar, inspired by their
bishop, the colourful and controversial Frank Weston (1871–
1924), made up packages of necessities and comforts for
them. And so, said King-Hall, "the *Hyacinth*, laden with all
the prettiest frills and furbelows, both outer and inner, of
the Zanzibar ladies, called off Dar-es-Salaam and sent them
to their fellow-countrywomen." The admiral included a box
of chocolates for Governor Schnee's British-born wife "as
a small token of friendliness from an ex-fellow-country-
man." Frau Schnee gave them to the mission ladies.

British civilians, like the German authorities, feared that
the war would provoke tribal uprisings. Colonists pon-
dered the effect on Africans of seeing white men fighting
each other. However, except for minor outbursts in remote
areas, there were no incidents that caused serious concern.
No major tribe on either side rose in revolt. Most tribesmen gave aid to one side or the other, sometimes to both.
For the British the only disturbing event was a small uprising in Nyasaland [Malawi], a colony five times larger than
Wales, about the size of the state of Maine, where the entire
white population barely exceeded 800. Here John Chilembwe, a mission-educated African, came back from an
American university to which he had been sent and began
preaching his own religion, "Ethiopianism," which seemed

to translate as Africa for the Africans and death to all whites.

On the evening of 23 January 1915 his followers attacked an estate belonging to Livingstone Bruce, a grandson of Dr. David Livingstone. Living in houses on the estate were three men, three women, and five children. The three men were killed, one being decapitated by an axe in the presence of his wife; the women and children were carried off. One of the women, aided by her African servant, managed to escape. Barefoot and in her nightdress, she fled through the bush to a neighboring planter, who sounded the alarm.

A double company of the KAR dispatched to the scene marched 87 miles in 47 hours, but was forestalled by 40 British volunteers and 100 KAR recruits under Captain L. E. Triscott, who rescued the women and children.

In one small township that was attacked by Chilembwe's followers, a wounded German lieutenant was being held prisoner. The Great War was for a time forgotten as the lieutenant assumed military command and organized the town's defences. It was a case, said one of the participants, of "instinctively white men first."

The entire uprising was quickly suppressed. Chilembwe was killed on 3 February and some twenty of his followers were soon after hanged; another 400 were imprisoned.

The Europeans were not above encouraging Africans to take violent action against tribes across the frontier. In the area east of Lake Victoria the British recruited an irregular unit which became known as the Skin Corps—its members' skins constituting their sole uniforms. They were mostly wild Masai, who wanted no pay but expected to be able to rustle their enemies' cattle. To qualify for enlistment a tribesman had to possess a rifle and bandolier, which were usually obtained by killing a German askari. Each man who was accepted came accompanied by a brother or other male relative, who stayed close by his side and claimed reversion rights to the rifle and bandolier in case their owner fell in battle. The corps was organized and led by Major J. J. Drought, an English farmer in British East Africa, who was described as being "a god to these wild savages; a man of great character, great shrewdness, and great courage."

More than once the members of the Skin Corps proved their worth. They were particularly adept at ambushing German raiding parties, and they excelled at raiding the Wassukuma, a tribe rich in cattle who inhabited an area across the border in German territory. But the Wassukuma also knew a thing or two about cattle lifting. They once made a major raid with the aid of some German detachments and returned with a large number of cattle. They also laid out in a neat row in front of a German police post 96 severed Masai heads.

On Christmas Day, 1915, Major Drought and Captain Meinertzhagen with fifteen of Drought's Skin Corps crossed the frontier, carrying only rucksacks, rifles, and ammunition. Germans often became sentimental, relaxed, and lax at Christmas. Drought's patrol found an outpost with pitched tents, fires burning, and no sentries. Meinertzhagen described what happened in his diary:

> We rushed them silently from not more than a few paces. We used bayonets only and I think we each got our man. Drought got three, a great effort. I rushed into the officer's tent where I found a stout German on a camp bed. On a table was a most excellent Christmas dinner. I covered him with my rifle and shouted to him to hold his hands up. He at once groped under his pillow and I had to shoot, killing him at once. My shot was the only one fired. We now found we had seven unwounded prisoners, two wounded, and fifteen killed, a great haul. I at once tied up the prisoners whilst Drought did what he could for the wounded. . . . Drought said he was hungry, so was I, and why waste that good dinner? So we set to and had one of the best though gruesome dinners I have ever had, including an excellent Xmas pudding. The fat German dead in bed did not disturb us in the least nor restrain our appetites.

chapter 16

1915: Alarums and Excursions

Although there were no major land battles on either the northern or southern fronts in 1915 and the main action on the coast was the seige of the *Königsberg* in the Rufiji, still, there were patrols, raids, some small but vicious fights, probes and preparations. There were also feints and frights. The most dangerous, or at least the most alarming to the British, was the fighting at Jassin (Jassini or Yasini), a small fishing village beside a palm oil and sisal plantation on the coast just two miles inside German East Africa, only fifty miles south of Mombasa. It was an unhealthy area: malaria was rife, tsetse fly plentiful, and the heat and humidity stifling, almost unbearable.

On Christmas morning, 1914, the British captured Jassin with little opposition and then garrisoned it with three companies of Indian infantry under the command of Colonel Ragbit Singh. On 12 January 1915 the Germans countered with a surprise attack, which was initially repulsed. On 18 January, with Lettow-Vorbeck in personal command, another attempt was made, but this was an enterprise that received an initial setback in the shape of a mutiny.

German askaris were allowed to bring their women to war with them. They cooked, tended wounds, carried the family's possessions, and cared for the sexual needs of their men. On the coast the *Schutztruppe* had a company of Arabs who preferred boys to women. Lettow-Vorbeck did not object to pederasts as long as they were good soldiers. ("With these simple people," he said, "whose predilection for their ancient traditions and customs is further confirmed by Islam and who are very proud and vain, it is particularly difficult to interfere with such customs.") However, for the sortie into the coastal swamps surrounding Jassin, supply problems were anticipated and he ordered that the boys be left behind. The Arabs loudly protested; they demanded their discharges, and when these were refused them, they bolted. Many were shot down by loyal askaris as they fled.

Not to be deterred, Lettow-Vorbeck attacked with nine companies and surrounded Jassin. But its Indian garrison stoutly defended itself. The German askaris, mired in the steaming slime of the swamp, were so miserable that some of Lettow-Vorbeck's officers urged him to give up the attempt. But Lettow-Vorbeck was an officer with imagination, and while he could see the misery of his own troops, he could also imagine the sensations of his enemy, shut up in their fortifications, "without water, and having to carry on all the usual occupations of everyday existence in a confined space, in a burning sun, and under hostile fire." He was convinced that if his men held on resolutely, they could win. He was right.

Tighe had dispatched a relief force, the 3rd KAR, but the defenders of Jassin had no way of knowing it. Colonel Rahbir Singh had been killed, supplies of ammunition were running low, and there seemed no hope of relief. Only some forty Gurkhas in a detached factory building had finally managed to fight their way free. After forty-eight hours, Captain G.J.G. Hanson, now in command, raised the white flag. The relief column arrived an hour too late and was met by a fierce fire from the victorious German force.

The 3rd KAR had made a valiant effort to rescue the besieged Indians and Gurkhas at Jassin, but were forced to fall back. There had been individual acts of bravery. A sergeant won a Distinguished Conduct Medal and a machine gunner named Charles Mathews (an African Christian) with the 3rd KAR succeeded in bringing away his 40-pound machine gun; he apologized to his officer for having left behind the 45-pound tripod. It was men such as these that the British were unconscionably slow to recruit in numbers.

At battle's end Lettow-Vorbeck paraded his prisoners and commended them for their gallant defence. The wounded he saw transported in rickshaws to Tanga. He returned the arms of Hanson and the other officers after they gave their parole not to fight again against Germany and that evening he gave them dinner. In spite of a wounded arm, he was in a jovial mood. Not only had he won a close, hard-fought little battle, but in his pocket was a recently received message from the Kaiser praising his defence of Tanga.

For the British the affair at Jassin was a gloomy beginning to a year that seemed to have no prospects for brighter events. As the *Official History* later noted: "The morale of the British forces undoubtedly had been shaken and they were not likely to be capable of passing to the offensive for some time to come." The Jassin fiasco infuriated Kitchener, who said it was a mistake "to suppose that offensive operations are necessary" and he advised Nairobi to "give up risky expeditions in East Africa."

Lettow-Vorbeck had won another victory, but it had been an expensive one—too expensive, considering his circumstances. It was of the very essence of the war being fought in East Africa that German losses, whether in defeats or victories, were for the most part irreplaceable and thus more grievous for their cause than were those of the British. This was particularly true of the losses among the professional German officers, and at Jassin Lettow-Vorbeck had lost six of them, including his adjutant and friend, Captain Alexander von Hammerstein, who was mortally wounded in the abdomen and died a hideous, lingering death in the mud of a mangrove swamp. "The death of this excellent officer tore a gap in the ranks of our staff which was hard to fill," Lettow-Vorbeck said. His askaris had also expended 200,000 rounds of small arms ammunition, and this, too, he could ill-afford to lose.

He had learned his lesson. Jassin had shown him that:

> such heavy losses as we . . . had suffered could only be borne in exceptional cases. We had to economize our forces to last out a long war. . . . The need to strike great blows exceptionally, and to restrict myself to guerrilla warfare, was evidently imperative.

June 1915 saw a British victory on the shores of Lake Victoria, but one that shed little glory on the victors. At Kisumu a British force under Brigadier General James M. Stewart was loaded aboard four old lake steamers. Stewart was a man with a kindly face and the air of a scholar. "A great gentleman, great charm," said Meinertzhagen, "but a hopeless, rotten soldier." His command on this occasion included the 2nd North Lancs, the 25th Royal Fusiliers, three companies of the 3rd KAR, the 29th Punjabis, a section of the East African Regiment, and a section (two guns) of the 28th Mountain Battery—in all, about 2,000 men. Their destination was the town of Bukoba, a small port in a saucer-shaped depression at the eastern end of the lake in German East Africa. Bukoba had stores, warehouses, and a powerful wireless station with a 200-foot tower. It may well have been of some strategic importance, but the main purpose of the expedition appears to have been, as Tighe said, "to help maintain the spirits of the British troops."

Although Stewart hoped to surprise the Germans, his ships were not blacked out and he had chosen a moonlit night for his attack. At one o'clock on the morning of 22 June, just as the troops were about to disembark, rockets lit up the sky all along the coast. Stewart decided to postpone the assault until daylight. Shortly after sunup he landed his strike force—the North Lancs and the 25th Fusiliers—at the foot of a steep cliff three miles north of the town. The landing was unopposed, for the Germans, never supposing that the British would land at such an unprepossessing spot, had only a 30-man cossack post there. The cliff was a formidable obstacle and difficult to scale, but it was somehow negotiated.

The Germans, although inferior in numbers, occupied well-chosen positions. As the British advanced, they came under a hot fire from small arms and a field gun. Casualties mounted, one being the admired sergeant-major of the Fusiliers. Frederick Courteny Selous, the sexagenarian Fusilier lieutenant, had served in the Matabele wars of the 1890s, but this was his first experience of fighting a well-disciplined, well-armed enemy. He remembered his sensations on this day:

> The machine guns were going too with their wicked rattle, and bullets from the snipers' rifles came with an unpleasant sound. . . . I thought, as I lay there only a yard away from the blood-stained corpse of poor Sergeant-Major Bottomly, listening to the peculiar noise of each kind of projectile . . . that I could recall various half-hours of my life passed amidst pleasanter surroundings.

The North Lancashires were ordered to turn the German left flank. They were slow and the ubiquitous Meinertzhagen was sent to prod them. He found Lieutenant Colonel C.E.A. Jourdain "shaking like a blanc-mange, terrified of casualties and thought he had the whole German Army opposed to him." As he refused to go forward, Meinertzhagen heliographed Stewart that the Lancashires were unopposed but were anchored where they were owing to "the incompetence of their commander." Jourdain received a preemptory order to advance and finally did so.

By nightfall the British were still a mile from the town. No one had eaten all day and no food was issued that evening. The exhausted, hungry men spent a miserable night bivouacking in the bush; few were able to sleep.

The fight commenced again the next morning, but by one o'clock in the afternoon the German field gun had been silenced and the Germans were retreating through the banana plantations south of Bukoba. The British rushed in, tore down the flag of the Imperial Eagle from the small fort, and ran up the Union Jack. Sappers blew up the tower of the wireless station and the German arsenal. The British had now only to bury their eight or ten dead, tend to their wounded and depart, but Colonel Driscoll asked permission for the troops to loot the town and Stewart gave his consent, adding that there must be no violence or drunkenness. Stewart was an experienced Indian Army officer who had seen service on the North-West Frontier and in China; he knew that most of his European troops were not well-disciplined. To give permission for them to loot Bukoba was unconscionable.

The little expeditionary force dissolved into a drunken mob. Homes and shops were broken into; soldiers pranced about in German dress uniforms, pickelhaubes clapped on their heads. The African carriers, caught up in the spirit of vandalism, forced themselves into women's underclothes and paraded about smoking Henry Clay cigars. Officers joined other ranks in the revelry. A parrot whose only words were "Ach du schwein" was appropriated by a major. Civilians were hassled; women were violated. Meinertzhagen viewed the scenes of debauchery and drunkenness with shame, wondering what Lettow-Vorbeck and his officers would think.

Some of the looters were scandalized, as people often are when they pry into the private lives of others, by their glimpses of the Germans' sex lives. One soldier discovered companion photographs of the German commandant: in the first he stood resplendent in full dress uniform beside a woman (his wife?) who was completely naked; in the second, the same woman stood fully dressed in formal attire beside the naked commandant.

Stewart's after action report made no mention of the looting and violence, but it did include this pious paragraph:

Owing to the enemy selecting his gun positions at mission stations some damage may have been done to these buildings, but
it is believed that no shell touched a mission building.

At six o'clock in the morning the British started to re-
embark, but it took eight hours to gather everyone up and
get the soldiers and their loot on board. The one legitimate
war trophy, the German field gun, was so carelessly lashed
to the deck that it rolled off into several fathoms of water.

Lieutenant Selous, who loyally but unconvincingly
claimed that he "saw no drunkenness amongst our men,"
was disappointed by the cold reception given the heroes of
Bukoba when they returned to Nairobi:

One would have thought that as our men had come out from
England to fight for East Africa, and that as we had just returned
from a successful attack on an enemy stronghold, and as our
time of arrival in Nairobi had been telegraphed on ahead, that
something might have been done by the townspeople on behalf
of our tired and hungry men. . . . But not a bite of food for man
or officer was to be had on our arrival. . . . Not even hot water
could be obtained to make tea with.

However, the press in Europe and the United States made
much of the affair, and the regimental history of the Royal
Fusiliers described the action as "one of the few incidents
which were wholly satisfactory during the campaign." Former president Theodore Roosevelt congratulated his friend
Selous on "a first class little fight at Bukoba."

In July, another minor offensive operation was launched,
an attack upon Mbuyuni, a small hill in the shadow of Kilimanjaro. Mbuyuni was a more important objective than
Kuboka, being ten miles east of Taveta in the gateway to
German East Africa astride the Taveta-Voi road, but as Tighe
lacked both the force and the authority from the War Office
to press on for the capture of Taveta or to begin a major
drive into the enemy's territory, the strategic reason for
this minicampaign is obscure. It was obscure at the time.
Lieutenant the Lord Cranworth, a volunteer with Cole's

Scouts, pointed out: "Certainly had we been successful, we must have returned to our starting place."

For reasons not readily discernable, British generals have always delighted in using as many different regiments and races as they can assemble for any operation. For the attack on Mbuyuni, Brigadier General Wilfred Malleson managed to include an ill-assorted group of regulars and volunteers, Englishmen, Africans, Rhodesians, and Indians in a force of only about 1,300 men.

"Malleson is a bad man, clever as a monkey but hopelessly unreliable," wrote Meinertzhagen, adding, "He is by far the cleverest out here, but having spent all his service in an Ordnance Office, knows little about active operations. . . . He [is] unreliable, unscrupulous . . . with no knowledge of command." Malleson was indeed ignorant of command responsibilities, and he was unpopular with other officers, many of whom considered him an ill-mannered bully, but, although a staff officer for most of his career, he had not spent all his time in an ordnance office; among other assignments, he had once been an intelligence officer, and thus knew something of Meinertzhagen's duties.

Early on the morning of 14 July 1915 Malleson's force in two columns reached an open valley facing a ridge along which the German 10th Field Company was strongly entrenched. There was no communication between the two British columns. The flanking column, led by Cole's scouts and two companies of the KAR, approached in the dark and came quite close to the German position before it was stopped by heavy rifle and machine gun fire. The main column was brought to a halt before it could properly deploy. A frontal attack was attempted and failed.

Malleson started to pull back, and this retrograde movement panicked the 29th Punjabis and the carriers. A considerable amount of ammunition was lost and the North Lancashires abandoned one of their machine guns. The despised KAR effectively covered the withdrawal and eventually marched into camp with all their equipment and carrying their dead. The British suffered 10 percent casualties, not all inflicted by the enemy. Some thirty men of the 29th Punjabis suffered wounds in the left hand—the usual symptom of a self-inflicted wound.

The official communique described the battle of Mbuyuni as "a success . . . not out of proportion to the casualties inflicted on us." Lord Cransworth, reading this, commented: "It was very consoling therefore to know that someone besides the enemy was satisfied."

On 20 September a column under Lieutenant Colonel Francis Jollie of the 28th Indian Light Cavalry tried an attack on Longido with a mixed force that included the 3rd KAR, which suffered 41 casualties. Three of the KAR's dead were men who were successively shot down while carrying an unfurled flag. This was the last time any unit of the King's African Rifles carried a flag into action. Jollie's attack was still another miserable failure.

In August a well-fortified British post on an isolated hill south of Voi was surprised and captured by the Germans. This extended the danger zone of the Uganda Railway by another thirty miles. The British had found it hard enough to guard their railway, running as it did so close to the border.

In the small raids that came to supply most of the action on the northern frontier, the Germans proved themselves the most imaginative and daring. In detachments of eight to ten, Europeans and Africans, they circled round the British camps and, making use of telephone equipment captured at Tanga, tapped the British lines and ambushed columns of ox wagons or isolated detachments. Brigadier General Malleson was ambushed in this fashion and escaped only through the bravery of Sepoy Sabadai Ghulam Haidar of the 130th King George's Own Baluchis (Jacob Rifles), who lost his life covering his retreat, giving him time to speed to safety in his motorcar. Haidar was recommended for the Victoria Cross, but it was denied him.

Near Longido one day the horses and mules of the EAMR were put out to graze with a single horse guard. Three Europeans strolled up to him, took him prisoner, and made off with fifty-three good horses and mules. The wretched guard was left tied to his own saddle on the ground. The raid was brought off, said one of the EAMR troopers admiringly, "with the utmost coolness and impertinence, in the full light of day, at a spot close to the main road where our people were constantly passing." The animals enabled Lettow-Vorbeck to form another mounted company.

Another party of four Germans and six askaris met with less success. They rode to the Bura Hills, where the British had a dam and a pumping station, and sociably took tea with the lone guard before tying him to his chair while they dynamited the dam and the waterworks, which were put out of commission for three weeks. One of the Germans was wounded by the blasting and they were too slow getting away. All were captured. Tighe, who had taken over command from Wapshare in April, wanted to execute them. The War Office forbade it.

The most persistent German activity and the most worrisome and annoying to the British was the series of relentless attacks upon the Uganda Railway. In one two-month period between March and May, thirty-two trains and nine bridges were blown up by German raiders. In July 1915, the railway was successfully attacked five times in one week. German patrols first operated in the Tsavo area west of Voi (famous for the numbers and ferocity of its lions), but they soon extended into the area east of Voi and crossed the unexplored Taru desert, a barren, arid waste. The patrols were small: usually only one or two Europeans with two to four askaris and five to seven carriers. They had to slip past British patrols and sentries, and they were sometimes betrayed by natives.

Most patrols reached their objectives, though they were frequently absent for a fortnight. Marching for hours each day under boiling suns took its toll. Men were sometimes reduced to drinking their own urine. If a man fell sick or was severely wounded, it was often impossible to carry him back, although it was occasionally done. To be left behind meant capture or worse, to make a meal for a lion or another

A German patrol setting off on a raid on the Uganda Railway

wild beast. Germans and askaris alike understood this, yet many who could not go on handed their rifles and ammunition to comrades so that at least these could be saved.

The first patrols, arriving at the Uganda Railway half starved and dehydrated, were often captured, but in the course of the year the Germans improved their techniques and began sending out fighting patrols with machine guns.

Usually the raiding parties went north from German posts on the frontier, did their work and quickly returned. One resourceful party, however, discovered a water hole north of the railway line and, after blowing up some rolling stock, returned to it and settled in comfortably for a few days while British patrols combed the area south of the line looking for them.

Germans and askaris alike eagerly volunteered for these patrols, Lettow-Vorbeck said: "The influence of these expeditions on the self-reliance and enterprise of both Europeans and natives was so great that it would be difficult to find a force imbued with a better spirit."

The Germans improved on the quality of their mines as time went on. When the British began pushing empty trucks ahead of their locomotives, they devised mines that would only explode after a certain number of wheels had passed over them. "There was an abundance of dynamite to be had on the plantations," said Lettow-Vorbeck, "but the demolition charges captured at Tanga were much more effective."

Lettow-Vorbeck himself went out on at least one patrol, taking with him three German sergeants, a few askaris, and some carriers. They made a six-day march to the railway and successfully blew up a locomotive using an electric detonator, but their carriers, left in the rear, fled on hearing the explosion, leaving the water bags, leaking and mostly empty, on the ground.

It was a hard return march. Little water was found along the way and no fruit trees or berry bushes. One of the sergeants accidently shot himself in the leg and had to be carried by the askaris. They moved only by night, navigating by the stars, and, with luck, in time came upon a German outpost.

Patrols of Germans and British alike played cat-and-mouse in the thick bush of the Tsavo, not only with each other, but with wild beasts as well. Colonel Josiah Wedgewood, a direct descendant of the founder of the famous pottery firm who was among those who fought in East Africa, said it was like fighting in a zoo. Lions and other beasts of prey disputed water holes with sentries and patrols. In the first eighteen months of war the British lost thirty men killed by wild animals, principally lions and rhinos.

A company of the KAR on patrol was put to flight by the charges of three rhinos. Once when British and German patrols were exchanging fire, a rhinoceros launched an attack on the British and scattered them; it then turned and, with perfect impartiality, charged the Germans, sending them flying. Having proved himself the victor in this fight, the still enraged beast wheeled and charged a group of Masai tribesmen who had been merely interested spectators of the action, killing one.

A female rhinoceros and her calf stampeded an Indian guard post near a Tsavo River bridge. Twenty shots were fired at the duo without a hit being made. Most bridge guards, found by Imperial Service troops, were regarded by the British as worse than useless. Ill-trained and undisciplined, they lounged about unarmed in unfortified camps. Often neglecting to clear fields of fire, they were easy targets for German patrols.

Except for the Gurkhas in the Kashmiri Rifles and the Jats in the Bhurtpore infantry, the Imperial Service troops— from Jhind, Kaparthala, Fardkot, Gwalior, and Ranpur— were despised. There were many tales of their unreliability. A picket of one such unit, brigaded with the EAMR, reported back in camp at Namanga one evening that they had been driven in by an enemy force advancing from the heights above. All ranks stood to arms through the night and British units on either side were alerted. There was no attack. Patrols sent out next morning found everything peaceful, except for a troops of hostile baboons.

On 20 April a German patrol attacked the bridge at Mile-post 218 on the Uganda Railway. It was guarded by elements of the 98th Indian Infantry from Hyderabad, who were inattentive and walking about unarmed when the German patrol struck. Offering no resistance, they were quickly rounded up and disarmed by the Germans, who were then free to blow up the bridge at their leisure. When the patrol departed, it carried off the sepoys' rifles and ammunition, but left its prisoners unharmed, doubtless thinking it better to have such troops as enemies.

Indians of all classes suffered from the low repute of the Imperial Service troops. Some were said to be in correspondence with "the seditious party in India." When two sowars of the 17th Indian Cavalry (formerly 17th Bengal Lancers) deserted to the enemy, the reputation of their countrymen reached its nadir. Even Indian civilians were suspect. Wood to fuel the locomotives was supplied by Indian contractors who, with their African labourers, lived along the tracks. They were often accused of giving aid and comfort to raiding parties. Probably many of them did, for as Brigadier General Charles Pears Fendall said, "It is a little difficult to see what an unarmed Indian is to do when a German with a party of armed men come to his hut and demand water and shelter."

As the number of raids on the railway increased, the British grew increasingly frustrated. They sent out night patrols, but these sometimes fired on each other. They used armoured trains, but they were never, it seemed, at the right place at the right time. Bridge guards were either too lax or too nervous, sometimes shooting at everything that moved. All along the line the bush was burned back fifty to one hundred yards, but this did little to deter the raiders. The imaginative Meinertzhagen put dead birds around water holes and posted signs saying **POISONED.** "This simple ruse has kept enemy patrols from using wells and it rendered some eighty miles of railway absolutely secure from attack," he said. Not for long enough.

Some armoured motorcars arrived in August and they were sometimes sent out on patrols. At first the German askaris were terrified by these mechanical monsters, but it was not long before they were fearlessly attacking them. In one encounter five German askaris were captured and brought back to camp in an armoured car. According to W. Whittal, who witnessed their arrival, the askaris came into camp

> full of hilarity and enormously pleased at the new experience. . . . They had enjoyed their first ride so much, in spite of the untoward circumstances that had been responsible for it, that they absolutely refused to get off the car and had to be removed by main force.

Small British successes were few and attacks on the railway increased. German morale continued to climb and British morale to sink. Brigadier General J.H.V. Crowe admitted that by the end of 1915, "The morale of our men was none of the best, partly owing to the state of health, partly to their previous lack of success, and in a measure to the defensive attitude adopted."

On the Southern Front British morale was somewhat higher. There were numerous small affairs, mostly raids back and forth across the porous border, but neither side gained much of an advantage, nor did either side know much of what the other was doing. At one point Captain C. W. Barton, marching north to attack the Germans, and Baron von Longenaue with 300 men marching south to attack the British, passed within a few hundred yards of each other.

On 26 February a British patrol under J. J. McCarthy killed one ruga-ruga and captured several others. On 17 March a German patrol crashed into another patrol led by McCarthy and each side lost one officer and one askari. On 17 April a detachment of the Northern Rhodesia Rifles and Northern Rhodesia Police, all under Major Boyd Cunningham, captured a German stockade 35 miles east of Fife; Lieutenant S. Irvine, a well-known local settler who led the attack and was the first to enter the stockade, was mortally wounded.

In June 1915 the Germans attacked the fort at Saisi, located at the fork of the Sasai and Mambala rivers. It was garrisoned with 400 Rhodesians and some Belgian troops from the Congo (Zaire) under Major J. J. O'Sullevan. The first attack was repulsed, as was a second larger attack by 1,500 or 2,000 or 3,000 German troops (accounts differ), including 400 Europeans and a company of Arabs. Unable to take the fort by storm, they laid siege to it. By the third day of the siege the defenders were short of fuel, ammunition, and water.

All their oxen, goats, and mules had been killed by a German 12-pounder shooting shrapnel. But water was the major problem. There was no well inside the fort, so at night waterbottles were tied together and packed in grass to muffle any sound and parties of men carried them to one or other of the rivers. "When they started firing," O'Sullevan recounted, "the watering parties lay down, for firing at night is invariably high, and when the firing ceased the water party stole water, but sometimes we could not get any, despite trying in both directions [in both rivers], so we remained thirsty until the next night, for it was absolutely impossible to get any in the daytime."

On the fourth day the Germans, under a white flag, sent a formal demand for the fort's surrender. Major O'Sullevan refused. (The officer who went out to meet the white flag was fired on, but the Germans quickly sent a formal apology. "The conduct of the war in this sector was courteous," said one Rhodesian later.) The Allied force in the fort was almost at the end of its tether when, on the eighth day, the Germans gave up the siege and withdrew. Major O'Sullevan was awarded the D.S.O. for his stout defence.

The Rhodesians were good soldiers in spite of their indifference to normal military discipline, and, although there were few of them, Rhodesia contributed a higher percentage of its white manpower to the war than any other segment of the empire: 6,831 out of a total of about 25,000, and of these 732 were killed. The Northern Rhodesia Rifles, which had been raised by Major Boyd Cunningham (described by *The Times* as "a noted big-game hunter, administrator, and transport expert") had fought well, but for unfathomable reasons the regiment was disbanded at the end of 1915, its members being given honourable discharges. Some returned to their farms, some went to England to enlist in other regiments and to fight in France, some later enlisted in other Rhodesian units, such as Murray's Column, and one man, Lieutenant Arthur Darville Dudley, a slightly built, energetic man, rode 200 miles on a bicycle along roads and native paths to join the Naval Africa Expedition, one of the most extraordinary undertakings in a campaign that was already a curiosity.

17

The True African Queens

Lake Tanganyika, 12,700 square miles of water, is the second largest lake in Africa, after Lake Victoria. Its 4,700-foot depth makes it the deepest lake in Africa and the second deepest (after Lake Baikal) in the world. It is further distinguished by being the longest lake in the world, stretching 420 miles north and south, although only ten to thirty miles wide. The Lukuga River is its only outlet, and as this is frequently silted up, sometimes for years, the level of the lake varies enormously. Its fauna is rich, for it has an extraordinary number of fish and other animal species peculiar to itself: seventy-five percent of its more than 400 species are endemic. Hippopotamuses and crocodiles abound, including the rare sharp-snouted crocodile. The first Europeans to see the lake were Richard Francis Burton and John Hanning Speke in 1858.

Flanking this long, slim body of water at the time of the Great War were the colonies of two European powers: German East Africa on the east and the Belgian Congo on the west; in the southwest corner, a bit of the shore was shared with Northern Rhodesia (Zambia). At the beginning of the war the Germans had two gunboats on the lake, the *Hedwig von Wissmann*, 100 tons, and the smaller *Kingani*, 45 tons. Another ship, the *Graf von Götzen*, 800 tons, was under construction. (It was launched on 9 June 1915, but this was unknown to the British Admiralty.)

On 22 August 1914 the *Hedwig von Wissmann* opened hostilities on the lake by attacking the unarmed Belgian steamer *Alexandre del Commune*, 90 tons, damaging her severely. The Belgians managed to beach the ship and attempted to repair her, but on 9 October the Germans sent a landing party to explode charges in her hold. Then with German thoroughness the *Hedwig von Wissmann* shelled her into a hopeless wreck. It was these aggressive actions which finally convinced the Belgians that the neutrality of the conventional basin of the Congo was a fiction that could not be preserved and they joined France and Britain in carrying on the Great War in Africa.

In terms of overall strategy, it was probably not wise of the Germans to provoke the Belgians into making war in this part of the world so soon, but in local terms Germany's aggressions are understandable, for the stakes were high. The *Alexandre del Commune* was the only Allied vessel on the lake that could have been armed to become a threat, and thus was the only obstacle to Germany's absolute and complete supremacy on Lake Tanganyika.

Just to be sure of their control, the Germans also towed away and sank the *Cecil Rhodes*, an old British steamer lying without engines on a beach at Kasakalawe Bay at the south end of the lake. Nearby was the wreck of the *Good News*, which had been sent out by the London Missionary Society in 1886, the first steamer on the lake. For good measure they blasted its rusty hull into scrap.

Adding to the insecurities of the Belgians on the western shore was the fact that many of the local tribes on their side of the lake, particularly the Ba-HoloHolo, entertained German sympathies. German raiders could anticipate willing guides and German intelligence officers received timely information about Belgian military activities. The Belgians had failed to endear themselves to their African subjects in this area, and here more than anywhere else in sub-Saharan Africa, there seemed a real danger of a serious tribal revolt. In March 1915 they hanged a goodly number of BaHoloHolo, and this quietened them somewhat, but the psychological effect of German control of the lake was a potent factor in a potentially explosive situation. What happened on Lake Tanganyika and around its shores could have a dramatic effect upon the East African Campaign.

An Englishman named John R. Lee, a big game hunter and prospector who had served with Rimington's Scouts in the Boer War and had later served as an officer with the Canadian Scouts, was in the lake region of Central Africa when the war began and through his friendship with various African chiefs he became intimately acquainted with the problems and dangers to Britain's chief ally on Lake Tanganyika. A practical as well as an intelligent man, he devised a scheme for wresting control of the lake from the Germans. He returned to England where, on 21 April 1915, he met with Sir Henry Jackson, the First Sea Lord, and laid before him a venturesome project.

The Admiralty did not possess a chart of Lake Tanganyika, but a map of Africa was found and with its help Lee explained how a large motorboat could be carried from England to Cape Town (6,100 miles), and from there be transported 1,800 miles by rail to Elizabethville (Lubumbashi), capital of Katanga Province in the Belgian Congo (Shaba Region in Zaire), and thence 142 miles to the village of Fungurume, thirty miles northwest of Jadotville (Panda-Likasi), where the railway came to an end. From this point on the route would be difficult but not, Lee was convinced, impossible. The boat could be dragged in a trailer by teams of oxen, crews of Africans and traction engines for 120 miles, through bush, savannah, and over the Mitumba mountain range to Sankisia, where it could again be loaded on a train and carried a mere fifteen miles to Bukama on the Lualaba River (upper Congo). It could then be floated down the Lualaba to Kabalo. From here the last 175 miles could be covered by rail to Lukuga (later Albert-ville and now Kalemie) on the shore of Lake Tanganyika.

Lee's scheme was carefully thought out and he had answers to all the questions put to him by Sir Henry and his staff. The boat could not be carried in pieces and assem-bled on the lake shore, it was said, because the Ba-Holo-Holo would tell the Germans, who would destroy it before it could be assembled and launched. It was best to launch the boat from Belgian rather than Rhodesian territory because Northern Rhodesia was too far away (200 miles) from the German naval base at Kingoma. Lee admitted that traction engines had never been where he proposed to use them, but he felt confident that if used in the dry season—April to October—there would be no serious difficulty.

With astonishing and unaccustomed speed, the Admi-ralty gave its approval. The very next day Sir Henry wrote that "it is both the duty and the tradition of the Royal Navy to engage the enemy wherever there is water to float a ship." With these brave, fatuous sentiments Lee's expedition, or, as it was officially designated, the Naval Africa Expedition, was launched. The appositely named Admiral Sir David Gamble was put in charge of the arrangements and Sir David directed that two boats instead of one be sent. Lee was given the rank of Lieutenant Commander in the Royal Naval Volunteer Reserve, but it was thought only proper that a regular naval officer, an R.N., be in command with Lee as his second. To this Lee agreed. It was a fateful mis-take.

The Admiralty approved several of Lee's recommenda-tions for officers, including a couple of men from the 25th Royal Fusiliers, who were duly released from the army and commissioned in the navy. Qualified petty officers and technical ratings were assigned. Weapons and equipment were provided and Lee set out to find suitable vessels. He located two launches that seemed ideal. They had been built for the Greek Air Force (incredible as that may seem at this early date), but like the *Severn* and the *Mersey* they had been commandeered by the Royal Navy before they could be delivered. They were forty-foot motor launches with eight-foot beams, built of 3/8-inch mahogany. Their 100 h.p. engines drove twin screws through the water at nineteen knots.

Although all agreed that the expedition should be commanded by a regular naval officer, there was some difficulty in finding one, for there was a great reluctance to appoint an officer already serving at sea and all the best officers were. Reasoning that an officer in the Royal Marines would be suitable for what could be considered an amphibious operation, Gamble approached a major he knew in the Intelligence Division, but the major declined the appointment; such an expedition, he said, was "an impossible adventure." At an adjoining desk sat Lieutenant Commander Geoffrey B. Spicer-Simson, R.N., who, the moment the major declined, popped up and volunteered. Gamble was taken by surprise, but he consulted Sir Henry Jackson and on 26 April Spicer-Simson was offered the appointment, which carried the temporary rank of commander.

His prewar career in the navy had not been distinguished. A coveted promotion to commander had long eluded him. He had once briefly commanded a destroyer, but his career suffered a setback when he collided with and sank a liberty boat. After two dockside watchkeeping jobs and the realization that he was the oldest lieutenant commander in the Royal Navy, he began to refer to himself as being beached. But then he accepted an appointment of the Colonial Office to command a survey ship on the Gambia River in West Africa. He survived four years of this life and then returned to Britain just days before the declaration of war.

Naval officers were in short supply, particularly regulars, so after a brief tour on board a contraband control vessel, Spicer-Simson was promoted to Senior Naval Officer of the Downs Boarding Flotilla, which put him in charge of two gunboats and six boarding tugs operating out of Ramsgate. His lagging career seemed to have taken a turn for the better. But less than a fortnight after taking up his new command, one of his gunboats, anchored just where he had ordered her to anchor, was torpedoed in broad daylight and sank within twenty minutes. At the time Spicer-Simson was ashore entertaining some ladies at a hotel. He quite soon found himself behind the desk in the dusty little Admiralty office from which Admiral Gamble plucked him.

The new commander was something of a linguist and spoke excellent French, a desirable skill as he would need to cooperate with the Belgian authorities. He had previously served in Africa; he had commanded small ships; and he was a career officer. On the surface he seemed an entirely suitable choice. But it was a curious fish the Admiralty had hauled in for this extraordinary enterprise.

A large, muscular, round-shouldered man with thin, close-cropped hair, a Van Dyke beard, and light grey eyes, he affected a nasal drawl that many found irritating. He relished telling stories of his exploits in exotic lands. Some were near incredible; in all, he emerged as the hero. He indulged in a proclivity for browbeating waiters and others serving on lower rungs of life than his own. As those who accompanied him on the Naval Africa Expedition were to discover, their commander possessed other personality traits that were, to say the least, odd.

The blessings of the Colonial Office, the War Office, the Belgian government, and General Tighe in East Africa (who revealed himself as woefully ignorant of the situation on the lake) were all eventually bestowed, and on 22 May 1915 Lee sailed for South Africa to make the necessary arrangements. He took with him a petty officer named Frank Magee, a broad-faced, stocky former journalist who had worked as a reporter in Tripoli and South Africa.

The launches Lee had found bore numbers. "As they are not convicts, you had better find names for them," ordered Admiral Jackson, so Spicer-Simson decided to name them "Dog" and "Cat." When Sir Henry strongly objected to these names, he christened them *Mimi* and *Toutou*, to which, strangely, the Admiralty had no objection. He explained to his men that the names stood for "meeow" and "bow-wow." The ratings called them "Mimmie" and "Tow-Tow."

When the launches were adapted to accomodate three-pounder guns, they drew four inches more water and their speed was reduced to fifteen knots, but they were still believed to be faster than the fastest German gunboat. Messrs. Thorneycroft, who had built them, turned out trailers with solid rubber tyres to carry them.

Dr. H. M. Hanschell, senior demonstrator at the School of Tropical Medicine, was selected as the expedition's surgeon and was given a commission. He well knew the dangers and diseases to which the members of the expedition would be exposed, but the Royal Navy's medical supply system baffled and finally bested him. He knew that medical supplies and equipment for the tropics, packed in zinc-lined boxed of a size and weight that could be carried on a bearer's head, could be obtained from the Royal Army Medical Corps, so he suggested to the elderly surgeon captain at the Admiralty whom he had been told to consult that it might be a good idea to talk with the army's doctors. But the elderly surgeon captain merely looked at him and said, "I understand that you are joining the *navy*."

"Yes, I hope so, sir," Hanschell replied. "But the matter is very urgent. . . ."

"I am aware that it is urgent, thank you," said the surgeon captain. "Now go do as I say. Sit on a park bench and draw up a list of your requirements. And remember, you are in the *navy*." He then stood up, held out his hand, and said, "Good luck."

Hanschell took his problem to Spicer-Simson, who simply laughed and assured him, "It will turn out all right." This was to be Spicer-Simson's reaction to most of the expedition's problems. Curiously, he was usually right. The following day Hanschell was handed a printed list of medical stores supplied to gunboats on the West Africa station. It was dated 1898. Hanschell picked his way through it, adding a microscope, surgical instruments, and some modern drugs.

To protect against insects, scratches, and fungal infection, he recommended protective clothing. Spicer-Simson agreed with him on principle, but he had himself designed a special officers' uniform for ceremonial occasions: an airy light grey-blue shirt, blue necktie, naval cap badges, army badges of rank, and all worn with a silver-topped black cane and a sword.

On 15 June 1915 the little expedition set sail with its launches, guns, ammunition, goods, and gear on the *Llanstephen Castle*, a passenger liner bound for South Africa. Some of the passengers strongly objected, as well they might, to a naval expedition on board a civilian liner in time of war, but both Spicer-Simson and the ship's captain airily dismissed their protests. The British in the Great War never hesitated to put munitions and military matérial aboard passenger ships, even those carrying women and children.

When Hanschell discovered that none of the medical supplies he had ordered had been put aboard, he rushed to Spicer-Simson in a panic, but the commander was unperturbed. "We don't need more than a little quinine, do we? I never had more than that on the Yangtse or in Gambia. We can buy some in Cape Town. The bar's open—come and have a drink!"

To Hanschell's relief, just at the sea reach a launch pulled alongside with his missing medical supplies. A jumble of cardboard boxes, badly tied packages, and odd crates were dumped on the deck. There was no time to check them, but he signed a receipt. On examination he found that only a fraction of his order was included. There were no surgical instruments and little of value except an excellent microscope. Fortunately, Hanschell had brought along serums and vaccines from his London hospital. He was able to vaccinate the expedition against small pox and inoculate them against typhoid.

Spicer Simson was soon regaling the passengers with his stories: how he shot an enormous rhino on the banks of the Gambia—where no rhino has ever been seen—and how he tracked and shot a waterbuck (usually about the size of a pony) and carried it back to camp on his shoulders. On board the *Llanstephan Castle* was the astronomer royal from Cape Town, whom Spicer-Simson did not scruple to correct when one evening he was talking about the stars to a group of passengers. "He'd make a damned poor navigating officer," sneered Spicer-Simson. When he overheard some of his men speaking of "Lee's expedition," he called them together and put them straight: it was *his* expedition.

In Cape Town Hanschell was able to buy the medicines and supplies he needed and to see them packed in carrier sizes in water-proof and ant-proof containers. He had time to spare, for the expedition's advance was delayed by the Admiralty, which had received a report from a Belgian engineer who claimed that the launches could never be carried over the Mitumba mountain range. Spicer-Simson was instructed to wait until Lee had surveyed the route.

Before Lee could complete his work, his reputation was sabotaged by Sub-Lieutenant Douglas Edward Hope, a man whom Spicer-Simson had known for seventeen years and had recommended for his appointment. Hope had served in the Bechuanaland Police, the British South African Police, and as a lieutenant in the North Staffordshire Regiment during the Boer War. In addition, he had been to sea and held a mate's ticket. He was unknown to other members of the expedition because he had been sent ahead with orders to report to Lee and assist him. He did nothing of the kind.

Instead of joining Lee, Hope went only so far as Eliza-bethville, from which place he sent a flurry of telegrams in all directions accusing Lee and Magee of having been picked up drunk by the police, of disclosing the purpose of the expedition, and of insulting Belgian authorities. He added that Lee was well known to be an unreliable character and that the expedition had lost much prestige. The Belgian vice-governor, he claimed, would like to have him recalled.

Lee, who knew nothing of the mischief being made by Hope, telegraphed Spicer-Simson on 16 July that he had found a practicable route and that he had started work to improve it. Two days later Spicer-Simson wired the Admiralty that the route to Sankisia was feasible, implying that he himself had surveyed it, and adding that as Lee could not be found, Hope should be promoted to lieutenant and take Lee's place as advance man. The launches and the rest of the expedition he ordered to entrain and proceed north.

The expedition reached Elizabethville on 26 July and the next day Lee and Magee came out of the bush to report progress. Lee had surveyed and blazed the entire route. He had put hundreds of Africans to work clearing and leveling the track, blowing up boulders, and building dumps of firewood for the traction engines. He had also explored alternate routes and signed contracts with labour contractors. When he had turned over all of his maps and contracts, Spicer-Simson informed him of the charges against him and ordered him back to Cape Town to await further orders from the Admiralty. Seven years later, Frank Magee, writing about the expedition for *The National Geographic Magazine* (October 1922) said:

> About this time we lost our guide and the originator of the expedition Lieutenant (sic) Lee, sunstroke and fever obliging him to go to the hospital.

On Lee's departure, Spicer-Simson announced that Magee was promoted to Warrant Officer. However, as Hope had tarred Magee with the same brush as Lee, he neglected to inform the Admiralty of this personnel action. Exactly what sort of an understanding Spicer-Simson worked out with Magee, or whether or not there was an understanding, is unknown.

The morale of most members of the expedition was dampened by Lee's abrupt departure, but Spicer-Simson was in high spirits. At a party given for the officers by some fifteen British residents of Elizabethville, he was in fine fettle, telling stories of his strength and agility as a youth and of how he had shot a man-eating tiger in China. To the intense embarrassment of his officers, he also insisted on singing all the verses and choruses of "Swanee River."

The railway ended at a place called Fungurume, which the Naval Africa Expedition reached the first week in August. Here they were joined by Lieutenant Arthur Dudley, a former Rhodesia Rifles officer. Dudley had seen service in the Boer War and he held papers as a second mate. He was an energetic, conscientious man and Spicer-Simson made him his executive officer.

The two traction engines arrived on 15 August. They were "road locomotives" with large steel-straked wheels, high smoke-stacks and canopies that sheltered both drivers and engines. Each pulled a ten-ton trailer that could carry its wood. Although the chief driver confidently stated that his machines could go anywhere, one of them almost went through the first of some 150 bridges the expedition would have to build and cross. It took nine hours for the "locos" and the launches to cross the first stream. Then one of the locos tumbled sideways over an embankment and there was an even longer delay getting it upright and on the path again. Added to other difficulties was the discovery that both of the specially constructed trailers were buckling under the weight of the launches. On 28 August, when only thirty miles from Fungurume, they completely collapsed.

The two trailers of the locos were adapted to carry the launches, but the delay was worrisome, for the rainy season was approaching and heavy rains could, and probably would, sink the expedition in mud. Throughout all of these difficulties and apprehensions Spicer-Simson remained calm and confident, undismayed by present difficulties or thoughts of future problems. Micawber-like, he trusted to his luck, sure that something would turn up—as, indeed, frequently happened. On 2 September the launches had been manoeuvred onto the adapted trailers; on the same day, three teams of eight pairs of oxen arrived, and by first light the next morning the expedition was again on the move. That day it travelled six miles.

Through country infested with tsetse fly and disease-carrying ticks the expedition hauled its loads up hills and across streams, using the locos, oxen, and the raw muscle of

Water being carried to the traction engine that carried boats overland to Lake Tanganika

hundreds of Africans. The climb up the Mitumba range was arduous and the task of bringing the launches safely down the other side was even more so. But all engineering difficulties were overcome, thanks principally to the efforts and the ingenuity of Sub-Lieutenant A. E. Wainwright, a former locomotive engineer and construction worker who had emigrated to Rhodesia, where he had become a prosperous landowner. When water was in such short supply that the locos' boilers silted up with sand and men and beasts were thirsty, search parties were sent out in all directions. All returned empty-handed save Wainwright, who came back leading a procession of 150 women, each carrying a water jug on her head.

At last, on 28 September, the expedition reached Sankisia, a wretched little village that served as the terminus for a narrow-gauge railway that was to carry them to Bukama, only fifteen miles away. Thanks largely to the work done by Lee in finding the best route, they were making good progress and the worst was behind them. This was apparent to everyone, but Spicer-Simson's reports abused Lee for his choice of route. The Admiralty was pleased with his progress and Admiral Gamble praised Spicer-Simson's patience, resourcefulness, and determination.

It took only two hours to cover the fifteen miles to Bukama, a small town on the east bank of the Lualaba, but the expected steamer to carry them down river was not waiting. Its captain sent word from Musanga, fifty miles away, that the Lualaba at Bukama was too shallow for his ship. The river was, in fact, the lowest it had been in six years. It was then decided to float the launches down to Musanga. Empty petrol tins were attached to the underside of each launch to increase buoyancy, and on 6 September they started downstream, pulled by barges rowed and poled by Africans. Spicer-Simson had wisely engaged a pilot, Captain Jens G. Mauritzen, who proved invaluable; supplies were carried in dozens of dugout canoes.

In spite of frequent groundings on sandbars, *Mimi* and *Toutou* arrived at Musanga, where a Belgian river steamer awaited them. The launches were hauled aboard and on 16 October the steamer left port, loaded not only with the expedition's men and matériel, but with African civilians, East European traders, some prisoners in chains with their guards, along with chickens, goats, elephant tusks, provisions, crates, boxes and bags; spare space was filled with stacks of wood for the steamer's furnaces. The steamer was soon grounded and the expedition transferred to another ship. On 22 October it reached Kabalo, railhead for the tracks that ran to Lukuga on Lake Tanganyika.

At Kabalo the egregious Lieutenant Hope joined the expedition, but his stay was brief. He had outlived his usefulness and he displayed an irritating habit of disregarding orders. Spicer-Simson discharged him, accusing him of drunkenness and insulting Belgians—the same charges Hope had leveled against Lee.

The departure of Hope was also explained by Magee as due to sunstroke, although, in fact, no member of the expedition was felled by the sun or suffered any serious disease. This remarkable record was due in large part to the efforts of the conscientious and energetic Dr. Hanschell, who even burned down government buildings if they were infested with ticks, lice, or fleas and there was danger of them being used by his charges.

The railway did not quite reach the lake, but stopped three miles short of Lukuga at Makala. Here the launches were off-loaded and hidden until a safe harbour could be found for them. Commandant (Major) Stinghlamber, the senior Belgian officer at Lukuga, gave the expedition a correct but unenthusiastic welcome. As Commander Spicer-Simson was one grade higher in rank, a controversy was at once begun as to who was, or ought to be, in charge.

Some of Stinghlamber's officers confessed to expedition members that they had given them no better than a hundred-to-one chance of success. Spicer-Simson took for himself full credit for the achievement and he was soon trotting out his stories for the Belgians. He was even reminded of a new one about how he had once commanded a destroyer that sank a German cruiser.

Not long after the expedition settled into newly built huts on top of a bluff overlooking the lake, he took to flying a vice-admiral's flag and wearing a skirt. It was not a sarong or a kilt, but a skirt: "I designed it myself," he said proudly. "My wife makes 'em for me." At the same time, against the advice of Hanschell, he took to rolling up his sleeves, exposing arms and legs that were completely covered by elaborate tattoos, a display which impressed the Africans enormously. The Belgians disparagingly referred to him as *Le commandant à la jupe*. Spicer-Simson did not object to *jupe* (skirt), but he did object to being called *commandant* (major). He demanded that he be addressed as "*mon colonel*."

The rains were late and the first shower did not fall until 7 November, but soon after came the first real tropical storm. Magee described it:

> It broke over our camp in a hurricane of wind accompanied by ear-splitting bursts of thunder and vivid lightning, which illu-

minated the country for miles around. The lake itself became a raging sea, enormous breakers rolling up and crashing on the shore, uprooting trees, and demolishing native huts.

The tornado persuaded Spicer-Simson to pressure Stinghlamber into constructing a safe harbour for the launches and tons of rock were hauled in to construct breakwaters. Meanwhile, *Mimi* and *Toutou* were kept ashore until all was ready for them.

In the first week in December there were visits from the German gunboat *Kingani* and shots were exchanged. The Germans had, of course, heard of the British Naval Africa Expedition crashing through the Congo, but they did not believe, or could not believe, that the British would succeed in dragging vessels large enough to be a threat to them across the mountains and through the bush of the Congo to the shores of Lake Tanganyika. What worried Lieutenant Commander Gustav Zimmer, the senior German naval officer on the lake, was the rumour that the Belgians were building a new warship. The information he received from the Ba-HoloHolo was not now as dependable as it had formerly been. Indeed, it was true that at Kabalo, the railhead on the Lualaba, the rusting pieces of the *Baron Dhanis* were resting. The Belgians hoped that some day it would be safe to bring them to the lake and assemble the steamer. But that time had not yet arrived.

Lieutenant Job Odebrecht, captain of the *Hedwig von Wissmann*, had made a daring reconnaissance of the port at Lukuga in a dinghy, but of course he found nothing. Then Lieutenant Rosenthal, late of the *Königsberg* and now captain of the *Kingani*, swam ashore to reconnoitre, and on his second night, 2 December, discovered the British launches. When he swam back to where he had left his ship, he found it gone. His shipmates had given him up for lost; he could only turn back to shore, where he was soon captured. By this time Spicer-Simson's relations with the Belgians had reached low ebb and, to his fury, he was not permitted to question Rosenthal before he was sent away.

The *Kingari* captured in action December 26, 1915 and renamed *Fifi*

In the first weeks of December storms lashed the coast and heavy seas pounded the new harbour, carrying away eighty yards of breakwater. Nevertheless, on 22 December *Toutou* was brought out of hiding and slid into the water. *Mimi* followed the next day. The 3-pounder guns were soon mounted, tanks were filled with petrol, and the engines tested. On Christmas Day a test run was made and each gun was fired once.

In his story for *The National Geographic* Magee wrote: "We kept Christmas in the good old-fashioned style," but in fact there was no Christmas celebration of any sort. One of the ratings who decorated his hut was berated by Spicer-Simson, who bawled, "What's this? A whorehouse? Take all that down and burn it."

At 7.15 am on 26 December, a Sunday, Spicer-Simson received a report from Belgian lookouts that an enemy vessel was twenty miles away and approaching. He kept the information to himself and ate breakfast without passing it on to his officers. At 9.30, as usual, officers and ratings were paraded for inspection and church service. Spicer-Simson was reading aloud from the prayer book when an

African ran up to him with a message, which he glanced at, stuffed in his pocket and went on reading. Soon his officers, who stood facing the ratings, could see the *Kingani*, 45 tons, the smallest of the German gunboats, rounding a point of land.

Only when the service was over did Spicer-Simson order the chief petty officer to dismiss the men and man the launches, adding "Hands clean into fighting rig" (ordering men into clean clothes to reduce the danger of sepsis in case of wounds). The ratings, already in their cleanest Sunday best, quickly changed into old clothes, many not at all clean, and raced down the path to the launches in the harbour. Spicer-Simson followed at a stately pace.

Dudley took charge of *Toutou* and Spicer-Simson commanded *Mimi*. It was a clear, bright day, but the wind was rising and the lake was becoming increasingly choppy. Thousands of Africans lined the bluff overlooking the harbour and lake, and covered every hill along the coast. The Belgians and British left ashore also watched anxiously as the two launches roared out of the harbour for their first battle for the control of Lake Tanganyika.

18

The Battles for Lake Tanganyika

Now was the time to see if this quixotic enterprise was worth the energy and expense expended on it; whether the frail wooden launches were strong enough to survive Tanganyika's storms and the German guns; and whether the men whom Dr. Hanschell had nursed and cursed to bring them still healthy to this remote spot in the middle of Africa were indeed the right men to wrest control of the lake from the Germans. And certainly now was the time to see if the eccentric, tattooed, skirt-wearing Commander Geoffrey B. Spicer-Simson could do more than tell tall stories, whether his performance could match his jactation.

The *Kingani,* unaware of her danger, moved sedately along the coast. Spicer-Simson waited until she was close enough for him to slide between her and the German base at Kigoma. He ordered Dudley in *Toutou* to attack her port quarter while he came in on the starboard side. A Belgian motorboat, the *Netta,* was instructed to stay out of the action but to be on hand to pick up survivors in case either launch was hit.

The launches moved well out into the lake and then turned sharply to overhaul the *Kingani*, whose sailors were inspecting the shore line. Suddenly the German captain spied them, their white ensigns fluttering bravely against the backdrop of the green hills beyond. *"Die Engländer sind hier!"* he shouted and swung hard to port. The Germans' one gun, a 6-pounder so mounted that it could only fire forward, was of heavier metal than the 3-pounders on the British launches and it opened fire on *Mimi*, the nearest attacker, before *Mimi* was close enough to reply. A single hit would have blown the launch out of the water. But the lake was choppy now and all the vessels bobbed and rolled. Smoke poured from the *Kingani*'s single funnel as it developed top speed.

At 11.47 A.M. *Mimi* and *Toutou* came within 2,000 yards and were able to return the German fire, but this also brought the British within rifle and machine gun range. Zigzagging, they kept up a continual fire. The fight was soon ended. The *Kingani*'s foredeck exploded in flames. Her colours were hauled down and someone was seen waving a white cloth.

With a huge, taciturn ex-lance corporal at the wheel, the *Mimi* headed straight for the crippled ship. The ex-corporal, plucked out of an officers' training camp by Spicer-Simson, had seen action in France where he lost a finger at Ypres, but he had never been to sea and knew nothing about boats, as he now demonstrated. He rammed the *Kingani* amidships. Spicer-Simson was sent sprawling across the deck. Belgian officers watching the action through glasses from the bluff roared with laughter, and one burst out, "The gallant captain has rammed his prize!"

With her bow badly damaged, *Mimi* backed off and ran for home, where she was quickly beached. Spicer-Simson stepped ashore and stood in a daze, silent and unsmiling amidst the crowd of cheering Africans, Belgians, and Britons who ran to congratulate him. Belgian buglers sounded off and a shore battery banged a salute. Dr. Hanschell thought he probably could not take in the fact that after years of pretension he had at last truly become a hero. True, he had had much luck, but every commander needs that. He had indeed brought these launches here to the heart of Africa, launched them on this great inland lake, and forced the surrender of a German gunboat. The responsibility had been his; he now deserved the glory and acclaim.

Behind him on the water limped his prize, the *Kingani*. Dudley had come alongside her, taken off two survivors, put a prize crew aboard, and run up the white ensign above the German colours—as when a prize is taken on the high seas. The *Kingani* was listing badly and taking in water through a shell hole on its port side. Three Germans—the captain and two sailors—had been blown to bits; their blood was splattered over deck and bulkhead. The captain's mangled torso, his thigh ripped off at the hip, leaned crazily against the gun shield. Nearby, clean and unharmed, was a tethered goat that bleated in protest when the British seamen climbed aboard.

A young British petty officer took the wheel and steered for the shore. He ran her aground and she settled in seven feet of water, keeling over somewhat on her starboard side. Then the petty officer, pale and shaking, his nostrils filled with the smell of burnt powder and blood, fainted.

Spicer-Simson soon recovered and was his old self again. Two shells had struck the *Kingani*, but he claimed twelve hits—all from *Mimi*'s gun under his direction. Going over his prize, he stopped to take a ring from the finger of the dead captain and put it on his own.

Eleven of the *Kingani*'s survivors were assembled: three Germans (one the chief engineer) and eight African deck hands and servants. The chief engineer, who spoke English, revealed that none of the officers had any idea that the Royal Navy was on the lake. They had heard that the British were trying to drag boats over the Mitumba range, but had discounted the report as being improbable. Their chief concern, he said, was that the Belgians would assemble and launch the *Baron Dhanis*.

The German dead were given a military funeral, and then a guard was placed over their graves. This was a necessity, the Belgians insisted, because some of their askaris came from cannibalistic tribes and might want to exhume and consume the dead. Immediately after the service, two of the British sailors approached Dr. Hanschell with two small bottles filled with the blood of the German captain. One bottle had a piece of the captain's finger as well. They wanted to know how to preserve these souvenirs and keep them "fresh." Hanschell added thynol to the bottles.

Spicer-Simson had taken the captain's ring. The sailors had taken his blood. Soldiers had to be discouraged from eating the remains. War on the shores of Lake Tanganyika had taken on a distinctly barbaric cast.

The eleven captured survivors of the *Kingani* were marched away to a Belgian prison; the goat was claimed by the ratings and became a pet and mascot. One other member of the crew, Fundi, an African stoker, had leaped overboard and managed to reach shore. The expedition's African servants had found and hidden him. He was discovered by a couple of British officers, who learned that he was clever with his hands. Spicer-Simson, when asked if he could be kept and put to work, readily gave his permission, delighted thus to outwit the Belgians and cheat them of their prisoner.

In due course a wireless message arrived: "His Majesty the King desires to express his appreciation of the wonderful work carried out by his most remote expedition." Highly gratified, Spicer-Simson read it aloud to all hands. He soon learned that he had been made a substantive commander, his date of rank to be the date of the battle. Dudley was also promoted, becoming a full lieutenant.

In some cultures madness is taken for holiness. As Spicer-Simson grew more eccentric, more of the Ba-HoloHolo and other tribesmen had come to revere him. With the sinking of the *Kingani* his apotheosis was complete. Many knelt and clapped their hands or threw themselves on the ground and trickled sand through their hair when he passed by. The tattooed snakes curling up his arms added to his lustre, particularly when he took to semaphoring to or from the launches, even though no one, not even the signalman, could read his messages. The Ba-HoloHolo believed he was calling to his ju-ju to deliver another German ship into his hands. Perhaps he was doing something like that.

The tribesmen particularly relished seeing their god bathe, which he did with considerable ceremony. At four o'clock every Wednesday and Saturday his African servant set up a green canvas tub and filled it with cans of steaming water while a growing crowd jostled for the best seats around it on the ground. A bath mat was spread; a stool was placed beside the tub and on it were set a bottle of vermouth and a glass; the water was tested with the servant's finger and adjusted to the right temperature; then Spicer-Simson was informed that his bath was ready.

The god himself emerged from his hut wearing only slippers and a towel draped around his waist, every inch of his torso covered with tattooed beasts, birds, reptiles, flowers, and insects. He stood for a moment smoking a cigarette in a long holder while his audience clapped. When silence fell, he raised his arms and, flexing his muscles, sent the tattooed snakes writhing. Then, handing his cigarette holder to his servant, he stepped into the bath. He scrubbed vigorously, using a heavily scented soap that perfumed the air. When completely lathered, he stood up while his servant rinsed him with buckets of cold water. He then dried himself, wrapped the towel around his waist, and lit another cigarette while his servant poured him a glass of vermouth, which he drank appreciatively. The bath rite finished, he strode back into his hut to the cheers of his devotees.

A local priest, a Belgian White Fathers missionary who came regularly to beg for quinine, declared that Spicer-Simson was "demoralizing Africa." Although his influence was hardly that great, that pernicious, or that extensive, his fame certainly spread fast. He was called by tribesmen Bwana Chifunga-tumbo, which might be roughly translated as Lord Belly-Cloth. They had seen him come with his smoke-and-fire locos; they saw other white men jump when he spoke; and they knew that with two small boats he had conquered the *Kingani*, taking white men prisoners and dyeing the deck with blood.

Back in the bush the Ba-HoloHolo formed little clay statues of Spicer-Simson—"and very good likenesses too," according to Frank Magee. Dr. Hanschell found one that stood two feet high on a small altar surrounded by feathers, snake skins, and round stones covered with blood.

German intelligence on Belgian activities withered. The Ba-HoloHolo switched their allegiance from the Germans to the skirted British god, the new master of the lake. The Belgians obtained an extra bonus from the expedition: they no longer had to fear an uprising. The Germans, kept in the dark, still did not know about *Mimi* and *Toutou*, nor did they know what had happened to the *Kingani*.

Second to Spicer-Simson in the local sights were the seaplanes, which arrived shortly after the British victory. They came packed in crates and were assembled at Tongwe, a Belgian post twenty-five miles south of Lukuga. Magee described the effect when the first Short hydroplane flew over Lukuga:

> Suddenly the seaplanes shot into view out of the clouds, describing circles and going through sundry evolutions over the camp. The native stood spell-bound, gazing upward with arms extended, eyes bulging and mouths agape.
>
> The airman then made a sudden dive downward that broke the spell. The savages bounded off into the bush, terror lending wings to their progress. Mothers snatched up their pickaninnies and dived for the shelter of kraals, shrieking at the top of their voices. It was real pandemonium.

When the *Kingani* was hauled out of the water, the expedition's engineer constructed a forge and made a suitable patch for the shell hole in her hull. She was re-floated and the engines put into running order. A 12-pounder gun intended for the *Baron Dhanis* was mounted forward, although it was too large for the ship, twelve feet long, whilst the *Kingani* measured only forty-five feet. Unless it was pointed straight ahead it could not be fired without risk of capsizing the ship with the recoil. A 3-pounder was mounted aft and the ship was renamed by Spicer-Simson HMS *Fifi*— a fitting match for *Mimi* and *Toutou*. Thus *Fifi* became the first captured German warship to take its place on the list of the Royal Navy.

The Belgians now felt it was safe to assemble the *Baron Dhanis*, 1,500 tons, and it was brought up in sections by rail from Kabalo. The *Alexandre del Commune*, almost a total wreck, was patched up, re-fitted, and re-christened the *Vengeur*. The Belgians also had a squarish ten-ton river barge, appositely named *Dix Tonne*, armed with a 57 mm and a 47 mm gun, that could only move at six knots, but it was part of the little Allied fleet that was growing on Lake Tanganyika. After a lengthy correspondence between the British and Belgian governments, it was finally agreed that a Belgian officer would command on shore and Spicer-Simson would command all the Allied vessels on the lake.

The *Kingani*'s original gun was actually a British 6-pounder which Max Loof had taken off of the *City of Winchester*, along with 200 rounds of ammunition, at the beginning of the war. With the demise of the *Königsberg*, it had been sent to Kigoma and mounted on the *Kingani*. This gun and its ammunition were now transferred to the *Vengeur*.

On 9 February in the early hours of the morning the *Hedwig von Wissmann* was sighted steaming down the coast on the same course the *Kingani* had taken. At 100 tons she was more than twice the size of metamorphosed *Fifi*, and she carried two 6-pounders forward and a revolving Hotchkiss aft but she was reputed to be one knot slower than the smaller ship.

The crews of the Belgian and British vessels raced for the harbour. *Fifi* raised full steam and *Mimi*'s motors were turned over. (Toutou was again out of action, having been tossed against a breakwater during a storm a few weeks earlier.) *Fifi*, *Mimi*, *Dix Tonne*, and a small vedette boat left the harbour at 7.45 A.M. to do battle. Spicer-Spencer was

in *Fifi* and Wainwright, the former locomotive driver, commanded *Mimi*. It was a grey overcast day, but the lake was
smooth.

The *Hedwig von Wissmann* was about six miles away from
Spicer-Simson's little flotilla when at 9.30 she turned sharply
to port and fled. Both *Fifi* and the German poured oil on
their logs to obtain maximum speed. In the bowels of *Fifi*,
Fundi, the captured stoker, furiously stoked the furnaces
for the boilers of his new masters, but with the added
armament *Fifi* could not work up enough speed to keep up
and so fell back. The German was soon only a smudge on
the horizon, but Spicer-Simson ordered his gunner to open
fire. The recoil of the ten-pounder almost stopped the ship,
but Spicer-Simson ordered the firing to continue.

At this rate the *Hedwig von Wissmann* would escape—or
would rendezvous with the *Graf von Götzen*, 800 tons. A
meeting had, in fact been arranged, and had it taken place
the odds would have changed dramatically in the Germans' favour, for the *Graf von Götzen* carried one of the
Königsberg's 105 mm guns. But *Mimi* had the speed to catch
the German steamer and it now roared past the slower *Fifi*
in spite of Spicer-Simson's furious wig-wagging for her to
turn back. Wainwright simply ignored the commander's
frantic arm waving, which in any case he could not read.

At 3,000 yards Wainwright, keeping astern of the *Hedwig
von Wissmann*, opened fire. Some of his shells struck home,
but they did only superficial damage. As long as she was
fleeing, the German could only reply with her smaller
Hotchkiss; when she swung round to put her six-pounders
into action, she lost passage and *Fifi* drew closer. A single
hit from a six-pounder would have meant the end of *Mimi*,
but Wainwright managed to skip out of harm's way and
stay astern.

The *Fifi* now began to catch up. She continued to fire and
she was within range, but as no one on board could see
where the shots were falling, there was small chance of a
hit. Wainwright, however, could see that all of the shots
were over, and he dropped back to report this. Coming

abreast of *Fifi* he had first to endure a torrent of abuse from Spicer-Simson before he could call back the needed spotting information.

The *Hedwig von Wissmann*, now at bay, was a good target for *Fifi's* twelve-pounder, but Spicer-Simson had shot away almost all of his ammunition. Only three shells were left. And the next round misfired. With the unexploded shell in the gun, firing had to be postponed for twenty minutes, until it was safe to open the breach and remove the defective round and dump it overboard. When a fresh shell was shoved into the breech, the gunner took careful aim and, with skill and luck, sent it crashing through the hull to explode in the engine room. Water poured in and the *Hedwig von Wissmann*, enveloped in smoke and flames, began to sink.

Her sailors tried to launch a boat, but it sank. Men leaped frantically over her side into the water and within minutes the *Hedwig von Wissmann* slid bow first to the bottom of the lake. It was 11.15 A.M. The British ships picked up the bobbing survivors, though Spicer-Simson delayed the *Fifi's* mercy mission to turn back and pick up a German flag locker he had spied among the flotsom. In it was found, to his great delight, a large Imperial German naval ensign, the first ever captured.

Of the rescued crew, an able seaman originally on the *Königsberg* was the only man wounded, and Dr. Hanschell operated at once, amputating two fingers and a half of a third. The captain of the *Hedwig von Wissmann*, Lieutenant Job Odebrecht, was paroled and invited to dine with the British officers. As he had lost his shirt and boots, Hanschell generously provided him with both.

The Admiralty was most pleased with Spicer-Simson's successes. In his after action report he credited himself with having order *Mimi* forward, and he praised Wainwright for his faithful execution of his orders. Admiral Sir Henry Jackson, lost in admiration of this splendid officer, said, "I doubt whether any one tactical operation of such miniature proportions has exercised so important an influence on enemy operations."

The day after the battle the *Graf von Götzen* appeared off Lukuga looking for some sign of the *Hedwig von Wissmann*. Spicer-Simson, standing on his verandah, watched it intently through his glasses, while Dudley, beside him, pleaded with him to order an attack. In the harbour, *Fifi* was getting up steam and *Mimi* was preparing for battle, but Spicer-Simson let the moment pass. The *Graf von Götzen* looked formidable; he had already earned his place in history. While Dudley argued, the *Graf von Götzen* altered course and disappeared.

Twice more in the days ahead the *Graf von Götzen* steamed within sight of Lukuga without a shot being fired. Officers and ratings were disappointed and disgruntled; morale drooped and respect for their commanding officer sank.

On 21 February Spicer-Simson left Lukuga. He announced that he was going to see if any other vessels on the Congo River were suitable for his use on the lake, but he was gone an unconscionably long time. It is not entirely clear where he went or what he was doing, at one point he was staying with the British consul at Boma, at the mouth of the Congo, about 1,600 miles from Lukuga. Wainwright was left in charge, but he was under orders not to attack the *Graf von Götzen* unless Lukuga itself was attacked.

The sinking of the *Hedwig von Wissmann* had been acclaimed in Europe and at the British headquarters at Nairobi, for it had been this ship which had symbolized German power on Lake Tanganyika. The high commands in London and Nairobi either did not know about, or perhaps dismissed the importance of, the *Graf von Götzen*. As a result of Spicer-Simson's successes it was now declared that "active cooperation with the Belgian forces has become a practical possibility."

The Belgians were eager to cooperate. Commandant Stinghlamber had been replaced by Lieutenant Colonel Moulaert, who had made the mistake of speaking rudely to Spicer-Simson on their first meeting. Moulaert was ordered by General Charles Tombeur, the senior Belgian officer in the Congo, to coordinate plans with his British counterpart for the final conquest of the lake area as part of a joint British-Belgian advance into German East Africa from the northwest. It was an order impossible to obey, for Spicer-Simson was not there and no one knew where to find him.

However, on 12 May, after an absence of nearly three months, he returned to Lukuga. By this time the impatient Tombeur had ordered Moulaert to complete the Allied conquest with or without the British, but Spicer-Simson returned in time to thwart any unilateral action and to tell the unfortunate Moulaert that he, Spicer-Simson, was in charge of the Allied flotilla on the lake and that he would make his own plans without reference to the Belgian commander.

Instead of attacking the *Graf von Götzen*, Spicer-Simson began an acrimonious exchange of letters, reports and telegrams, a controversy that stemmed from his refusal to cooperate with Moulaert. He then ignored all Belgian plans and the joint Anglo-Belgian offensive at the north end of the lake and sailed south with *Mimi, Fifi, Vengeur*, and the now repaired *Toutou*. His declared purpose was to support an advance by Brigadier General Northy, the new British commander on the Southern Front.

There was indeed some action in this area. In Rhodesia two companies of the British South African Police (BSAP) and a large number of volunteers, most of whom were tough, independent-minded Rhodesian settlers' Some of whom were men discharged after the disbandment of the 1st Rhodesia Regiment, formed a unit known simply as Murray's Column after its commander, Lieutenant Colonel Ronald Ernest ("Kaffir") Murray. These were not men who took easily to discipline and, as one Rhodesian noted, relations between them and the regular forces were "sometimes not what they should be." In June 1916 Murray's Column moved north to attack Bismarckburg at the south end of the lake where the Germans had built a Beau Geste–style fort with crenelated walls.

The attack was not without incident. The Rhodesians may have been a rough and ready lot, but they possessed their own sense of chivalry. Only one man at a time was allowed to fire at the Germans and the African askaris who could sometimes be seen darting from place to place on the walls, and it was thought unsporting to use a machine gun.

On 8 June a British askari was sent to the fort under a white flag to demand its surrender, but the Germans, sitting comfortably behind their stout walls, declined to give it up. On his way back with the German reply, the askari encountered a group of BSAP troopers and Dr. J. M. Harold, a former Irish international rugby player. He informed them, or they thought he informed them, that the Germans *had* surrendered. The doctor and the troopers therefore sauntered up to the fort and knocked on the door, a thick wooden affair studded with iron and loopholed. It was opened by the fort's commandant, Lieutenant Hasslacher, who asked politely in excellent English: "What can I do for you, gentlemen?"

"Oh, just coming in," said Dr. Harold casually.

"How do you mean—just coming in?"

"Well, you've surrendered."

"I've done nothing of the sort," said Hasslacher indignantly. "You are my prisoners."

There was a second of stunned silence. "Like hell we are!" bellowed the doctor. "You're ours! Grab him!"

Lieutenant Hasslacher was seized and carried off, pursued by a storm of bullets from his soldiers on the walls of the fort. Some of the BSAP troopers were wounded—one through the cheek and another through the thigh, and a Rhodesian lieutenant was mortally wounded in the groin—but they were carried along. All tumbled into a protective gully, where in spite of a covering fire from their comrades in Murray's Column, they were pinned down. Hasslacher then made a proposal: he would order his men to cease fire if the doctor would allow him to return to the fort. The doctor agreed. Hasslacher held up a white handkerchief, blew a blast on his whistle, and the firing stopped. A party from the fort ran out with lemonade and bandages. Stretcher bearers ran out from the British lines. Captain R.W.M. Langham, a Rhodesian officer who witnessed the scene, said,

'I don't imagine that many actions have been terminated by a whistle like a Football Association Cup-tie." That night the Germans slipped out of the fort and escaped.

In this as in so many other actions in this campaign, there is no use asking *why*. Why wasn't an officer sent as a *parlementaire* to demand the fort's surrender? The doctor might have been wearing a Red Cross brassard on his arm, but why didn't the Germans shoot the BSAP troopers when they strolled up to the fort? Why did the askari say that the fort had surrendered when it had not? Or had he been misunderstood? Why did the doctor, of all people, go to the fort? How did the Germans manage to make what one historian called a "miraculous" escape? The answer to all such questions except the last have long been lost in the African interior. It is now known how the Germans managed their miraculous escape.

Spicer-Simson's flotilla had arrived at Kituta (no longer found on most maps) in Northern Rhodesia after a stormy voyage. They anchored on 26 May and there met up with Murray's Column just as it was about to move on Bismarckburg. Murray was surprised to see the flotilla and its skirted, tattooed commander, for he had received no orders or information concerning him. Initially he could see nothing that the flotilla could do for him; on second thought, he asked Spicer-Simson to make sure that the Germans did not escape by way of the lake.

Accordingly, Spicer-Simson took the flotilla to Bismackburg, and there he could see the picturesque fort on the hill, a small European settlement, an African village, and the harbour which sheltered several large canoes and three dhows, sailing vessels of about 100 tons each which were used to carry troops and supplies up and down the coast.

The officers in the flotilla assumed that he would go in and sink the canoes and dhows, preventing the Germans from escaping in them, but Spicer-Simson ruled otherwise. He feared the guns of the fort. Dudley and Wainwright argued with him, and Dudley volunteered to go in unsupported, but he was adamant. He sailed back to Kituta without firing a shot. He seemed to feel that he had done enough, and that he need not again risk his skin or his reputation in further enterprises of doubtful success.

It was known that Murray's Column was advancing and everyone in the flotilla assumed that they would certainly play a part in the final assault, acting as Murray's left flank on the water. But the ships stayed anchored at Kituta and the crews lived ashore. Not until the morning of 9 June, the day after the final assault, did Spicer-Simson take his flotilla back to Bismarckburg. They arrived to find the Union Jack flying from the fort and the dhows and canoes gone. Thus the "miraculous escape" of the Germans from Bismarckburg.

Spicer-Simson now found himself face to face with the Rhodesians, a different breed from the Belgians or the men of the Royal Navy. Laughter and jeers greeted the flotilla as it entered Bismarckburg's harbour, and a Rhodesian called out, "Where the hell were you navy chaps last night?"

Spicer-Simson ordered Dudley and Hanschell to accompany him as he stepped ashore wearing his gold-braided cap, blue flannel shirt, and his skirt. He asked a young Rhodesian officer to take him to Murray, but he merely pointed to the fort and said, "Straight up there. You can't miss it. Just follow your nose." Spicer-Simson's face flushed, but he said nothing. Marching up to the fort he was greeted with whistles and ribald laughter: "Kiss me, Gertie!" and "Oh! la! la!" and "Chase me, Charlie!"

At the fort he went in alone to face the wrath of Colonel Murray and emerged pale and shaken, holding out his hands in front of him as though he had been suddenly struck blind. "Kaffir" Murray was not the type of man to take kindly to those who failed him and robbed him of the fruits of victory.

Whatever Murray said to him was devastating. The flotilla was wanted to help mop up small German posts on the lake shore. He sent Wainwright and Dudley to handle this work while he lay on his cot, a beaten man. When Dr. Hanschell suggested that he be invalided home, he leaped at the chance and was soon back in England, explaining that he had suffered from malaria, dysentry, and numerous other tropical diseases. He also claimed that the *Graf von Götzen* had refused to come out and fight—a version that was incorporated into the *Official History*.

Meanwhile, the British seaplanes, manned by Belgian pilots and observers, flew to Kigoma to bomb the *Graf von Götzen* and on 10 June 1916 they claimed to have hit her. They had not. It scarcely mattered, for on Lettow-Vorbeck's orders, the ship's 105 mm *Königsberg* gun had been removed and turned over to the *Schutztruppe*.

As far as is known, no bomb from any aircraft ever touched a German ship on Lake Tanganyika, but Jan Smuts, who certainly should have known better, thought so, and even after the war he more than once said that "German armed vessels on the lake had been bombed and destroyed by seaplanes." Smuts, it seems, was completely ignorant of Spicer-Simson's contribution to the campaign. In the end, the Germans themselves took the *Graf von Götzen* out of commission. As General Tambeur's forces were approaching Kigoma, they sank her just offshore, having first carefully greased her engines and vital parts so that after Germany won the war she could be re-floated. [This proved convenient for the British, who re-floated her and used her on the lake into the 1960s.]

All twenty-eight members of the Naval Africa Expedition returned to England alive. Spicer-Simson was awarded the Distinguished Service Order; three of his officers received the Distinguished Service Cross, including Dr. Hanschell; and six ratings were awarded the Distinguished Conduct Medal. In addition, Spicer-Simson, who had been mentioned in dispatches four times, was created a Commander of the Crown of Belgium and awarded the Belgian Croix de Guerre with three palms. No medals and no recognition of any description was given John R. Lee, originator of the project.

When the admirals at the Admiralty had the time to study all of Spicer-Simson's reports and letters and to make some comparisons of accounts, it became evident, as Admiral Gamble concluded, that Spicer-Simson's "tactless behaviour might have contributed to a serious disaster." And when it became known how he had shirked his duty at Bismarckburg, his further advance in the navy was blocked forever. He was returned to the Intelligence Department and found himself in the same dusty office at the same desk next to the same Royal Marines major. He was now a commander with a chest full of ribbons, but he was working at his former inglorious tasks. Nevertheless, within a few weeks his spirits rose and he returned to his usual state of self-assurance.

Although he had been found out by his fellow officers on the expedition, by the Admiralty, and probably by others who had seen him at close range, he was still the popular hero. Versions of the story of the expedition were told over and over again in newspapers and magazines: 'The Jules Verne Expedition," "The Strangest Story of the War," "Nelson Touch on African Lake," and "Commander Spicer-Simsons (sic) Exploits on Lake Tanganyika." In the popular press he became the hero he always claimed to be.

In time, other members of the expedition told their stories and Peter Shankland put them together in an excellent account of what he called the "Phantom Flotilla." In summing up he had this to say of Commander Spicer-Simson:

> He had created a hero-image of himself that history had accepted. This was not to be explained by any logic. His appeal was to the irrational in all men, to what they wanted to believe. He was still the Little Clay God of the Ba-holo-holo.

CHAPTER

19

Smuts Takes Command

Early in May 1915 General Sir Horace Smith-Dorrien, fifty-seven years old, was relieved of his command of the Second Army on the Western Front and sent home by General Sir John French, the commander-in-chief. In June he was given command of the First Army for Home Defence. It was hardly a fitting appointment for an active full general. But on 12 November 1915 the subcommittee of the Committee for Imperial Defence recommended that German East Africa be conquered "with as little delay as possible," and in the following month General Smith-Dorrien was selected to command the British forces in East Africa.

It was Smith-Dorrien's understanding, and indeed the intent of the committee, that the forces in British East Africa would be considerably augmented, but Lord Kitchener, the Secretary for War, disapproved of sideshows in Africa and he refused to part with the necessary men, guns, and gear. The matter was finally submitted to the prime minister and Asquith eventually approved of sending a British brigade, a South African brigade, 2,000 mounted Boers, a couple of battalions of Indian infantry, and twenty-five guns to East Africa, which at this point was held by two British battalions, a brigade of the King's African Rifles, about 9,000 Indian troops, and a handful of colonial volunteers.

The War Office wanted the campaign to begin in March, but Smith-Dorrien demurred. His plan was to hold Lettow-Vorbeck in check until after the rains and in the meantime carefully to build up his army so that all would be ready and in place when he launched his attack. He selected his staff in London, sent them off to East Africa, and on Christmas Eve 1915, he embarked for Cape Town to confer with Botha and Smuts about the South African troops they were to supply. On his first day at sea he fell ill with a chill, which soon developed into pneumonia. When the ship docked at Cape Town he was taken immediately to a hospital. There his recovery seemed assured until he insisted on leaving and picking up his work before he was well enough. In consequence, he suffered a relapse so severe that he was forced to abandon all hope of undertaking a campaign in East Africa and he returned to England. Perhaps it was just as well.

Before leaving London, Smith-Dorrien had drawn up an appreciation of the situation in East Africa as he saw it. From this it is obvious that he viewed the projected campaign as being governed by the same factors as the war he had experienced on the Western Front in Europe, one in which numbers of soldiers, big guns, vast quantities of ammunition, and large stocks of materiel were vital factors; he could not imagine a war in which military strength counted less than able carriers, quinine, and knowledge of bushcraft.

Winston Churchill had hoped to become governor of British East Africa and Commander-in-Chief of the army there. His naval career—four years as First Lord of the Admiralty—had come to an inglorious end in 1915 with the disastrous Dardenelles campaign, of which he had been the chief advocate. Although he had recommended himself for the governorship and for Smith-Dorrien's place, the prime minister did not approve. By the end of the year he was a mere major in a yeomanry battalion in France. The man selected to replace Smith-Dorrien, Jan Smuts, seemed an improbable choice, a man who only thirteen years before had been a rebel in arms, the leader of a rag-tag group of less than 200 guerrillas fighting against the British Empire.

Jan Christian Smuts (1870–1950), son of an Afrikaner farmer, had not attended school until he was twelve years old, but he soon caught up with and surpassed his fellow students. After graduation from Victoria college in Stellenbosch, he won a scholarship to Cambridge, where he placed first in both parts of the law tripos—and in his spare time wrote a treatise on Walt Whitman. He was a loner. He played no sport and made few friends. He was admitted to the Middle Temple but in 1895 returned to practice law in South Africa.

In the course of his life Smuts hitched his wagon to two successive stars. The first was Paul Kruger, President of the Transvaal, who appointed him state's attorney at the age of twenty-eight. When Kruger left South Africa during the Boer War, Smuts found his second star in Louis Botha, who was distinguishing himself as a Boer general. In 1911, when the Union of South Africa was formed from the four colonies, Botha became prime minister and Smuts became a leading member of his cabinet. The personalities of the two men could not have been more different, but they complemented each other perfectly, and each recognized, admired, and utilized the talents of the other. During the Boer War Smuts had been a bold and resourceful guerrilla leader on a small scale. He had taken only a small part in the South-West Africa Campaign; he had stayed home most of the time to mind the store while Botha went to fight the Germans. Now, it seemed, it was his turn. Overnight he became, at age forty-six, the youngest lieutenant general in the British army and in charge of what became one of the most arduous campaigns in British military history.

The appointment surprised many and dismayed some. Brigadier General J.H.V. Crowe remarked, "It was a bold stroke to entrust command of those bodies of troops and the carrying out of those operations to a man who was not a soldier, who had practically no experience in handling any considerable force." Others, perhaps remembering Lloyd George's aphorism that "there is no profession where experience and training count less in comparison with judgment and flair," were sanguine.

Smuts arrived at Mombasa on 19 February 1916—just one week after still another miserable military failure. Brigadier General Wilfred Malleson, probably the least competent general in Africa, had led some 6,000 men with 18 guns and 41 machine guns in an attack upon the German positions at Salaita, near Taveta, one of the principal jumping-off points for German attacks on the Uganda Railway. The Germans, under Major Georg Kraut, were ensconced in well-constructed, well-placed entrenchments in dense bush on an isolated hill in a bit of British territory they had wrested from the British on 5 December 1915. Kraut had on the hill about 1,300 men, two small field guns, and twenty-one machine guns.

Malleson's little army was a mixture of Indians, Africans, Englishmen, Rhodesians, and South Africans. The newly arrived South Africans were green troops; most had had little training. They were long on hubris and short of experience.

Lieutenant H. Walter Stockdale had almost missed the war when the 6th South African Infantry embarked at Durban on 9 January, for he lingered too long over his farewells; the ship was already fifteen feet from the quay when he managed to push his way through the crowd and with a desperate running jump, cleared the gap, to the cheers of the soldiers aboard and the leave-takers on the quay. (A couple months later he was in the hospital with an injured knee after stepping in an "elephant hole.")

Two young soldiers in B Company, 6th South African Infantry, innocent of war's realities, had passed their time during the slow voyage up the coast by tossing messages in bottles overboard. Each message meticulously included their names, their unit, the name of their ship, and, for good measure, the number of soldiers on board. Some of their bottles were found a year later, washed ashore on Mafia Island. They were astonished by the repercussions.

Malleson launched his attack on Salaita at eight o'clock on the morning of 12 February, the day Smuts left South Africa. He opened with a heavy bombardment of what he believed to be the German trenches. A few days earlier the newly formed 26th Squadron (South Africa) of the royal Flying Corps in its first flight over the German positions had reported trenches on the crest of the hill and nothing more. It was these dummy trenches which Malleson's guns pounded with shrapnel and high explosive shells. The *Schutztruppen* were cleverly concealed at the foot.

When the British infantry began its advance it was met by accurate fire from two field guns and the South Africans came under heavy machine gun fire. It proved too much for the green South African troops. They wavered, and when Kraut sent his screaming askaris at them in a furious bayonet charge, they broke and bolted, not stopping until they reached the Serengeti Plain.

The South Africans suffered a loss of 132 or 138 or 170 men. And a loss of their *amour propre*. They had arrived in East Africa with all of their prejudices intact and had been in the habit of referring to the Indians as coolies. Many had professed to be offended by the prospect of fighting alongside them. But their rout at Salaita had been covered by the 130th Baluchis, who had also been subjected to heavy fire and a German bayonet charge but had held firm. A story, perhaps apocryphal and certainly denied later by South African historians, relates that on the day after the battle the South Africans were sent their abandoned machine gun lashed to a mule with a note that said, "With the compliments of the 130th Baluchis. May we request that you no longer refer to our people as coolies."

The after action report of the battle could be used as a model for all generals reporting unpleasant military experiences:

The enemy was found to be in force and counter-attacked vigorously. General Malleson was forced to withdraw to Serengeti, but much useful information had been gained and the South African infantry had learned some valuable lessons in bush fighting, and also had an opportunity of estimating the fighting qualities of the enemy.

Yes, indeed.

As soon as Smuts disembarked at Mombasa he set off for headquarters in Nairobi, where he made a brief stay, refusing all official receptions. He then hurried south to make a personal reconnaissance of the front in the Serengeti area. General Tighe had drawn up a plan for an attack on German East Africa in this sector, and Smuts endorsed his plan with only minor changes.

Considerable staff difficulties had arisen. Tighe had his own staff, of course, and confusion enough ensued when the staff Smith-Dorrien had selected in England arrived at Nairobi. Now Smuts arrived with his South Africans. To this was added the long-standing confusion caused by the different methods of Colonial, Indian, and War Office administrators.

Smith-Dorrien's staff officers were unknown to Smuts and they expected to be sacked, but most were kept on. Smuts had brought along John Johnson Collyer to be his chief of staff, but he was anxious that everything should be done along War Office lines, and Smith-Dorrien's selections could do it as his South Africans could not. In any case, Smuts was more concerned about the capabilities of his subordinate commanders. Keeping most of the English staff was a wise move. (Among those staff officers who did depart, although not immediately, was Captain Meinertzhagen.) Even so, it was a long time before the British army in East Africa was properly administered—and there were those who plausibly argued that it never was.

Smuts wasted little time sorting out staff problems. As Dolby said, "The real history of the war begins with Smuts; for, prior to his coming, we were merely at war; but when he came we began to fight." On 5 March he launched a two-pronged attack in the Kilimanjaro area: Stewart marched to Longido and then southeast around the base of Kiliman-

jaro while Tighe approached west and north of Kilimanjaro, through Salaita and Tavetta. Smuts's aim was to get
on the road and the railway beyond Moshi in time to cut
off the retreat of the forces under Major Kraut in the Arusha area. The principal geographical objective was Moshi,
a market town for European colonists and the terminus of
the Northern Railway that ran to Tanga. The more important strategic objective was the capture or defeat in battle
of Kraut's force.

The British badly needed a victory *somewhere* in the world.
The BEF had experienced a disaster at Loos on the Western
Front; Gallipoli was a hideous stalemate; and there had
been a singular lack of success in Mesopotamia. Smuts
gratified the Cabinet and the War Office by attacking at
once, without waiting for the rains to come and go, as Smith-
Dorrien had intended. He now had in hand, in addition to
the troops that had been in East Africa, a South African
expeditionary force under Brigadier General J. L. van
Deventer that consisted of two infantry brigades; a mounted
brigade; a battalion of "coloured" troops (men of mixed
white, black, and Hottentot blood) known as the Cape Corps;
five batteries of artillery; a squadron of the Royal Flying
Corps (RFC); and various ancillary units—in all 27,350
combatants with 71 field guns and 123 machine guns.

The South Africans added to the variegated cultural mixture of the troops in East Africa. Robert Dolby, who served
in the campaign, remarked that "since Alexander of Mace-
donia descended upon the plains of India, there can never
have been so strange and heterogeneous an army as this."
East Africa was to witness the largest assortment of races,
tribes, and nationalities ever to be involved in a single
campaign in modern history.

The diversity of the British forces can perhaps best be
illustrated by looking at three battalions from three conti-
nents, all of which were to earn high marks for their long
service and were to sustain appalling casualties before the
end of the campaign.

The 2nd Rhodesian Regiment and the 25th Battalion of

the Royal Fusiliers arrived early in 1915; the 129th Baluch Regiment (later the 4th Battalion of the Duke of Connaught's Own 10th Baluch Regiment) arrived in January 1916. The splendid services of these battalions in East Africa lay in the future and could not easily have been predicted when they arrived.

The 2nd Rhodesia Regiment had been hurriedly raised. A few of its members had served with the 1st Rhodesia Regiment in South-West Africa, but most were recruits who had been promised that they would see active service and told that it was better to serve in their own colony's regiment than to go to Europe and serve with strangers. The 2nd Rhodesians, although a white unit, wisely recruited thirty African scouts. After eight months of training, almost none of which was to be of the slightest use to them in East Africa, they were shipped off, 600 strong, up the coast to Mombasa.

The 25th Royal Fusiliers, one of the most colourful battalions to serve in the Great War, was raised and led by Lieutenant Colonel Daniel Patrick Driscoll, fifty-five years old, who had served in the Upper Burma Rifles and had won the Distinguished Service Order leading Driscoll's Scouts in the Boer War. The battalion liked to call itself the Legion of Frontiersmen, and perhaps no battalion had ever before been so filled with a like collection of adventurers.

Included were a number of big game hunters, the most famous being sixty-four-year-old Lieutenant (later captain) Frederick Courteny Selous. One of his fellow officers said of him: "His endurance and marching powers were extraordinary. Quiet and modest, he was nobly self-effacing, and had the humility that is part of every great man's make up." Indeed, he was universally admired. Even Meintertzhagen respected him, and former President Theodore Roosevelt once said, "There was never a more welcome guest at the White House than Selous." Another officer in the battalion was William Northrup, an American millionaire and owner of a large farm in East Africa. A huge man, he wore a 64-inch sword belt around the center of his 336-pound frame.

Angus Buchanan, a naturalist who had been collecting specimens in a remote corner of Hudson's Bay when the war began, hurried to England to enlist in the Frontiersmen. Advancing through all ranks, he was a captain within eighteen months. Cherry Kearton, a noted photographer, also enlisted, as did an opera singer, a Buckingham Palace footman, several American cowboys (all said to have come from Texas), some Russians who had escaped from exile in Siberia, a former Honduran general (who rose to the rank of sergeant), several veterans of the French Foreign Legion and the Spanish-American War, stock exchange clerks, a lighthouse keeper from Scotland, a circus clown, an Artic explorer, and a lion tamer who professed to be afraid of lions.

In East Africa the Frontiersmen were known as the "old and bold," for many, like Selous were overage for hard soldiering and on their chests they wore the medal ribbons of other wars and distant campaigns. The 25th Fusiliers was the only battalion ever sent out from England for active service without preliminary training. It was a large battalion, leaving England 1,166 strong; it landed at Mombasa on 6 May 1915. Less than four months later one of its officers, thirty-year-old Lieutenant Wilber Taylor Dartnell, an Australian, won a Victoria Cross. A patrol he was leading near Maktau was ambushed; fourteen of his men fell. Although wounded in the leg, he ordered the remainder of his men to leave him. He covered their retreat and was last seen firing at the advancing enemy askaris.

At the beginning of the war the 129th Baluchis was a one battalion regiment composed of two companies of Punjabi Muslims and six companies of Pathans (one of Mohmands, two of Afridis, and three of Mahsuds). It was sent to Europe and arrived in September 1914, the first Indian unit to land in France. It was quickly shoved to the front and Captain P.H.C. Vincent had the unfortunate distinction of being the first Indian Army officer killed in the war. In its first ten days in the line—at Hollebeke in the Ypres sector—it lost half of its British officers, nearly a third of its Indian officers and other ranks. One of its sepoys, Khudadad Khan, won the Victoria Cross, the first native-born Indian to do so.*

In spite of reinforcements, a survivor, writing two months later, said, "We have now practically no men left." Indeed, losses almost equalled the original strength of the unit. The 129th Baluchis had been a fine battalion, but it had been blown away.

Good battalions, once lost, cannot easily or quickly be reconstructed, nor can the esprit of its members be instantly revived. With almost no rest, the battalion was thrust back into trenches near Givenchy where, at nine o'clock in the morning on 19 December, the Germans exploded several huge mines under trenches held by the Sirhand Brigade. The entire brigade was routed, and it is not to be wondered at that the 129th was the first to break. Their panic spread to other Indian units. Many threw away their rifles in their terror as they fled. When halted they declared that all their officers were dead. Many were.

Just ten days before this disaster it had been learned that of the 1,848 sepoys admitted to hospital for wounds up to 3 November, 1,049 (57%) suffered from hand wounds, and hand wounds, particularly those in the left hand, were considered almost sure signs that the wound was self-inflicted. By 14 August 1915 the 129th Baluchis had sustained 318 casualties from hand wounds.*

The demoralized Baluchis were withdrawn from the line. It was proposed to send the battalion to fight the Turks, but the troops, being Muslims, baulked at fighting their co-religionists. To demonstrate their seriousness, they murdered one of their British officers. They came to believe that the Germans were Muslims, and many proclaimed that they

---

* Indians only became eligible to receive the Victoria Cross in 1911.
* For comparison: the most hand wounds in any British battalion were 54 in the Connaught Rangers.

would not fight Germans either. The most radical and fanatical members of the battalion were removed and the rest shipped off to East Africa. Their reputation preceeded them, and one disgusted British officer wrote: "We were, of course, delighted to have troops that could not be retained at home and were considered too uncertain for another front, especially as the men insisted they would never fight Germans."

In spite of its unsavoury reputation, the 129th developed into a first-class fighting unit again. The discovery that the Germans ate *schweinfleisch* destroyed the notion that they were Muslims. Dr. Brett Young spoke of them as being "lean and lithe" and of possessing "splendid physique," and he added that one "need not wish to be in a tight corner with better men." Other British officers came to echo his sentiments. They were known to use less ammunition than anyone else and to produce more corpses.

The battalion also acquired a reputation for fighting patrols that were so vigorous that their claims were sometimes met with skepticism. A havildar (sergeant) whose report on the success of a patrol was met with less than full belief by his commanding officer, returned from his next patrol and reported having killed a German officer, a noncommissioned officer, a sentry, and a bugler. "Here," he said, laying the evidence before his officer, "is the officer's revolver, the naik's (corporal's) stripes, the sentry's rifle, and the bugler's bugle. So now perhaps you will believe my first story."

The extraordinary number of races, tribes, and nationalities grew even more elaborate when later in the campaign units from the Gold Coast and Nigeria were added and the Portuguese entered the war.

Voi, a town of the Uganda Railway only sixty miles from the German frontier, was built up as a staging area. An airfield was constructed at Mbuyuni. Salaita was reconnoitred by Pretorius, the elephant hunter, who reported to Smuts that it was "a little desert where there is not a drop of water to be found, and the Germans are getting their supply from Taveta, a town eight miles away." He recommended by-passing Salaita and capturing Taveta. It was sound advice, but it was not taken. Salaita was attacked after a long artillery bombardment—and found deserted. The Germans, well aware of the vulnerability of their position, had evacuated it and pulled back beyond the Lumi River. Smuts marched on and Longido was taken without opposition. On 13 March he entered Moshi. He had reached his geographical objective, but no masses of German troops had been taken. The pincer movement had pinched no one.

Smuts's intended envelopment was to be repeated time and time again—and always with the same result. His campaign in East Africa was a series of frustrating attempts to surround Lettow-Vorbeck's main force or to bring him to fight a decisive battle. He never succeeded. Each time they tried the British were convinced that they would bring Lettow-Vorbeck to bay, and each time he eluded them. He always retreated in the face of overwhelming force, but not before it was necessary, and it was never easy to assemble the required force at the needed point. Smuts and the commanders-in-chief who followed him captured territory, but none succeeded in defeating the wily Lettow-Vorbeck. The British imagined that he would fight to the end to defend the colony's major cities and railways, but he had no intention of doing so. His aim remained to suck British forces into the East African vortex "in the greatest possible strength, and thus be diverted from other more important theatres of war."

Even so, Smuts's successes sounded good in reports to London. The territory he captured could be measured in miles; progress on the Western Front, if any, was measured in yards. He had swiftly recovered the British territory lost at the beginning of the war and he had pushed his way into the interior of German East Africa. Under Smuts, all fighting would be done on the enemy's soil.

In the advance on Moshi the British witnessed impressive examples of German ingenuity in making do with what was available. Wire from plantation fences had been used

Bridge on the Morogoro-Tabora (Central) Railway destroyed by the Germans in 1916

as telegraph lines and broken off necks of beer bottles had been used as insulators. They noted too that the wires had been strung from tree tops or extremely tall poles to avoid being broken by giraffes. Along the railways they saw examples of German thoroughness, for as the Germans retreated, they took up the tracks, fish plates, and even bolts. What could not be carried away was destroyed; no bridge was left standing.

Initially, in most areas of British East Africa the alarms of war did little to alter the normal course of life. At the Missioni Consolata, an Italian mission station, Smuts's victories were eclipsed by a conquest which Father C. Cagnolo found of far greater importance:

> A striking event happened on January 14th 1916, which became a matter of discussion and thought all over the country, and filled with new courage the missionaries far and near: the Baptism and Christian wedding of the great chief Karoli.

Karoli gave up some sixty wives to settle for one, and he allowed himself to be baptized "Joseph." Father Cagnolo dubbed him "the Great Constantine of Kenya." Later in the war, even the Italian missionaries would be enlisted to assist the warriors, the Great Constantine forgotten.

Lettow-Vorbeck saw clearly the course of the campaign, in which he would play hare to Smuts's hounds. Others, less percipient, anticipated victories. On 27 January 1916, the Kaiser's birthday, Governor Schnee travelled to Dar-es-Salaam to take the salute at a parade and to deliver a rousing speech praising the *Schutztruppe* and the "brilliant leadership" of its commander. He sent a copy of his address to Lettow-Vorbeck, who snorted, "Good! At last he has accepted the fact that we are at war. I hope he will speak as resolutely six weeks from now, when the military situation may not be so healthy for us."

Well prepared, Lettow-Vorbeck did not find Smuts's advance daunting; he calmly moved his headquarters down the railway line to Kahe and made himself comfortable in a plantation. It was decidedly cramped but, he said, "I myself was lucky enough to find a comfortable shake-down on a sofa, with the cloth off the dining-table. Telephone messages came in day and night without ceasing; but they did not prevent us from making the material side of our existence comfortable." He confidently expected Smuts to move down the railway after him and he made adequate preparations to meet him, including an elaborate installation for one of *Königsberg*'s guns.

As anticipated, Smuts began an advance down the Usambara Railway to Kahe on 18 March. It was not in Lettow-Vorbeck's character or in his plans merely to flee from Smuts. He intended to give black eyes and bloody noses to his pursuers, and this he did—over and over again, for almost invariably he had the advantage of selecting where he wanted to fight, and when.

Smuts found the Germans in force in strong defensive positions with each flank resting on two deep, fast-flowing, crocodile-infested rivers. Brush was cleared in wide belts to give good fields of fire for the German Maxims. The *Königsberg* gun was well sited to cause maximum destruction.

With poor intelligence and inadequate maps the British

pushed forward, taking heavy casualties. Nightfall found them short of their objectives and they dug in as best they could with bayonets, knives, and their bare hands. Throughout a miserable night the wounded called out for stretchers and doctors; all were hungry, thirsty, and physically spent. Captain Angus Buchanan of the 25th Royal Fusiliers said, "In that bush forest, after dark, wandering parties, unfamiliar with the encampment as it lay after the battle, seemed to be looking for every regiment, and water cart, and doctor in creation." The next day they made an exhausting flanking movement—and found nothing but a few abandoned telephone lines swinging in the wind. The Germans had vanished. Lettow-Vorbeck had no intention of exposing his troops to a last-stand engagement when they could easily fall back to new positions. The British were allowed to enter Kahe without opposition. It, too, was empty. Anything of use had been carried off or destroyed. Here, however, the British made their first capture of one of the *Königsberg*'s ten guns. It had been rendered unserviceable and tumbled in the weeds.

In the wake of his initial victories Smuts took the opportunity to sack three of his generals: Malleson, Stewart, and Tighe. He wanted a new team. Malleson, responsible for what Smuts called the "Salaita fiasco," had more than once proved himself an incompetent commander. The end came when, at the height of a battle, he reported himself too sick with dysentery to continue in command. Meinertzhagen saw him leave the field in a motorcar, "reclining on a soft cushion and smoking a cigarette." Stewart, not really a bad general, was not a good one either, and Smuts blamed his slowness for the escape of Major Kraut's forces. [Stewart eventually became governor of Aden.] Tighe was a good garden variety general, though he was said to drink more than was good for him, and he had not blotted his copybook; it was, after all, essentially his plan which Smuts had used to achieve his initial success, but Smuts wanted better men, his own men, in the chief commands. He saw that Tighe was awarded a knighthood before being sent away. Smuts was then free to form three divisions: two under trusted and proven Afrinkaners, "Jaap" van Deventer and "Coen" Brits; the third under Brigadier General A. R. Hoskins, DSO, a Staff College graduate and former inspector general of the King's African Rifles.

Coenraad ("Coen") Brits, forty-seven, was a tough-talking, hard-drinking, crude but effective warrior. He had been a general in the Boer War and had helped Botha suppress the rebellion of 1914. When mobilizing troops to fight in South-West Africa, he sent a telegram to Botha: "Mobilization complete. Who must I fight? The English or the Germans?" He was once fined for using bad language in a public place, and he habitually greeted friends by slashing them with the sjambok, the heavy hippopotmus hide cattle whip he was never without. It was said that the harder he hit the better he liked his victim. "If that's true," said one, "he must have liked me very much." Deneys Reitz, a friend from Boer War days, saw him in East Africa:

> He held the rank of Brigadier General. Around the gilt oak leaves on each gorget tab were twined sprigs of forget-me-nots, embroidered in vivid purple. Thinking this was some new insignia of officer I asked him what it meant. Looking down affectionately at the ornaments the old man said that his wife had worked the flowers upon his uniform to remind him of her while he was at war. We could not help smiling, but we liked him the more for his naive simplicity.

Louis Jacob ("Jaap") van Deventer, thirty-nine, had served under Smuts in the Boer War and had taken part in his daring raid into Cape Colony. A big man with long moustaches and a goatee, he spoke in a husky voice, the legacy of a British bullet which had pierced his throat. Meinertzhagen wrote:

> He is cunning as an old fox and does not make up his mind till the last moment. Then he acts like lightning; up to that moment he appears dense and slow. To him a decision is final; there is no swerving, no delay, no alteration of plan. . . . He experiences

some difficulty in not realizing that he is the hunter and not the hunted, for during the Boer War he was accustomed to the latter role. . . . The old man has a wonderful eye for country and relies largely on manoeuvre, which appears to suit the peculiar Dutch temperament.

General C. P. Fendall knew him well:

He was a big man morally as well as physically. Extraordinarily clear-headed, he always saw the point of an argument at once, and could and did look at all sides of every question. He had a very high standard by which he judged the conduct of all men.

Unaccustomed to speaking English, he avoided it where possible. He was a popular general and earned the respect of all, even his English staff, whom he had no notion of how to make use. Under van Deventer there was no red tape and, unfortunately for historians, few records.

Arthur Reginald Hoskins, commissioned in the North Stafforshire Regiment in 1891 at the age of twenty, was a more conventional British officer. He had seen active service under Kitchener in the Sudan, in South Africa during the Boer War, and in the campaign against the "Mad Mullah" in Somaliland in 1903.

Smuts now had good experienced men in key command positions. He would need them, for in the next few months he was to encounter four major surprises. The first, and most discomfiting, was the discovery that Lettow-Vorbeck possessed a mind as brilliant as his own, and in military matters was his superior, a fact he could never bring himself to admit, although he admired his genius. After the war the two men were to become friends.

The superior fighting qualities of the German askaris was also a surprise. These "damned kaffirs," as Smuts called them, had been well trained and disciplined by German officers and NCOs, and they were, at least initially, man for man, better soldiers for bush fighting than the British, Indians, or South Africans. It took the British an unconscionably long time to realize that African tribesmen could be turned into first-class soldiers, particularly for bush warfare, and Smuts never really accepted the fact, though he was forced to concede that the German askaris knew their trade.

The third and most devastating surprise for Smuts was the discovery that the greatest enemy his troops faced was not the Germans with their clever commander and well-drilled askaris, but infections and diseases carried by germs and worms, by tsetse flies, and a myriad of other insects. These decimated his army; they almost completely destroyed it.

Smuts's fourth surprise hit him with such force that its power and influence could not be denied: the rains. He later admitted his astonishment:

> I had read about it, and I had heard more; but the reality surpassed the worst I had read or heard. For weeks the rain came down ceaselessly, pitiless, sometimes three inches in twenty-four hours until all the hollows became rivers, all the low lying valleys became lakes, the bridges disappeared, and all roads dissolved in mud. All communications came to an end, and even Moses himself in the desert had not such a commissariat situation as faced me.

He had thought he could go on fighting through the rainy season. If the troops in Europe could fight in the mud of Flanders, he reasoned, his men could slog through sodden bush in East Africa; it was a notion that caused his men much needless suffering.

As the rains normally begin in March, Smuts was lucky to have made his first successful forward movement just before the delayed rainy season began. The capture of Kahe was the last action before the heavens opened, the rains descended, and wild beasts, Africans, Asians, and Europeans sought shelter from its pitiless, unceasing downpour.

chapter 20

On the Road to
Morogoro

D ay and night the rain drummed on leaves and ground
and roofs. Paths became streams, valleys became
lakes; bridges and roads were swept away; every river and
stream was in flood; trees dripped unceasingly, mud coated
the ground and all who tried to walk on it; damp clothing,
wet blankets, soggy food, rusting metal, and mildewed
webbing added to the misery. No one was ever dry. The
heavy rains lasted for two months, but to wait for them to
end would cause a delay Smuts could not tolerate. He had
a plan for the next stage of his invasion and he was eager
to put his troops in motion.

When the Germans retired from Kahe the British conquest of the Kilimanjaro–Meru area was complete. Smuts's
sharp little eighteen-day campaign had put into British
hands one of the most fertile and healthy districts in the
colony. Kitchener thought that Smuts should now stop: He
had eliminated the danger of an invasion of British East
Africa and there was no real purpose to be served by the
conquest of a colony which would fall into Allied Hands

after the war in any case. But Kitchener was losing his influence in the councils of war and his views were not shared by Smuts and those in London who saw an opportunity to win stunning victories in Africa with which to counterbalance the lack of success in Europe.

Generals try to outguess each other. Smuts thought that Lettow-Vorbeck would reason that he intended to pursue him southeast down the Usambara Railway. But Smuts wrote in a dispatch: "Merely to follow the enemy in his very mobile retreat might prove an endless game. . . . In view of the size of the country it was therefore necessary to invade it from various points with columns strong enough to deal with any combination that could be brought against them."

Brigadier General Northey, the new commander in Rhodesia, was to push up into the southern part of German East Africa; Brigadier General Crewe was to cooperate with the Belgians in an invasion of the populous northwest corner of the colony. As for Smuts himself, he intended to push southeast down the Usambara Railway in the direction of Tanga, turn south towards Handeni and then on to the key town of Morogoro, about one hundred miles east of Dar-es-Salaam on the Central Railway which linked Dar-es-Salaam with Lake Tanganyika. Meanwhile, further east, van Deventer's division was to push south across the Masai plain with the key road junction of Kondoa Irangi as his first objective, and then push on to get astride the all-important Central Railway. Smuts had hopes that the Portuguese, who had declared war on Germany on 9 March 1916, would attack German East Africa from the southeast, as he urged them to do.

Smuts was too impatient; he could not wait for the rains to stop. He had been told—erroneously—that the rainy season was most violent in the Kilimanjaro area and that further south it was not nearly so bad. His informants were pro-German Afrikaners whose aversion to the British was such that after the Boer War they had left South Africa to make new lives for themselves in German East Africa rather than live under British rule. Why Smuts trusted them is something of a mystery. He usually took intelligence reports with a grain of salt, but he believed the Boer farmers and stated confidently in a dispatch that "the rains would not seriously interfere with military operations." Perhaps he simply believed what he wanted to believe. In any case, the rains did hinder operations and his soldiers marched and fought through the worst rainy season within living memory.

In the last week of March he ordered van Deventer's 2nd Division to prepare to march on Kondoa Irangi, 250 miles east of Dar-es-Salaam and 150 miles south of Moshi. On 3 April the 1,200 men of the Mounted Brigade splashed out of Arusha in a pouring rain for Kondoa Irangi, about a hundred miles away in a straight line and perhaps twice that for van Deventer's troopers. They were followed soon after by the 3rd South African Infantry Brigade. It was the beginning of a march which has been called "one of the outstanding feats of the First World War" and "one of the most notable and determined adventures of the First world War." Everything, including the colony's infrastructure, conspired to make it arduous. The railways and most of the roads and paths ran east and west, between the Indian Ocean and Lake Tanganyika, while the course of the campaign was from north to south.

The Mounted Brigade (three regiments of cavalry and mounted infantry) advanced thirty-five miles over rough country in forty-eight hours, before they found their way blocked by Captain Paul Rothert with the 28th Field Company ensconced on a rocky elevation called Lolkisale, which commanded the only spring in the area. The troopers were dead tired and ravenously hungry, but they surrounded the hill and pushed home a hard charging attack. The hill was stoutly defended until Rothert fell seriously wounded; then most of the askaris lost heart and surrendered. This was the first serious defeat for the *Schutztruppe*, the first time a unit had surrendered.

Such small victories were rare; the usual pattern was as van Deventer described in a report to Smuts:

The fighting consisted of the enemy receiving our advanced guard with one of several ambushes then falling back on a well-prepared position, and retiring from that on to further well-selected ambush places and positions. All the time our less advanced troops were subjected to vigorous shelling by means of long-range naval guns.

Within a fortnight van Deventer's Mounted Brigade was reduced by casualties—mostly from disease, starvation, and sheer exhaustion—from 1,200 to 800 effectives. A week later, when van Deventer finally reached Kondoa Irangi, he had only 600 reasonably fit men still able to do duty.

The drenched South African infantry, following in the wake of the Mounted Brigade, plodded painfully through "black cotton" mud and slithered on the red laterite slides. Their route was strewn with the unburied and putrefying corpses of hundreds of van Deventer's horses, donkeys, and mules killed by the tsetse flies that had swarmed out of the thorn trees to attack them. Of the brigade's 3,894 horses and mules, 1,639 died on the march. The infantry called their carcasses "van Deventer's milestones," but Captain F. H. Acutt, a South African artilleryman, said that this was a misnomer, for "the average interval between stinking, dead carcasses was 100 yards." One sick infantryman wrote: "We lay there in the mud and retched from the stench of dead animals and watched the rats crawl over us."

The commissary problems were enormous. Half rations soon gave way to even smaller portions. Some starving soldiers lived for a time on groundnuts and paw-paws. Motorcars and lorries simply sank into the mud, as did the supply wagons. Wireless sets broke down, telephone wires snapped, dispatch riders were unable to move; communication was just barely possible by using mounted messengers. Field hospitals established en route overflowed with patients and rainwater.

Kondoa Irangi, the first major objective, revealed itself to be a small town nestled in a narrow valley 85 miles north of the Central Railway. It had been a German food depot and boasted a wireless station, but the town had been partially burned before the Germans left. Nearby, however, was a most welcome sight: a herd of 800 cattle. In the hills to the south, barring the route to the Central Railway lay a strong German force of nearly 4,000 men under Major Kraut, and van Deventer was too weak to drive them away.

Eleven days after the arrival of the Mounted Brigade—if such it could still be called—the infantry trudged in to Kondoa Irangi. The men were in wretched condition, suffering from malaria and dysentery, covered with sores and infected scratches and cuts. The 129th Baluchis had only 158 fit men. The 2nd Rhodesian, which only three months before had left Salisbury 600 strong, was now reduced to 50 effectives. Dr. Francis Brett Young, their doctor, recorded that "their machine guns had been turned in to Ordnance for want of gunners and pestilence had swept away the lives of all transport animals."

As the seriously sick and the wounded could not be evacuated during the rains, conditions at Kondoa Irangi were appalling. An English officer wrote:

> With only just sufficient lift on the road to keep up a restricted supply of rations it was impossible to send up hospitals. Field ambulances had to do the work of stationary hospitals; clothing and equipment could not be sent up in anything like sufficient quantities. . . . A certain amount of food was available from the country round, but the arrangements for getting it in, and distributing it were bad. . . . As time went on the ration improved a little, but the men never got the full ration to which they were entitled during the two months they were there.

On 3 June van Deventer reported to Smuts:

> Following is the present situation in my division. Today 711 sick in hospital and 320 in convalescent camp. Lack of strengthening foods such as oatmeal, bacon, jam, cheese, milk, ect. renders it almost hopeless to expect convalescents to get fit for active duty. . . . Empty lorries returning is the only means of evacuating our sick. The majority of our men are lying on the ground in tent hospitals as there are no stretchers avail-

able. Infantry regiments for the most part arrived here without blankets—dearth of boots, clothing, soap—the very poor rations are the cause of the very heavy sick rate. . . . If immediate steps are not taken the situation will daily become worse . . . the animals are weak . . . arrangements will collapse.

This gloomy report fell into the hands of Lettow-Vorbeck and doubtless gave him much comfort and encouragement. He did not allow his enemies any rest and made frequent attacks on them.

Deneys Reitz came upon Piet Swart at Kondoa Irangi. He had been a farm hand in South Africa and was now with the Mounted Brigade:

> He was haggard from fever, he had starved and suffered and was in rags, but he held an original view of the campaign, for when I asked him whether he regretted having come, he said No: he had travelled in a ship, he had seen aeroplanes and Kilimanjaro and elephants, and if his parents wanted to see all this it would cost them fifty pounds.

Later Reitz found him lying dead by a river with a bullet between his eyes. Beside him was his dead horse.

The Germans had a small six-pounder at Kondoa Irangi; it was mounted on a frame so that it could easily be carried from place to place by askaris. They would fire a half-dozen rounds and then pick it up and move elsewhere. The South Africans laughed at it and mockingly called it Big Bertha. Several attempts to capture it failed. Reitz and two others stalked it one day, and after an exhausting uphill approach they found the gun emplacement. The gun was gone but the German commander had left a note: "15 rupees for the bluddy Englisch!"

There is an oft-repeated story that dates from this period of the campaign concerning a British officer who was shot, captured, and sent to a hospital in Dar-es-Salaam where he was nursed by the wife of the German officer who had shot him. One version identified the German officer as Lieutenant von Ruckteschell, who for a time served as Lettow-Vorbeck's adjutant. The British officer is usually identified as a Major Buller, whom Lettow-Vorbeck believed to be the son of the famous Boer War general, Sir Redvers Buller, but Sir Redvers had no son. A romantic ending is sometimes supplied: when the German officer was killed, the British officer married his widow, who had nursed him back to health. One would like to believe there was some basis for this story. Perhaps there was.

Van Deventer, stalled at Kondoa Irangi, had 3,000 troops in hand after the arrival of all his infantry, but he was still outnumbered. It was the first and only time in the campaign that the Germans enjoyed a numerical superiority in any area. Kraut had 4,000 men well dug in. He could not be moved, but neither could he rout the British. Kraut also had several of the *Königsberg*'s guns; when van Deventer demanded artillery to respond, he was sent a couple guns salvaged from *Pegasus* in Zanzibar's harbour.

The rains fell upon the Germans as well as the British, but the Germans, working on interior lines, did not lack for food, clothing, and other supplies, and Germans and their askaris were inured to the climate. Still, life was not easy. When Lettow-Vorbeck set off on a 140-mile trip to Kimamba on the Central Railway, he set out by motorcar, but was forced to switch to a horse, and finally entered Kimamba on foot. Governor Schnee came from Tabora to meet him and to express his extreme displeasure at the course of the campaign. He demanded that Lettow-Vorbeck account for the "disaster" at Kilimanjaro and to explain what he was doing to assure the safety and well-being of the colonists and natives. In reply, Lettow-Vorbeck gave him a lecture on the military facts of life and suggested that he return to Tabora, where perhaps he was needed.

On the ninth and tenth of May the Germans launched four serious attacks on the British forces at Kondoa Irangi, the heaviest weight falling on the 11th and 12th South African Infantry. The attacks, which lasted from 7.30 P.M. on the ninth until 3.15 A.M. on the tenth, constituted the first and last time that the *Schutztruppe* took the offensive against any large segment of Smuts's army.

During a desperate fight on the 9th Meinertzhagen performed his last bloody exploit in Africa when a German
struck him a heavy blow on the shoulder:

> He was carrying a knobkerrie which I finally wrenched from
> his hand, got my knee well into his stomach and then set to on
> his head with the knobkerrie until he was silent. I was furious
> with him for hitting me on the shoulder.

Next day he learned that he had beaten to death Captain
Friedrich von Kornatzki.

In spite of some tense moments, the South Africans held
in the face of the determined attacks and soon after van
Deventer was astonished to discover that the Germans had
simply faded away. Even so, it was not until the end of
June that the British were fit enough to resume the offensive. Smuts, however, did not wait for van Deventer. On 22
May he began his push down the Usambara Railway towards
Tanga. He launched a two-pronged attack, with his main
force under Brigadier General J. A. Hannyngton (who had
commanded the 129th Baluchis in Flanders and had brought
them to Africa) moving straight down the railway line at
the rate of two miles a day; a second, smaller force, under
Brigadier General John Alexander Sheppard, moved
southeast along the left bank of the Pangani river and then,
near Korogwe, turned south towards Handeni. At first all
went swimmingly and the British encountered little opposition. Smuts reported to London that "the rapidity of our
advance exceeded my best expectations." On 19 June elements of Sheppard's column marched into Handeni.

The fertile Usambara highlands, where most of the German colonists had settled, were undefended and fell as a
plum into the British lap. Amani and its research station
was captured by a British priest named Pearce, now an
intelligence officer on Smuts's staff, who before the war had
been a missionary in the area. With a squad of sepoys he
simply walked into his old district, greeting people along

the way. The tribesmen had been ordered to give warning if the enemy approached, but it never occurred to anyone to think of the familiar padre as an enemy. Professor A. Zimmermann, Director of the German Biological and Agricultural Institute and a botonist of wide repute, was astonished, while taking the air in the cool of the evening, to see a British officer and six Indian soldiers approach. "Professor Zimmermann, I presume?" said Pearce.

"True," Zimmermann replied, "but how did you get here?"

"Well, I walked from Monga. And now I take possession in the name of his Britannic Majesty."

Lettow-Vorbeck was now deprived of the services of the institute, which since the beginning of the war had developed sixty-seven *ersatz* products. It had even manufactured many items, including 15,200 bottles of "whisky substitute."

In spite of the loss of Amani, Lettow-Vorbeck began to receive in late April and early May a stream of fresh supplies borne on the heads of thousands of carriers, for another supply ship, the *Marie von Stettin*, had successfully run the blockade and reached East Africa on 17 April. Some six months earlier Governor Schnee, after conferring with Loof and Lettow-Vorbeck, had made up a want list of items, most of which were desperately needed, and entrusted it to a German of Baltic descent who held a Russian passport. He had made his way to Portuguese East Africa and thence to Germany. In Berlin the Ministry of Colonies wasted no time. The *Marie von Stettin* was fitted out in Hamburg and loaded to capacity.

German thoroughness was never more evident than in the preparation of the *Marie von Stettin*. The entire cargo, 1,500 tons, was packed in parcels of 60–65 pounds suitable to be carried on a carrier's head or shoulder. Included in the boxes and bales were medals for the German heroes, including Iron Crosses first class for Loof and Lettow-Vorbeck, and Iron Crosses of lesser classes for other soldiers and sailors. There were also four field howitzers, two mountain guns, ammunition (including shells for the *Kön-igsberg* guns), clothing, tobacco, sweets, gear and equipment of all sorts, medical supplies and other items needed to carry on the campaign. A double pontoon bridge for rapid unloading was also aboard.

After a two-month voyage the *Marie von Stettin* reached Sudi Mto, a bay just south of Lindi in the extreme southeastern corner of the colony. As she entered the bay she dropped mines in her wake—the only German mines ever used in East African waters. The Germans ashore were waiting. They had prepared defences and had assembled 50,000 carriers for the 500 mile trek north with the cargo. There was no quai, but the pontoon bridge was thrown from ship to shore and in just four days the entire cargo was unloaded.

British warships arrived too late, but they put twenty shells into the *Marie von Stettin*. They were not enough. Within a month the Germans had refloated her and on a moonless night she sailed past the two British patrol boats that were charged with watching her. When Admiral King-Hall, still fascinated by aircraft, arrived on the scene with a balloon, the *Marie von Stettin* was long gone.

Almost all of the desperately needed cargo reached its destination, but 200 carrier loads were intercepted by an intrepid Australian, Arnold Wienholt. He had been a Queensland cattleman and politician with a keen desire to hunt big game in Africa. "I have always thought that to shoot a lion was something quite worth doing," he once said. So he went to Africa and shot them. He found, however, that it was not a one-sided combat. When war began he was recovering from a mauling given him by a lion that had knocked him down and bitten him twelve times. In gnawing on his arm it had cracked the bones in his forearm, bitten his biceps to the bone, and mangled his wrist, splintering some of the small bones. When, with luck, he escaped, he washed his arm with carbolic soap, set it as best he could and lashed it to a pine board. Doctors told him that he would never have the full use of his arm; undeterred, he joined Smuts in East Africa as an intelligence scout and quickly made a name for himself.

Wienholt was leading a small party behind the German lines when he discovered the long procession of carriers bringing goods north from Sudi Mto Bay. Carefully choosing the right place, he cut the telephone lines and then stepped out on the path. With their broad hats and beards, Wienholt and his men were mistaken for Germans. An askari jumped up and saluted. "Jambo, bwana," he said.

"Jambo, askari," Wienholt replied. "Why have you not cleaned your rifle?" he demanded. When the astonished askari held it up, Wienholt seized it and hustled the man into the bush to be guarded by his own askaris while he started after a long line of carriers swinging away up the path with their loads. Shouting and cursing in German, he turned them back. As fast as the loads arrived they were thrown on a waiting bonfire. When the carriers were released from their loads, they were dispatched to gather more firewood. Clothing—mostly pants, as it happened—cases of schnapps, bags of rice, beans, flour, and sugar—all were burned. The last load to arrive proved to be sausages, and these were rescued for a feast later. Wienholt and his men then disappeared, leaving the carriers gaping on the road.

Smuts had reached Handeni, a milestone on the march to Morogoro, but it was an unhealthy place and its clammy buildings were infested with rats. When Sheppard's men took the town they found that Major Kraut had vacated the place only a few hours before, leaving behind several hundred African carriers who were dying of typhoid.

Smuts did not want to tarry at Handeni. Kraut's forces had retired to defensive positions on high ground near Makinda on the Lukigura River. To attack him Smuts formed a flying column under Sheppard that consisted of the 25th Royal Fusiliers (now numbering only 200 men), the 2nd Kashmiri Rifles, the 29th Punjabis, and the 5th and 6th South African Infantry. After a punishing march they arrived before the German positions. One Fusilier officer wrote: "I have never seen men more tired and woebegone than our men; they have been marching twenty-four and a half hours, kit-laden and without substantial food, and yet when they went into battle all fatigue was forgotten, they were careless of further physical trial."

The *Official History* waxed romantic over this battle:

> The Kashmiri Rifles headed by [Alexander] Kerr and valiantly commanded by Lieut.-Colonel Haidar Ali Khan, pushed to close range, preparing to charge. The companies extended into the bush were somewhat difficult to control, and the assault had not been launched when three companies of the 25/Royal Fusiliers under Major H.H.R. White, in all perhaps 150 strong, came up on the left flank, grasped the situation instantly, fixed bayonets and rushed forward, cheering. The Gurkhas and Dogras of the Kashmiri Rifles took up the cheering and charged in alongside the Fusiliers, sweeping over all opposition. Charging with them went the mountain battery. . . .

> For once—rarest of occurances in this particular campaign— the assault got home with the bayonet. The German machine guns and a field gun (nine in all) were carried, their detachments bayoneted and the weapons captured undamaged. The defending force was driven in utter rout from the ridge and down to the neighborhood of the bridge, where it came under fire of the 29th Punjabis, which Sheppard had pushed forward across the river, and its remnants scattered into the bush.

British casualties were 10 killed and 36 wounded; the Germans lost four Europeans and 30 Africans killed and 21 Germans and 32 askaris captured. Most of Kraut's force retreated to fight again another day.

There was a halt after the fight on the Lukigura. Louis Botha paid a flying visit to the troops in East Africa. Another mounted brigade disembarked at Mombasa. Smuts, his opinion of African soldiers changing, approved the doubling in size of the KAR to 380 officers and 8,100 other ranks. Three British warships bombarded Tanga, and on 3 July 500 Indian troops, most from the 5th Indian Light Infantry half of whom had mutinied at Singapore in 1915 and murdered some of their officers), landed and cautiously crept

Indian troops on the outskirts of Tanga on the day it was captured, 7 July 1916

into town. They had nothing to fear; there was no fighting; all the Europeans had evacuated the town.

The capture of Tanga and its port facilities eased the supply problem considerably. Had the British taken it earlier, as they could so easily have done, it would have gone far toward easing the logistics problems and thus relieving the suffering of the ragged, half-starved troops.

In the first six months of 1916 an increasing number of aircraft arrived in East Africa. Much was expected of British aviation. " 'Planes should prove of immense value to us out here now that they have landed in the country. The Germans have no machines and are very unlikely to succeed in securing any," wrote Captain Angus Buchan. "It is with great satisfaction that we see them pass over," wrote John Crowe, "and the explosion of the bombs in their camp was eagerly listened for. There was hardly a day the enemy was not visited." However inspiring the airplanes may have been, there is no evidence that any German or askari was ever injured by a British bomb.

It did not take long for German askaris to discover how harmless the airplanes really were. They were noisy and slow. There was always ample time to seek cover and the British aviators rarely saw an enemy soldier. As Lettow-Vorbeck said, "We had learned to make ourselves invisible." This was confirmed by Arnold Wienhold when for a time he was a prisoner of the Germans. He was being marched down a road when an airplane flew over and dropped small bombs: "The askaris made me step off the road with them, but otherwise took no notice, and continued to roll their cigarettes: so much for the yarns of the native terror of our '*indegi*' (bird)."

The British aircraft of RFC Squadron 26, which supported Smuts's advance, were eight BE2c* biplanes, frail, butterfly-looking craft rejected for use on the Western Front because they were so slow that they were easy targets for German anti-aircraft guns and pursuit planes. The aviators did not seem to be first-class either. One returned from a flight and "stated that he felt sure he had hit a train." Another was known to drink a quart of liquor daily and on one rare occasion when he was sober, his observer, Leo Walmsley, was "terrified because I could actually feel the trembling of his hand on the joystick." Flight Lieutenant W.D.M. ("Karamoja") Bell, an elephant hunter turned pilot, refused to fly with an observer because an observer would block his view when he swooped down to strafe German positions with his elephant gun.

The heaviest bomb the airplanes carried weighed only fifty pounds. These were high explosives, but pilots some-

---

* "BE" originally stood for "Blériot Experimental". No airplane used a British engine—most were Gnome or Renault—but later it was said that BE meant British Experimental.

times dropped smaller incendiary charges or darts. Airplanes could carry messages, and once a wounded man was transported—the first use of an airplane as an ambulance—but they were not really good for reconnaissance in a country where the bush was so dense, and they rarely hit anything with their bombs. Dropping incendiaries into areas between the lines and starting grass fires was their most successful offensive operation, but this could only be done when the area was covered with dry grass, where the lines were known and static, and when the wind was in the right direction and there was some confidence that it would not change—a combination of circumstances which rarely occurred.

It was difficult to find suitable places for aerodromes near enough to be useful to moving columns; maintenance was always a problem; weather conditions often made flying impossible; air-to-ground communication was limited almost entirely to dropping notes from airplanes. In short, the aircraft supplied to East Africa in 1915 and 1916 were not effective.

With Smuts at Handeni, Lettow-Vorbeck concentrated his forces on the Central Railway, principally at Morogoro, where he made his headquarters and took personal command, and at Kilosa, 150 miles west of Dar-es-Salaam, where Kraut made his headquarters. Smuts assumed that the Germans would defend the railway, but the wily Lettow-Vorbeck entertained no such intention. After the war he wrote:

> The enemy expected us to stand and fight a final decisive engagement near Morogoro . . . [but] to me this idea was never altogether intelligible. Being so very much the weaker party, it was surely madness to wait at this place the junction of the hostile columns.

Van Deventer, after finally building up a two-week supply of food and ammunition at Kondoa Irangi and waiting for the country to dry out somewhat, resumed his march to the Central Railway, his mounted brigade again leading the way and skirmishing with small patrols. Ten days later advanced elements of his force struck the railway at Dodoma, halfway between Tabora and Morogoro. The local governor surrendered without a shot being fired.

Van Deventer then moved southeast along the railway toward Kilosa, midway between Dodoma and Morogoro, reaching it on 22 August. He entered it unopposed and established his headquarters there. Since leaving Kondoa Irangi van Deventer's column had had a comparatively easy time. For Smuts, however, the last few miles to Morogoro were difficult ones. The country was mountainous, overgrown, and cut by ravines and rivers. Lettow-Vorbeck played his usual games, taking up strong natural positions and holding them just long enough to inflict casualties and delay progress.

Smuts hoped that his pincer movement—his own force and van Deventer's—would bring the Germans to fight a set battle that would be decisive, but already Lettow-Vorbeck was exploring the area south of the Central Railway, and he was removing his supply depots from Morogoro. When the 2nd Rhodesians and two companies of Baluchis entered Morogoro on 26 August, the German rear guard was just clearing out south of town, leaving behind the smoldering ruins of supplies they were forced to abandon amid the twisted rails and dynamited rolling stock of the railway.

Smuts had captured the Central Railway, but the undefeated *Schutztruppe*, very much a force in being, was still to be reckoned with. German East Africa was not yet conquered.

CHAPTER
21

The Capture of Tabora

While Smuts and van Deventer were plunging into the heart of German East Africa, the Belgians agitated for an offensive in which they could take part in that section of Central Africa which today comprises the countries of Rwanda and Burundi (then called Ruanda-Urundi). It is fertile land and one of the most populous areas of Africa. [Today more than ten million souls live there on only 33,670 square miles.] The people are mostly Hutu and the Hutu's traditional enemies and oppressors, the enormously tall Tutsi (or Watutsi). There are also several thousand Twa pigmies. For the most part, people live in family clusters on isolated hillsides. Rwanda is unique in having the highest population density in Africa without having any village life.

Talks on British-Belgian cooperation for an invasion of this area took place over several months in several countries. As soon as it became clear to the Belgians that the neutrality of the conventional basin of the Congo could not be maintained, they became eager to attack German East Africa. In part this was a desire to avenge the German attack on their homeland and the atrocities that were said to have been committed there. But to mount an invasion they needed British help, and in the first eighteen months of the war the British withheld it. The powers that be in London were reluctant to commit resources to this obscure part of the world—until the arrival of Smuts.

Britain had been a guarantor of Belgian sovereignty and had declared war when Germany invaded the country, but in Africa, where they were rivals for power and influence, there was considerable ill-feeling between Belgium and Britain. Spicer-Simson's claim that the Belgians failed to cooperate with him was readily believed in London because distrust of Belgium was so pervasive in British government circles.

Many Belgians believed that Britain wanted to take from them the mineral-rich Katanga region of the Congo. The British felt that the Belgians wanted to grab even more territory and that they already exercised too much influence in Central Africa. When the Belgians wanted to build the Katanga Railway, they claimed that the British were obstructive, as indeed they seem to have been. Britain forbade the export of rails to Katanga, claiming they were strategic materials, and she blocked the Belgians from using their sterling balance to buy rails in the United States. [Eventually the Belgians took the rails from German East Africa's Central Railway and bought rolling stock from the Rhodesian Railways.]

The absence of good relations between the two governments was also evident in the relations between the men on the spot in Africa. In Elizabethville the attorney general, Martin Ruthen, the unofficial leader of the Belgian community, was outspoken in his anti-British and anti-American sentiments. Most of the many Europeans and Americans in Katanga worked for the Union Miniére or the railway, and they were widely regarded by the Belgians as troublemakers, union organizers, and corrupters of the work ethic in honest Belgian workers. There was, in fact, almost a private war between the Belgians and the Anglo-American communities in Katanga.

With each side suspicious of the other's war aims, it was with difficulty that cooperation for a joint invasion effort and a drive on Tabora was agreed upon, and then, insisted the Belgians, it was to be "without prejudice to any post-bellum territorial claims." The ultimate objective of the campaign was to be Tabora, the German colony's largest inland town. Schnee had moved his government there and it was the headquarters of the *Schutztruppe's* Western Command. The Belgian military forces in the Congo were led by Baron Charles Henri Marie Ernest Tombeur; British forces in western British East Africa were led by Sir Charles Preston Crewe, a fifty-eight-year-old South African soldier and politician who had fought in the Boer War and had served in the cabinet of the Union of South Africa.

The Belgian colonial army, instituted in 1888, was called the Force Publique. It was manned by askaris under European officers, many of whom were Scandinavians. For the askaris, conditions were harsh; enlistment was for seven years; the pay was low and the discipline severe. Flogging was a common form of punishment. The askaris were recruited from some of the most primitive tribes and it was widely believed that many were cannibals. It was even rumoured that the authorities economized on food by feeding condemned prisoners to them. Not surprisingly three serious mutinies flared up in the first dozen years of the Force Publique's existence. For the invasion of German East Africa the British agreed to supply the Belgians with 5,000 carriers from Uganda, but many of these deserted, convinced that if food ran short they would be fed to the Belgian askaris.

Bickering, resentment, and distrust did not end with the decision to undertake a joint invasion of the Ruanda-Urundi area. General Tombeur and Sir Charles detested each other. They largely ignored each other's strategic goals and there was little communication between them.

In March 1916 Tombeur had just over 10,000 men organized into two brigades, one under Colonel Molitor and the other under Lieutenant Colonel F. V. Olsen, a Dane. They carried sixty machine guns and twelve field guns. Olsen set out from the Rusizi River, which connects Lake Kivu and Lake Tanganyika, while Molitor began his march further north in the magnificent country at the northern end of Lake Kivu that contains the Mountains of the Moon, one of the major sources of the Nile.

The German military commander in this corner of the colony was a remarkable soldier, Captain Max Witgens, who later in the war carried on his own independent campaign with uncommon success. He reported to General Kurt Wahle, who was in charge of Western Command and head-quartered at Tabora.

Throughout the first eighteen months of the war Witgens had carried out raids and inflicted minor defeats on the Belgians. Now, in the face of attacks by such overwhelming numbers under Crewe and Tombeur, he emulated Lettow-Vorbeck and Kraut, retreating as slowly as possible, always in good order, giving his enemies a bloody nose whenever opportunity presented itself.

On 8 June 1916 Olsen occupied Usumbura on the east side of the north end of Lake Tanganyika and then marched east to Kitega, capital of Urundi Province. In late June, Molitor's column, moving southeast, crossed the Kagera River, turned east towards Lake Victoria, and on 24 June engaged in a sharp flight. Three days later he reached the southwest corner of Lake Victoria.

Crewe planned to capture Mwanza, the key German port at the south end of Lake Victoria, but first he sent a flying column to capture (again) Bukoba on the western shore. Carew's column, consisting of 190 KAR, some Buganda Rifles, and a few scouts, carrying only two machine guns, made a dash through the bush, but they found Bukoba deserted. [After the war Captain Carew claimed to have been the only soldier in the Great War to have been wounded by an arrow—presumably one shot by a rugga-rugga.]

The main British force under Crewe sailed in a fleet of small craft from Kisumu and landed a few miles outside of Mwanza. There was a small, sharp battle, in which still another *Königsberg* gun took part. The Germans were prised from their positions and the British entered the town. Before retreating the Germans had been able to destroy their wireless masts but otherwise had done little damage. Crewe gathered up two companies of KAR and started in pursuit of the fleeing Germans, but he became bogged down in some marshland and the German rear guard gave him an uncomfortable time so he turned back to Mwanza.

The Belgians, who had been moving slowly and consolidating their positions, now began a rapid drive south towards Kigoma. Crewe also drove south. The advance became a race, but a race slowed by determined and skilled German resistance. Communication between Crewe and Tombeur all but ceased as they moved along their separate routes. The Belgians continued to advance in two columns, the first, under Olsen, moving down the east side of lake Tanganyika, taking Kigoma, the German's chief port on Lake Tanganyika, on 28 July, and on 2 August occupying Ujiji, where forty-five years earlier Henry M. Stanley had found Dr. David Livingstone, and where earlier still Richard Francis Burton and John Hanning Speke had been the first white men to see the lake. The Belgians now held the western terminus of the Central Railway, down which they moved, eastward toward Tabora. The Germans slowly fell back, destroying the railway as they retreated.

At Tabora, the new German capital, Schnee and his wife were ensconced in the governor's house, and Wahle, with about 5,000 men, was now concentrated there. The town sits on an open plain encircled by hills some ten miles distant. Wahle had fortified the hills and had put the town itself in a state of defence.

After ten days of hard fighting the Belgians entered Tabora on 19 September 1916. The Germans did not wait to be captured but retreated southeast in three columns: the principal one under Wahle himself; the others under Major von Langenn and Captain Witgens. The Belgians had no interest in pursuing Wahle; they had captured a vast tract of land with comparatively small loss (41 Europeans and

1,235 Africans), and they were content to rest on their laurels. And laurels there were.

King George V told Albert I, King of the Belgians: "I desire to tell Your Majesty how highly I appreciate the loyal cooperation given my troops during the long and hard operations in East Africa." King Albert told Tombeur and his troops that they had "upheld upon African soil the honour and reputation of our arms." Smuts, too, expressed his gratitude to Tombeur for his "cordial cooperation," though "cooperation" had been conspicuously absent. Tombeur was made a Commander of the Order of Leopold and Britain conferred a knighthood (K.C.M.G.) on him.

As for Sir John Crewe, a Belgian dispatch rider brought him the news that he was too late. He had encountered spirited opposition and difficult terraine; he limped into Tabora six days after Tombeur. Soon after, he retired to South Africa and resumed his political career.

Governor Schnee left with Wahle; henceforth he and his staff were carried along by the *Schutztruppe*, and he was a constant annoyance to Lettow-Vorbeck, whom he nagged, quizzed, and interfered with. He left his wife, Ada, behind in Tabora where she continued to live in the governor's house, for Tombeur was too gentlemanly to remove her. About 140 other women and a number of children were also left behind at Tabora, as were 2,000 prisoners of war—mostly British and Belgian with a few French, Italian, and Russian internees. Included were a hundred British missionaries and about thirty British women and children.

Although pictures taken of the prisoners and internees immediately after their release show them looking strong and fit, there were charges of abuse. *The Times* waxed wroth over what was considered the worst charge of ill-treatment:

In the treatment of British prisoners . . . a policy was followed deliberately calculated to lower the prestige of the race in the eyes of the natives. . . . British prisoners were made to drag a wagon loaded with government stores through the streets and were halted in the native market to afford opportunity for the negroes to come and jeer at them, while they saw them doing the work of oxen. At the same time instructions were sent that the men pulling the wagon were not to take the road past the governor's house as it offended his excellency to see men who were not decently dressed.

The wagon-pulling incident appears to have been an isolated instance, but there were variations of the oft-repeated story. Captain W. D. Downes reported that Europeans were forced to collect dry dung with their hands and load the cart. And "this was done notwithstanding the fact that there were many native prisoners available for this purpose."

The other side of this coin was the charge, believed in Germany, that the Belgians ill-treated German civilians after they captured Tabora. In reprisal, the Germans seized twenty-three prominent Belgian citizens and put them in an internment camp in Germany. Every war finds those who abuse prisoners of war or internees, but such individuals appear to have been rare in this campaign and it was never a policy on either side. The German civilians found at Tabora were not ill-treated. They were, however, fearful of the cannibalistic tendencies of the Belgian askaris and so requested internment in Europe; their request was granted and they were sent to France.

Dr. Holtom, who, it will be remembered, was left behind by his messmates in Dar-es-Salaam harbour, was imprisoned at Kilimatinde, about 160 miles east of Tabora and 60 miles west of Dodoma. Lieutenant Denis Cutler, the intrepid aviator of the Rufiji, was also there. Dr. Holtom had many complaints about the treatment he received. His pillow "was very thin and lumpy and not conducive to slumber." For a few days after his arrival he suffered because he did not have a "sleeping suit." A German woman cooked for the officers, but Holtom found the potatoes too small and the meat too tough, and "we never had rice pudding," he said. Servants waited on the officer prisoners, but only one was allotted for each six. Holtom was incensed. He demanded a servant of his own, and he made such a fuss that, incredibly, one was provided him. The prisoners were issued clothing, boots, underclothes, towels, and a safety razor, but Holtom found the razor "quite useless" and so grew a beard. Tea was served at four o'clock, but, Holtom complained, there was no bread unless some was saved from breakfast.

The Germans paid the officers: three rupees per day for lieutenants and captains and a half rupee more for field grade officers. [A rupee was worth 1s. 4d. at then current rates.] With this they could buy tea, tobacco, potted meats, newspapers, sugar, and even plum pudding and liquor. There was no roll call and prisoners could stroll outside the prison for an hour every evening. Holtom was even allowed to visit friends in town. It was hard to make a case for ill-treatment, but Holtom did his best.

The Germans asked him to tend to the ills of all the prisoners. He was willing to do this, but he thought himself "clearly entitled to some remuneration for attending the interned civilians, who had no claim on my gratuitous services other than those of bare humanity." The Germans told him he could charge the civilians if he liked, but that they would not pay him.

Christmas was celebrated in some style. Fellow prisoners, an English planter and his wife (the only woman), invited the doctor to dine with them. A small Christmas tree gleamed with candles and the table was decorated with bougainvillea. All dressed in their best. Whisky was served as an aperitif and dinner consisted of chicken, potato salad, and pickles; there was a Huntley and Palmer cake for desert and sardines for a savoury. "Not much of a Christmas dinner," sniffed Holtom.

When typhoid broke out at Kilimatinde the Germans brought in doctors. Although most of the soldiers in the camp had been inoculated, most of the sailors had not. In the royal Navy inoculation was "not a part of naval routine." Of the Germans on this occasion Holtom said, "I must in justice admit that in the matter of the typhoid outbreak they behaved with humanity, doing all in their power to make the sufferers comfortable and to ensure their recovery."

It was not difficult to escape from Kilimatinde and a few tried, but all were caught, betrayed to the Germans by tribesmen. In April 1916 the prisoners were transferred to Tabora and most were freed by the Belgians. At Tabora Holtom heard the famous story of the Europeans pulling the cart. "White men," he exclaimed, "pulling a truckload of stores or some German's luggage under a *native* guard! I confess that when I first heard of it I could not believe it. . . . Yet I was assured it was perfectly true."

Curiously, none of the prisoners was interrogated. Arnold Wienholt, caught behind the German lines, said, "It is only fair to mention that from Lettow-Vorbeck downwards no one ever appeared to have any idea of attempting to ask for information."

When the Allied prisoners were released at Tabora, they marched north to Mwanza and thence by ship to the western terminus of the Uganda Railway, by rail to Mombasa, and by ship to England. On their tramp north from Tabora the British proudly carried before them a huge Union Jack sewn from a blue skirt, a red tablecloth, and a white apron. Actually, they did not themselves carry the flag; they hired an African to carry it for them.

After the capture of Dodoma by van Deventer on 29 July, of Morogoro by Smuts on 26 August, and of Tabora by Tombeur on 19 September, it seemed to many that the East African campaign was practically over. Most of the seaports and lakeports had been captured and British warships patrolled the coasts; all the railways were in Allied hands; Rhodesian forces under Northey had pushed northward, and, in spite of the lack of cooperation on the part of Spicer-Simson, had captured Bismarckburg and Langenburg. Even the Portuguese, newest and least competent of allies, had timidly pushed a few troops over the Mozambique border into southeastern German East Africa. Lettow-Vorbeck was surrounded, it was said, by a "ring of steel," and there seemed not the slightest possibility of further aid from the Fatherland.

Of course, no one thought of zeppelins.

22

The True Enemy

"In this campaign the Hun have been the least of the malignant influences," wrote Dr. Robert Dolbey. "More from fever and dysentery, from biting flies, from ticks and crawling beasts have we suffered than from the bullets of the enemy." Indeed, it did not take a doctor to see this. "The real enemy was the climate, the wild regions, and the swamps and forests and scrub," wrote Deneys Reitz. Smuts's soldiers were in fact heavily engaged in fighting the myriad stinging, biting, burrowing, parasitic creatures of Central Africa and the many diseases and infections they brought. Lieutenant Colonel A. E. Capell of the 2nd Rhodesians wrote with feeling of the horror: "The yellow spectres of fever and dysentery stalked through the sweltering camp, entered the dug-outs and beckoned to their victims to come to the shell-rent hospital tent."

By July 1916 the ratio of non-battle casualties to battle casualties was 31.4 to 1. "I believe between October and December [1916] we evacuated between 12,000 and 15,000 patients, mostly malaria cases, from our hospitals and ambulances along the Central Railway," wrote Smuts.

This was not the kind of war the soldiers had bargained

for or wanted to fight. "To be killed or wounded while assaulting the enemy is to fall nobly," said W. S. Thatcher, "but to march indefinitely, burning with fever or racked with dysentery in a tropical sun until one dies or collapses on the roadside in a misery of pain and agony, is no whit less noble, though for this there are no decorations or mentions."

If officers were disheartened by the conditions of the East African Campaign, the spirits of the other ranks were distinctly lower. A 25th Fusilier expressed the sentiments of many when he said, "Ah, I wish to hell I was in France! There one lives like a gentleman and dies like a man. Here one lives like a pig and dies like a dog." And W. W. Campbell, a lorry driver, wrote:

> Distressed and depressed beyond measure, we felt that death and ugliness lurked everywhere. It was in the air we breathed, the water we drank, the sun that warmed out bodies; it crawled on the ground, dropped heavily from rain-sodden trees, hung suspended in the humid, reeking atmosphere. Every living thing went in fear of its life, or turned upon another in self-preservation. Human life itself was an embodiment of ignorance and suspicion. It permeated our very souls, turned bright thoughts into dark, and made one long for the fate that he feared.

By mid-1916 there was not a unit whose ranks had not been thinned by hideous diseases. The history of the 2nd Loyal North Lancashire Regiment was typical of the wastage. The battalion had arrived in East Africa at the end of 1914 with 832 men. By March 1915 it had been reinforced by drafts up to 901; 150 were in hospital. On 10 June it mustered only 350, and nine days later only 265. By 31 October it had admitted 836 men to hospital; only 258 had remained well. On 15 February 1916 it mustered 577, thanks to large drafts of fresh men, but it was down to 495 within a month. In April it was sent to South Africa to recuperate and refit. It returned in June with 531, but by December it was down to 345.

The 2nd Rhodesians lost only 36 men killed in battle, but

suffered 10,626 cases of sickness, 3,127 of which were malaria. By 21 December it had only 67 men still standing, of whom 37 were declared unfit. Although the West Coast Africans of the Nigerian and Gold Coast battalions—which landed in the last half of 1916—were better able to resist the diseases, their British officers tumbled rapidly. Christmas Day of 1916 found 42 Europeans in the 4th Nigerians; one year later there were nine, of whom three were regularly on the sick list. And this battalion was said to be "far better off in this respect than any other battalion in the brigade."

The 9th South African Infantry had few battle casualties, but it suffered horrendous losses. It arrived in East Africa on 14 February 1916 with 1,135 officers and men; by 25 October it had 116. A draft of 1,000 South Africans reached Korogwe safely, but of these only 330 reached Handeni, 40 miles away.

The Indians suffered as much as the Europeans. On 20 July 1916 the commander of the 129th Baluchis had only 200 men on duty and 800 in hospital. The 30th Punjabis arrived in late December 1916 with 530 fit men; one month later it was down to 230.

Among Africa's killer diseases, none was more prevalent than malaria. Almost every soldier who served in East Africa contracted some form of it. "Depressing it is," wrote a soldier with Murray's Column of his continual bouts of fever, "and I long for white sheets and home when I'm not up to the mark."

The dreaded blackwater fever, the most dangerous complication of malaria, takes its name from the deep red or black colour of the victim's urine. Its onset is usually sudden with temperatures climbing to 104° or 105° F. [40° or 40.6° C.], severe chills, nausea, headaches, and vomiting. Jaundice appears within a few hours and large amounts of hemoglobin are released; the body is dehydrated, increasing the chances of renal failure, which causes death in nearly half of all cases. Dr. Dolby found champagne "a great standby" and "blessed morphia brings ease of vomiting and is a priceless boon."

Malaria, carried by the female anopheles mosquito, is caused by sporozoa of the genus *Plasmodium*, four species of which may infect humans. Not until late in the campaign was there an agreed-upon policy for the prevention or treatment of malaria; then orders were issued that everyone must take five grains of quinine per day. When the senior medical officer at the military hospital at Dar-es-Salaam heard of this dosage, he exploded: "What nonsense! The only way to administer quinine is 20 grains on Saturday night and 30 grains the next night!"

Such a dosage could actually contribute to the complication of blackwater fever. A breakdown of the red corpuscles (hemolysis) occurs in all cases of malaria, but in blackwater fever white corpuscles break down as well. This is caused by a number of factors, including, ironically, sensitivity to quinine, the usual prophylaxis for malaria.

The army issue was quinine sulphate pills, but these were often in short supply. Lieutenant Colonel G.M.G. Molyneux, commanding the 6th South African Infantry, more attentive than most to medical and sanitary requirements, purchased at his own expense large quantities of quinine hydrochloride capsules, which were more soluable and more palatable.

German troops, in their high-necked uniforms, long-sleeved shirts, and long pants or breeches with putees, suffered less than the British from insects and the diseases they carried. Most of the British wore open-necked shirts with short sleeves, and many wore shorts.

Malaria is but one of the many diseases transmitted by mosquitoes, ticks, flies, fleas, and other insects in tropical Africa. Others are transmitted by food and water—particularly water. Inoculation for typhoid, or enteric fever, was known and many, but not all, soldiers in East Africa had received shots. Anti-enteric injections, given in two shots, were offered, but men could refuse them if they chose, and some did.

Many of the soldiers in East Africa suffered from, and some carried home with them, the insidious dracunuliasis, popularly known in Africa as guinea worm. It is believed that guinea worms were the "fiery serpents" that attacked the children of Israel during their stay near the Red Sea. [The worm is still endemic to the Gulf of Aqaba region.] Soldiers and carriers were infected when they drank unfiltered water containing *cyclopes* (water fleas) infected with *Dracunculus medinensis* larvae. When the *cyclops* is digested, the larvae penetrate the intestinal wall. Six weeks later they migrate to areas just under the skin where they mature into worms. The males die after fertilizing the females, who then burrow into connective tissue where their uteri become distended by some three million embryos in each.

About eight months after entering the human host, the pregnant female parasite usually bores her way to the legs, or sometimes the scrotum, of the host and nestles in the fibrous tunnel under the skin until, after about two to six months, she breaks through the skin to release larvae over a two-to-four-week period into water, which is needed to produce her vigorous uterine contractions. When the larvae are ingested by *cyclopes* and these are drunk, the process is repeated.

Guinea worm causes a painful and disabling illness, often accompanied by fever, dizziness, vomiting, diarrhea, intense itching, and other unpleasant symptoms. As many as fifty-six adult worms have been found in one person. Sometimes the female worms do not reach the skin; they then produce deep abscesses filled with larvae which can then invade other organs such as the genitals, lungs, eyes, and heart. Even joint spaces are sometimes penetrated, causing painful knee or ankle contractions and leaving the victim crippled.

The traditional therapy was to do nothing until the worm broke the skin and presented itself—usually twelve to fourteen months after infection, although they have been known to wait as long as fifteen years before appearing. Once the skin was broken the worm would be encouraged to present more of itself by frequent washing until a sliver of wood could be attached to one end. A few centimeters would then carefully and patiently be wound out each day for two or three weeks. However, until the uterus is emptied of its embryos, the worm resists extraction. In this process great care must to be taken that the delicate worm is not broken, for then the results can be disastrous: the young escape into the tissues, causing inflammation and fever, followed by painful abscesses and sometimes death from sepsis. Soldiers discovered that some Africans, with more experience in extracting worms than army doctors, were also more skilled.

The *cyclops* that carries the *Dracuncular medinensis* larvae is easily killed if the water in which it lives is boiled, or even heated, but the source of the worms was unknown, and in any event thirsty soldiers were careless. Hungry soldiers were also careless of what and how they ate, and dysentery was rife. Although not as deadly as blackwater fever, dysentery in its many forms, particularly amoebic and bacillary, is debilitating and can lead to death. Anyone who spent any time at all in the African interior caught it in some form, and in the East African campaign the rate was higher than in any other theatre in the Great War.

Almost everyone at one time or another suffered from chiggars [jiggers, sand fleas, chigoe]. Dr. Dolby said: "So great is this that at least five per cent of our army, both white and native, are constantly incapacitated. Hundreds of toenails have I removed for this cause alone. A corporal in the 25th Fusiliers wrote in his diary: "I took twelve jiggers out this morning—I think that is about the average each day!" One officer endured at a sitting the extraction of forty from one foot. Lieutenant W. S. Thatcher said, "It is extremely painful. . . . I have seen cases where all the toes have been eaten away, while the rest of the foot resembled a mass of dirty putrefying rags."

The chigger is a reddish-brown burrowing flea *(Tunga penetrans)* that originated in the American tropics but appeared in West Africa about 1870 and rapidly spread throughout tropical Africa. It prefers dry, sandy soil or dust and was found in most huts, stables, cattle pens, etc.. Impregnated females greedily attack warm-blooded creatures, even birds. The female secretes digestive enzymes that cause human skin cells to break down, forming tissue debris, and it is on this that she feeds. She then proceeds to ovulate, her abdomen distending to the size of a small pea from her developing eggs. For the victim there is intense itching and often secondary infection. The soles of the feet, skin between the toes and the roots of nails are favourite haunts, but they can also attack the armpit, face, scrotum, or penis.

The treatment was to enlarge the flea's entrance into the skin with a sharp and preferably clean needle, and then take out the entire insect. Some African women, from long practice, were found to be experts at this little operation. According to Arthur Martin, "It was only the surgery of the Africans that could be relied on. They were experts at incising with the crudest instruments—thorns perhaps—and digging out bags of eggs intact."

Army doctors, who in peacetime were not much respected by combatant officers, came into their own in East Africa. They had ample opportunity to exhibit their arrogance and they here commanded respect. Lieutenant R. C. Hill, commanding a Maxim gun section of the East African Mounted Rifles, was shot through the ankle joint while galloping his guns out of action under intense fire during the advance on Moshi. Beside him rode Captain C. J. Wilson, the unit's doctor. Hill called out to him, "Can I see you sometime when you are not busy?"

Perhaps all doctors at some time come to hate the sight of the sick. Dr. Francis Brett Young, himself ill with malaria, found sick sepoys draped in grey blankets "rather an irritating sight, for when an Indian is ill, no matter how little there may be the matter with him, he droops like a cut flower."

Doctors were often reluctant to give pain-killing drugs. A Canadian doctor in a base hospital remarked, "It's easy to get a reputation for kindness by being too complacent in giving way to requests for morphia. . . . This drug robs men of their appetite, keeps them thin, and prevents their wounds from healing." A subaltern in the 6th South African Infantry who was in the first painful and sever throes of amoebic dysentery consulted Captain H. Fayle, the regimental medical officer, and was given six small pills. The next day he reported with enthusiasm on their efficacy and asked for more, but was told: "I have nothing whatever that would be of the slightest good to you, not even a dose of Epsom salts. What I gave you was opium, and I am not giving you any more."

The subaltern lived with his amoebic dysentery, its blood and slime and pain, for three months until he could be put in hospital at Morogoro under the care of Sister Mabel Packard, one of the few nursing sisters in the interior. She had been with the Universities mission before the war and she simply continued her work, nursing Germans and Africans. She was pleased when the British arrived, although the Germans had treated her well and, as Arthur Martin remarked, "In a way it made little difference to her, she carried on as usual." To the British troops, however, her loving kindness and technical skills proved an inestimable blessing and she gained at least local fame as "The Angel of Morogoro." Many soldiers swore that they owed their lives to her careful nursing. She was the only English nursing sister, but not the only female nurse at Morogoro, for some German nurses were pressed into service. The medical facilities were really only those of a clearing station designed for not more than 200 patients, but it regularly operated as a stationary hospital and tried to care for 600.

The quality of medical service varied widely from nonexistent to splendid. In the interior the latter were found only in and around Nairobi at such places as Lady Colville's convalescent hospital. It was here that Arnold Wienholt, suffering from dysentery, was cared for, and he spoke of it as "a place so nicely run that a few weeks seemed to work miracles in us patients." When Dar-es-Salaam was captured most of the base hospitals were moved there; three large hospitals were established for Europeans, a tent hospital for the askaris, and even, eventually, one for carriers.

According to General Fendall, "The realization of the immense organization that would be necessary to deal with sick carriers came as a surprise." The heir-apparent to the throne of Uganda served as an officer in a corps of hospital orderlies at the carrier hospital, constructed of brushwood and placed outside town.

Hospital ships carried sick and wounded Indians back to India and British, South Africans and Rhodesians to South Africa or Britain. It was thought at first that all Europeans could be sent to South Africa for treatment and then returned to duty, but the doctors there were so appalled by the stream of diseased and wasted men sent to them that it was said they "acquired an exaggerated idea of the deadliness of the East African climate." Certainly few of the soldiers they treated were ever returned to duty. As a result, more convalescent camps were established in Kenya.

Few found fault with the hospitals at Dar-es-Salaam and Nairobi, but medical facilities in the interior of German East Africa left much to be desired. At Handeni a casualty clearing station was crammed into a small gaol where GOTT STRAFE ENGLAND remained painted on a wall. With the deterioration of the supply and distribution system came a shortage of medical supplies of all sorts, and there was much improvisation.

The declining quality of the medical services provided to the field force led to complaints and finger-pointing. After the war, Brigadier General J. J. Collyer, Smuts's chief of staff, speaking of the horrors of the advance from Morogoro to Kisaki, claimed that the sad state of the medical services was never brought to his or Smuts's attention, but this excuse is thin indeed, for everyone in touch with the field force was acutely aware that something was seriously wrong with the arrangements.

Many of the men bore their sufferings with remarkable fortitude. Sergeant Bill Eve of the 6th South African Infantry had been a locomotive driver before the war and was known as "Hell-fire Jack." At a small battle at Matamondo in August 1916 he received a frightful wound in his leg. As a surgeon worked on him by candlelight, he cracked jokes. He had hoped to fight in France after the East African Campaign; now he said, "This finishes me for France, sorr. I would sooner have broken a bottle of whisky than broken my leg." His leg was amputated.

Added to the burdens of the British medical services were the many sick and wounded Germans and their askaris that Lettow-Vorbeck left behind, confident they would be cared for by his enemies. Women and children were also left behind, and Captain W. D. Downes complained that "many of these same women were frequently most lax in their morals, and were a constant source of annoyance to the Provost-Marshal at base."

In mid-campaign there were 245 Royal Army Medical Corps doctors in East Africa and it was estimated that at least 200 more were needed. In the latter stages of the campaign Lettow-Vorbeck had only seven doctors, one of whom was actually a veterinarian, but he boasted that "the German medical staff may have been the best in the East Africa theatre," and he claimed that English soldiers preferred to be treated by German doctors:

> While the battlefield was being cleared, in which both English and German medical officers took part, wounded Englishmen begged to be treated by the German doctor. And later on, also, wounded men remarked that they hardly would have been cured if they had been treated by English medical personnel.

Such statements need to be accepted with some scepticism, for however good the doctors, the German medical facilities, particularly during the last two years of the war, were uncommonly primitive.

German operating theatres were usually newly-made grass huts. Serious operations, including several appendectomies (then still a serious operation), were performed in settings that were far from sterile. Used bandages were washed and re-used; compresses and dressings were made of beaten tree bark. Yet Lettow-Vorbeck maintained that his *Schutz-*

truppe had an "almost ridiculously low incidence of gangrene and tetanus."

The Germans no longer had the facilities and the knowledge of the doctors and professors at Amani, but they still had a chemist with them and they continued to improvise a number of medicines and salves. In addition to the vile-tasting "Lettow Schnapps," a quinine made from Peruvian bark, locally available material was pressed into service:

> Local plants and drugs yielded up, among other things, a disinfectant and digitalis and benzine substitutes, a synthetic immersion oil and a remedy for diarrhea whose effectiveness had been demonstrated by witch doctors. Ointment bases were made from hippo and elephant fat.

In spite of such makeshift medical arrangements, the Germans did seem to cope better than the British. Doctor Dolby could not understand it:

> To me it has been a source of surprise that the German, who consistently drinks beer in huge quantities, takes little or no exercise, and cohabits with the black women of the country extensively, should have performed such prodigies of endurance on trek in this campaign. One would have thought that the Englishman, who keeps his body fitter for games, eschews beer for his liver's sake, and finds that intimacy with the native population lowers his prestige, would have done far better in this war than the German. That in all fairness he has not done so.

One reason for the better condition of the Europeans in the *Schutztruppe* was that they were lavishly supplied with carriers. The German askaris, who brought their women to war to carry their gear and care for them, rarely carried more than their rifle and ammunition on the march. The British generally supplied one carrier for each European, while Lettow-Vorbeck generally allowed his Europeans seven or more each. During the most arduous part of the campaign he stirred up a "storm of indignation" when he issued orders limiting each European to only five carriers. His officers appealed to him "on the grounds of health and decency" to relent, but he himself set an example by making do with only four.

Captain A. W. Lloyd of the 25th Fusiliers had been a cartoonist for the *Sunday Times* before the war and on his return to England he published a book of cartoons about the British in East Africa called *Jambo: Or With Jannie in the Jungle*. In one cartoon, captioned "The Victor," he drew a famished British soldier struggling along with rifle, ammunition, pack and "billy can"; its companion piece, entitled "The Vanquished," pictured a plump and unencumbered German, smoking a cigar and swinging his sjambok, at the head of a file of seven carriers, one carrying a box labeled "delicatessen."

Among the British it was noted that the older men held up better than the younger to the hard marching, fatigue, loss of sleep, and reduced rations. Some argued that only men over twenty-five should be used in East Africa. Younger men were more fit, but they lacked the stamina and seemed to feel more keenly the rigours of the campaign. The sixty-five-year-old Selous was often cited. In Murray's Column, from which most men under twenty-five were invalided out in the first year, a man known as "Mac," who enlisted in 1915 at the age of sixty-two, fought for two years without ever reporting sick. Lettow-Vorbeck agreed that older men stood up better to the rough conditions. The South Africans in particular he thought were too young, were unaccustomed to the tropics, and "were extraordinarily careless about precautions against tropical diseases."

Captain Angus Buchanan was convinced that "at least half of the sickness was caused, directly or indirectly, from lack of full and proper nourishment for a prolonged period." Certainly food was the soldier's principal preoccupation and, as Buchanan said, "even when rations were full—and they were often not—our soldiers were always troubled with that subject throughout the East African Campaign." Game of any kind was shot when possible, and some grew to like the taste. (Hippopotamus meat was found to be "surprisingly tender and tasted like very sweet beef.") But a noisy army tramping through a wilderness sends game scurrying.

Men of the 6th South African Infantry were surprised one morning to be served a ration of meat for breakfast. Only after they had wolfed it down did they learn that they had eaten three of the pack donkeys. Lieutenant Colonel Molyneau had ordered them slaughtered in the middle of the night because, he said, "The men, like all soldiers of British nationality, were extremely soft-hearted in such matters."

Such care as was possible was taken to preserve the health of domestic animals. Each evening in the 3rd Battery, South African Field Artillery, the men were given five grains of quinine as a malaria preventative and the horses were each given five grains of arsenic in an effort to prevent trypanomiasia. One June evening the horses were given the quinine and the men the arsenic. Fortunately, the mistake was quickly discovered and salt water, soapy water, and any other kind of emetic that could be concocted was administered to the unfortunate gunners. They survived.

Only eighteen years before the outbreak of the Great War, Dr. David Bruce, working in South Africa, discovered that the tsetse fly carried the parasite *trypanosome* that causes what was called "cattle disease." There are about thirty species and subspecies of the fly, only one of which is capable of infecting humans with "sleeping sickness", but a decade before the war some 200,000 people died of this disease in just a three-year period in a single district of Uganda. However, in East Africa in 1914–18 it was primarily the animals which suffered from attacks of "fly."

The grey or brown tsetse, somewhat larger than a housefly, has wings that fold scissorwise. For some mysterious reason it inhabits well-defined belts of land that it refuses to leave. It feeds on blood every two or three days and will die of starvation if it cannot feed within ten or twelve days. It is said to hunt by sight and smell, but it will dive on anything that moves, including motorcars, trains, or boats.

Cattle and horses were the worst sufferers. Deneys Reitz was particularly affected by the loss of horses: "More than 30,000 of these dumb gentle brutes died here, and that part of me which loved and understood horses somewhat died too." Smut's chief of staff reported that "28,000 oxen died during the advance from Kahe to the Central Railway in three months. Later on in two months (September 15 to November 15) 19,000 horses, 10,000 mules, a further 11,000 oxen, and 2,500 donkeys died." Sadly, stricken animals were not killed. A South African gunner explained: "As animals were scarce and their lives so short, they could not be destroyed and released from their misery until they were beyond useful work."

The Germans had maps indicating the fly areas and the British were said to have seen these, but little use appears to have been made of them. Even today, at least half, and perhaps as much as two thirds, of mainland Tanzania is infested with tsetse fly, mostly the *Glossina moritans*, the cattle killer, but other types as well.

To many it seemed a bizarre place to fight a war: an untamed land of great beauty; of mountains, lakes and forests; teeming with a wide variety of wild animals; and alive with noxious insects and baneful germs. When all the surviving combatants had returned to their homes, the bugs and bacteria remained in possession of the field. Unconquered. The true victors of the East African Campaign.

23

The Pursuit of Lettow-Vorbeck

Having reached the Central Railway and having conquered half of the colony, Smuts ought to have given greater thought to his sick and exhausted soldiers and to his inefficient supply system. He ought to have called a halt. Even the *Official History* says:

> Viewing the campaign in retrospect it now seems, indeed, that at that stage he might with great advantage have contented himself with establishing his new bases at Dar-es-Salaam; restoring the railway and organizing his supply services on shorter, more manageable lines, meanwhile making his dispositions to end the campaign successfully by using the railway and the southern ports, by troops invigorated by rest.

So much for what Smuts should have done or might have done. Instead, he hatched another plan to catch Lettow-Vorbeck and again threw forward his exhausted, famished, disease-ridden troops.

Smuts made his headquarters in the pleasant town of

Morogoro, 115 miles west of Dar-es-Salaam, 1,700 feet above sea level, at the base of the northern slopes of the beautiful Uluguru Mountains. The Germans had destroyed or carried away everything of military value, but open spaces around the town were soon filled with tents for soldiers and carriers, hospitals, ordnance, engineering and supply depots, motorcar and lorry parks, repair shops and all the paraphernalia of a large military base in wartime. But Smuts could not even wait for his base to be established. He was eager—too eager—for action. He justified himself in a dispatch:

> I found many proofs of the precipitate flight and demoralized condition of the enemy forces, and I decided to continue the pursuit in spite of the fact that my forces and animals were worn out with the exertions of the last three weeks and that my transport had reached the extreme radius of action.

What Smuts mistook for enemy demoralization was merely the thorough destruction which the Germans deliberately left behind. There was no demoralization.

Smuts's plan called for still another envelopment operation, this time around the Uluguru Mountains in the hope of making a converging attack on the village of Kisaki on the Mgeta River. The troops boldly struck out, but they were short of blankets, food, carriers, and, most important of all, information as to where the enemy was to be found. All bridges had been blown, paths had been blocked, and then the rains came in persistent torrents. Smuts wrote to his wife on 3 September: "You cannot imagine how dangerous the rains became in this country. We are having a terribly hard time."

The historian of the King's African Rifles gives a succinct account:

> The painful story of the South African advance beyond Mlali can be told in a few words. It was made in two columns. One was intended to follow the valley of the Mgeta, but finding this

impossible struck through the hills further east. Neither column was in touch with the other, nor with headquarters, and on approaching the German boma [fort] west of Kisaki, each engaged the enemy independently. The columns thus failed to support one another, and as they were too depleted and exhausted to press home their attacks, for the first time in the campaign the enemy saw British troops retire.

Smuts appears not to have fully realized the importance of supplies. None of his troops was on more than half rations, and many were forced to do with considerably less. Some went for as long as thirty-six hours with no rations at all. Weakened by hunger, malaria and dysentery, men daily fell out on the line of march. Most staggered into camp hours later. But when the comrades of a man in the 6th South African Infantry reported that he had failed to show up, a stretcher party was sent back and found him dead. "There was nothing wrong with him," said the officer who examined the body. "Only starvation."

Still, Smuts's soldiers were expected to march and fight. Lettow-Vorbeck threw up ambushes and fought stubborn rear guard actions; there were innumerable vicious little battles. In one small fight in the Uluguru Mountains Lieutenant R. G. Glenday of the 3rd KAR charged three machine guns, engaged in a revolver duel at close range with a German officer, and was severely wounded, losing an arm. His only reward was a Military Cross.

Some were struck by the incongruities in their lives: death in a lovely landscape, for example. Doctor Young wrote after one small battle: "It was all ridiculous, you know, in that meadowland, on this summer day."

It could not be said that Smuts asked more of his men than he asked of himself. Deneys Reitz spoke of a visit that Smuts made to some of his troops: "He was thin and ill from malaria, but he spoke cheerfully. He told us that Roumania had joined the Allies,* and he gave us the latest news

---

* Rumania declared war on the Austro-Hungarian Empire on 26 August 1916.

from France. We had been in the wilds for so long that we had almost forgotten that there was another war."

The British now had about 80,000 men in the field. Lettow-Vorbeck had about 5,000 under his personal command; Wahle was retreating toward him with about 3,000 more; perhaps 1,500 men were in small scattered units. In the face of constant retreat and increasing hardships, Lettow-Vorbeck and his officers managed to maintain high morale among both German soldiers and African askaris.

Dar-es-Salaam was captured on 3 September, but it was hardly a glorious victory. Still, the Admiralty Prize Court awarded £ 100,000 in prize money. Lettow-Vorbeck had seen that it could not be defended, but he had made certain that it would be no easy matter for the British to make use of it. Max Loof and 125 of his sailors were left to blow up ships in port, the harbour facilities, the railway yard, locomotives, and all that might be of possible service and could not be removed. By deceiving the British, making them believe the town would be defended, he secured their help in the destructive process. A couple of the *Königsberg* guns were moved from place to place and fired under the direction of Lieutenant Richard Wenig, now hobbling on a wooden leg, but still serving his naval guns for the Fatherland. The deception succeeded, for as Loof said, the British "were always taken in by the clumsiest of ruses." One of the *Königsberg*'s guns was destroyed, but Wenig brought the other away. Left behind by the Germans were 370 civilians and 80 hospital patients for the British to look after.

Chasing Lettow-Vorbeck was a frustrating experience. C. J. Wilson wrote: "It was so intensely annoying, to be shelled day after day, week after week, by a fugitive enemy who ought at that stage of the campaign to have been almost at the end of his resources; while we, with the whole of the British Empire behind us, were powerless to retaliate."

The Germans seemed always to be more daring and more imaginative; they had a clearer idea of what was happening in the bush; they always chose the conditions under which they would fight. They sometimes delighted in rubbing salt in the wound. After one battle for a hillock, the KAR stormed the enemy's position to find that, as usual, the Germans had decamped. Nothing was left but a bantering note Captain Stemmermann had tucked in an empty champagne bottle. As the little group of British officers stood reading it, rain began to fall. One of them wrote that night in his diary: "Colonel furious, I furious, all of us wet and filthy."

To frustration was added the kind of ever-present danger that preys on men's nerves. Smuts wrote: "To march day by day, and week by week through the African jungle or high grass, in which vision is limited to a few yards, in which danger lurks near but seldom becomes visible, even when experienced, supplies a test to human nature often, in the long run, beyond human endurance."

In addition to all other difficulties, there were frequent attacks by bees, as at Tanga. On 7 September a British advance was held up when bees attacked the 6th South African Infantry. One company commander promised his men that if they just sat still the bees would not bother them. But the bees refused to discriminate and stung with ferocity those who sat and those who ran. Arthur Martin wrote:

> They were wearing shirts and shorts so worn that wherever creases had been formed, the cloth had been cut through. Their clothes were, in fact, merely hanging together. Thus the bees had access to all parts of the body. They crawled up the thighs, down the backs, under the arm pits, and so on. Many were seriously affected. The worst case was that of Cpl. J. H. McGreavey, who had to be carried off unconscious on a stretcher. Horses that did not get away were in several instances stung to death.

By September both sides had almost fought themselves to a standstill. Even Lettow-Vorbeck was in bad shape. His adjutant said of him:

> He has lost 12 kilos in the past two weeks and is yellow with fever, but he will not stop. He seems to live on coffee. But he

steams with energy and never complains of the excessive heat. I watched him coming back to camp today after twelve hours in the bush. He has climbed mountains, swam rivers, waded through quagmires and been badly stung by bees, but he is indefatigable. He arrived dragging his horse behind him, both of them footsore, and I am not sure which one more resembled a skeleton. One thing is certain. The horse will not last the next 24 hours, but the Colonel will.

He had also been badly bitten by sand flies and attacked by chiggers; his feet were pulpy masses of scabs and infected flesh and he could not bear even the straps of light sandals. His doctor was forced to remove two toenails; each evening his African cook cut out chiggers from his feet. His right eye had been scraped by elephant grass. He had broken his eyeglasses, and he was already half blind from a wound suffered in the Herero War in German South-West Africa.

In spite of all difficulties, the Germans managed to carry off most supplies in their retreat and to destroy what could not be removed. As the *Schutztruppen* fell back on the Mgeta River, they left behind at a placed called Kisaki, which had been a base and supply depot, a hospital full of sick for the British to care for. German forces were now reduced to 1,100 Europeans and 7,300 askaris with 73 machines guns, 16 field guns, and (still) four of the *Königsberg*'s 105 mm guns. It was a small army, but it was experienced, fit, and led by professional officers of ability. Its morale was high and it had complete faith in its debilitated, brilliant commander.

When the British reached Kisaki they found little of military value there. Smuts ordered his troops to press on, but they could not. The advance came to a halt. The *Official History* explained:

> His troops were at this time no longer in fighting condition. Increasingly exhausted by exertions of the preceeding weeks and the continuing shortage of supplies, their numbers depleted by sickness and almost at the end of their powers, they could do little more than hold their ground.

The soldiers' dreams were of food. Private Laurie Eyre of the 2nd Rhodesians wrote home: "I should like a real good meal again with vegetables, gravey, etc. I would give five rupees for a tin of condensed milk. Yesterday I got some tinned butter (a tablespoonful) to serve for two days; the first butter I have had for months." Captain Buchanan of the 25th Royal Fusiliers wrote that "those dark days at Kissaki cannot be surpassed and they were the days that found our spirits at lowest ebb."

Mangoes made a welcome addition to the slim diet, but they often caused digestive problems known as "mango belly." Captain Walter Douglas Downes in the Nigerian Brigade claimed to have eaten and "thoroughly enjoyed" such delicacies as monkey's brains on ration biscuit, bush rat pie, and "stewed hippo's sweetbreads." Many fell ill from eating unknown roots and berries. A donkey that had died of "horse sickness" and was buried, was dug up two days later and eaten. Near Mkindu a bridge tied together with rawhide was striped of its fastenings, which were cooked into a soup, leaving the bridge in "a very tattered state."

It was while his troops were stalled at Kissaki that Smuts sent Schnee a formal demand for surrender, agreeing to meet with him and Lettow-Vorbeck "at a time and place to be agreed upon." Lettow-Vorbeck was delighted: "General Smuts realized that his blow had failed . . . he had reached the end of his resources."

An extract from the British War Diary kept at "Advanced G.H.Q." written on 23 September 1916 reads:

> Very heavy rains are reported from all quarters, making the situation extremely serious. . . . All motor transport is at a standstill. . . . The troops in front have been on half rations for some time, and it was hoped to give them a rest and feed them well for the next two weeks, as they are all very weak from fever, lack of food, and continuous fighting. The rains have, however, put this out of the question, and the best that can be hoped—provided the rains hold off—is to prevent them from starving for the next week or ten days.

The rains did not hold off. The men continued to starve and to fall prey to diseases.

During the last three months of 1916 Smuts engaged in

no more offensive operations. He moved his headquarters to Dar-es-Salaam and worked to repair bridges and get the railways functioning again. He once more reorganized his army and ordered all those declared medically unfit to be sent home. The result was a mass exodus of white soldiers: 12,000 men, mostly South Africans, were sent away. When these wretched-looking young men reached South Africa, there was a public outcry. The Natal *Mercury*, among other newspapers, clamoured to know who was responsible for such an obvious failure to care for the troops; an inquiry was demanded. A newspaper reporter sent off to visit the camp of the 6th South African Infantry dubbed it "Starvation Camp," although this unit was, in fact, in better condition than most.

Coen Brits, now a major general, foolishly tried to deny that troops were on short rations or that men were starving. His statements had the effect of increasing the outcry and brought down a hornets' nest of criticism on his head. The government made strenuous efforts to still the clamour, for there was a need at the time to bolster recruitment.

Back in East Africa the white South Africans were replaced by black Africans from both sides of the continent, notably by a Nigerian brigade under Brigadier General F.H.B. Cunliffe, which arrived in the second week in December, and by the 2nd Gold Coast Regiment. Three other West African colonies also contributed men.

The Nigerian Brigade was to perform creditably in German East Africa—in spite of the incompetencies of the high command in West Africa which had dispatched it. With the British military's penchant for complicating the simple, no existing unit was sent. Instead, fifty-two men were taken from each company and lumped together to make new companies, which were linked in pairs, renumbered from one to sixteen, and then formed into four new battalions. The officers were also scrambled and some new arrivals who had never before served with African troops were posted to the brigade. This insured that the men would be serving in unfamiliar units under officers and non-commissioned officers who were strangers to them. Then, as if wishing to ensure lack of success, their familiar long Enfield rifles were taken from them at the last minute, and they were given the new short Enfield, which they were required to learn the use of while on shipboard. Lest somehow morale should still be high, they were put aboard their transports with not a single government official on hand to wish them luck.

Cunliffe, however, was an able commander, and when the transports landed at Durban, he put his men ashore for a few days and arranged something of a holiday for them. There were route marches, of course, to get the troopship kinks out, but there were also trips to the the zoo and elsewhere, including a visit to a "picture palace" where they watched a Charlie Chaplin film: "The men stood up in their places," said Captain Downes, "and shouted at the top of their voices when that wonderful little man managed simultaneously to hook by the neck and kick in the stomach a fat rival who aspired to the company of a charming, though rather eccentric young lady."

On landing at Dar-es-Salaam the Nigerians were sent at once to the front and within three weeks had suffered their first casualties. Within a month 400 were felled by pneumonia.

With the war half over, it was time to pass out some medals. One of the first British supply ships into Dar-es-Salaam brought a number of Russian decorations to be passed out to British commanders and heroes. No one really understood the hierarchy of Russian decorations and there was some friction among the generals as to who was getting the grandest. Van Deventer accepted the Order of St. Vladimir only after Smuts personally assured him it was the highest available. Smuts learned earlier than did Lettow-Vorbeck that the Kaiser had not forgotten him, and so, in this courteous war, he sent him a message of congratulations on being awarded the Prussian Order Pour le Merit, the famous "Blue Max," considered Germany's highest decoration.

Indian troops embarking for Kilwa, October 1917

Smuts fretted over the imposed inaction in the last quarter of 1916 and laid plans for still another pincer movement, which he was anxious to complete before the rains began in March. This time he sent a force under Brigadier General J. A. Hannyngton that consisted of the North Lancashires, two Indian battalions and two battalions of the KAR by ship to Kilwa, were they disembarked and moved inland in an attempt to get behind the enemy lines. Lettow-Vorbeck, aware of these moves and easily surmising Smuts's plan, drew back to the Rufiji. His main concern was the withdrawal of Wahle's three columns from Tabora, which were trying to join forces with Kraut in the fertile Mahenge area.

Kraut with about 2,000 men was now pressing on Northey's northernmost positions near Iringa in the Southern Highlands, 110 miles south of Dodoma. In late October the Germans cut off the town, ambushed a relief column and cut it to pieces, snapped up several supply dumps, raided Northey's line of communication, and then launched a vigorous attack on Iringa itself. But the Germans did not have it all their own way. The attack on Iringa failed; in the confused fighting in the bush, Wahle's columns lost touch with each other and one was trapped and forced to surrender. Casualties were high on both sides. In all, Wahle suffered about 750 casualties on his withdrawal from Tabora to the Mahenge area.

A small German force occupied a region between Tabora and Lake Ruka where there were neither British nor Belgian troops. It was some time before its existence became known, but on 22 November it was tracked down and trapped by Murray's Column; 7 German officers, 47 other Europeans, and 249 askaris surrendered. Small though it was, this was the best British victory since April, when van Deventer's Mounted Brigade had captured the 28th Field Company.

All of the German forces were now in the southern half of the colony. The columns led by Max Wintgens and Wahle himself joined Kraut in the Mahenge area and Wahle took command of the whole; Captain Theodor Tafel with a small force was on the Mgeta River; and Lettow-Vorbeck with the main force was in the southeast preparing to attack Kibata, near Kilwa, where the British had established a large base. Smuts also shifted the weight of his forces, ordering van Deventer to concentrate at Iringa and Northey at the village of Lupembe, a hundred miles east of the north end of Lake Nyasa; troops were also sent to reinforce Kilwa, where Hoskins took command.

For the first time, Lettow-Vorbeck began to have serious supply problems of his own. The area in the southeast into which his forces were being pushed was more primitive than the northern provinces and had so far been little affected by the war. Local planters and the civil authorities were not pleased to have the *Schutztruppe* among them and they resented their commandeering cattle and grain. The natives, too, were reluctant to sell their crops for German currency. It was not difficult for P. J. Pretorius, now a scout for Smuts, to assemble several of the chiefs and arrange for a coordinated uprising. For this feat he was awarded a bar to his Distinguished Service Order.

German and African discontent was overawed, but the fact was that there was not enough food to sustain large numbers of troops and carriers; the *Schutztruppe* had to move on. This became quite evident when, after six weeks of hard fighting that began on 6 December, Lettow-Vorbeck failed to take Kibata and lost the prize of the huge stacks of British supplies there. He therefore withdrew into a wilderness area just north of the Rufiji. By now, only the German force on the cultivated Mahenge plateau was still operating in a region where food supplies were plentiful.

In December 1916 Smuts launched an offensive designed to prevent a merger of the two main German forces and to trap Lettow-Vorbeck, or at least to bring him to that elusive decisive engagement which would end the campaign. Van Deventer, operating south of Iringa, was slowed by mountains covered with dense bush and valleys the rains had filled with water. He was late, and once again Lettow-Vorbeck slipped through his fingers, this time by crossing the Rufiji. As Lettow-Vorbeck once said, "There is always a way out, even of an apparently hopeless position, if the leader makes up his mind to face the risks."

Many people in Europe and the United States who were scarcely aware of the campaign in East Africa were reminded of it by the widely broadcast news of the death of Selous.

The 25th Battalion of the Royal Fusiliers, which had left London 1,166 strong, could on Christmas Day 1916 muster only 60 of its original complement, but among them was its oldest and most famous member: the sixty-five-year-old hunter and explorer Captain Frederick Courtney Selous. He had been on sick leave in England, but had returned on 16 December with a draft of 150 men. On 4 January, while leading a patrol, he stumbled upon a strong detachment of German askaris. In a brief fire fight he was shot through the mouth and died instantly.*

---

* The area where Selous fell was later made into a game reserve that bears his name.

On 20 January 1917 Smuts abruptly handed over his command to Major General A. Reginald Hoskins and departed for England, where he had been invited to attend the Imperial War Conference. At a stopover in South Africa six days later, he was quoted as saying that the back of German resistance had been broken and that the campaign would be brought to an end within a few months. This was certainly news to General Hoskins, and to every starving soldier in the bush.

By the time he reached England Smuts seemed ready to claim that the war in East Africa was actually over and that he had won it. Arnold Wienholt said, "I remember being distinctly annoyed by a letter from a friend, who asked me why I stayed on in East Africa on a 'back veld police patrolling job' now that the campaign was finished there."

On 20 March 1917 Lloyd George introduce Jan Smuts to the Imperial War Cabinet. He was, claimed Lloyd George, "One of the most brilliant generals in this war."

CHAPTER
24

New Leaders and a
New Phase

S ince Smuts in London was declaring that the war in
East Africa all but over, pressure was put on Hoskins
to hurry up and finish off the campaign; at the same time
he was confronted with a reluctance to give him the men
and supplies needed to make the attempt. Hoskins saw quite
clearly that Lettow-Vorbeck was not going to lie down and
roll over, and that a long hard campaign lay ahead. The
campaign was difficult to explain to anyone who was not a
part of it. After all, Smuts had captured all the railways,
all the ports, all the towns of any importance, and, except
in the Mahenge area, all of the fertile land in the colony.
What was left for Hoskins to do?

The British had won victory after victory, yet the campaign dragged on, and people wondered why. In May 1917
the Bulawayo *Chronicle* reprinted with obvious agreement
an article from the Johannesburg *Star* that said: "It is . . .
high time that someone brought these operations to an end.
The campaign in East Africa has been of the most prodigal
nature in money and in lives and constitutions."

Hoskins tried vainly to explain that the German army in the field had not been defeated, and that it consisted of tough professional soldiers led by a resourceful and determined commander. Adding to his troubles, the rains came early in 1917—only five days after Smuts left, in fact—and it was said that they were the worst within living memory. As Lieutenant Thatcher put it: "It rained steadily and heavily all the month of March and went on raining for two months after that." Colonel Richard Dobbs, A.Q.M.G., warned in a report: "I honestly cannot see how we are going to feed the troops in view of the weather and serious transport situation." Indeed, for a time supply arrangements broke down completely.

In spite of all his difficulties, Hoskins did make some progress. He was commander-in-chief for less than four months, but in that time he put in train some needed reforms, and he faced up to a fact which somehow seemed hard for British generals to swallow: that in East Africa black Africans made better soldiers than white Africans, Indians, or Europeans. One of Hoskins's first orders was for a rapid expansion of the KAR. Smuts had eventually increased its numbers to 8,000, but Hoskins tripled this figure; before the end of the war there were 35,000 engaged. They were, of course, officered by Europeans, and Hoskins, following the German example, increased the number of European NCOs in each battalion.

Although unable to get many reinforcements from outside Africa, Hoskins did manage to get more supplies and money for more carriers. And he strove to make all the staff work more efficient. A South African infantry officer noted the improvements: "One was struck by a new air of efficiency in the military arrangements, rations were generous, and all were fitted with clothing. Porters were supplied on a far more liberal scale than previously, and men could take 5½ times more personal kit than in the previous campaign. It appeared that after Major General Hoskins took command, far more attention was paid to the needs of men in the front line." More carriers were necessary, for the campaign was fought in increasingly wilder country with fewer roads, and these were available because compulsory service acts in Uganda and British East Africa authorized the virtual enslavement of tens of thousands.

In May 1917 Hoskins was relieved of his command and sent to Mesopotamia to command a division. He was replaced by van Deventer. In a way this was a curious choice, for almost all his staff and his subordinate commanders were English-speaking Britons, while van Deventer, whose mother tongue was Afrikaans, was loath to speak English and, at least initially, all of his orders, even to his staff, had to be translated. However, he saw clearly that his objective could not be a town or a geographical feature, but the destruction of the enemy forces in the field, and this could be done, as he said in a dispatch, only by "hard hitting and plenty of it." He was fortunate in that just as he took command the rains ceased and he was able to profit from the excellent preparations Hoskins had made. Even so, it was more than three months before he was completely ready for a major offensive.

In his birthday message the Kaiser referred to Lettow-Vorbeck and his men as a "small band of heroes." No mention was made of Schnee, who was still marching along with the main column. He struggled to maintain his authority and was a constant source of irritation to Lettow-Vorbeck, who resented his presence and that of his staff; he also complained of the number of carriers needed to transport their luggage and the amount of precious food that they consumed. Lettow-Vorbeck strove continually to shake off as many non-combatants as he could, but German refugees—women, children, and old men—continued to join him. When he finally ordered all women, including the wives of his officers, to leave or stay behind, there was an uproar in his camp. Schnee saw a chance to curry favour at the expense of his military commander and sided with the protestors. A meeting on the grounds of a field hospital ended only when a young nurse addressed the assembly:

van Deventer (on right)

In one of the wards this morning I heard a civilian patient crit-
icizing the wisdom of our glorious von Lettow for his insis-
tence on carrying on the war. One of the *Schutztruppe*, lying on
the bed beside him, badly wounded, leaned over and said:
"Anyone who is not for the commander now is a traitor to Germany and should be shot for it. If you were not a sick man, I
would shoot you myself. How dare you attack such a man. Von
Lettow is the brains of this campaign, but you sound to me like
the backside of it."

In a few days the European women were sent without incident across the river for the British to find and feed. The
African women were less compliant. Sent off under a German sergeant with three days' rations, they walked only a
few miles before they sat down and ate all their rations.
That done, they thrashed the sergeant and walked back to
their men. Lettow-Vorbeck surrendered.

General Crowe believed that the German officers retained
their hold on their askaris through their wives and children. "The wives of the askaris," he said, "apart from any
feeling of affection, practically represent their worldly pos-

sessions. They are the equivalent of so much solid cash and of so many head of cattle, and as long as they are behind them they had every inducement to remain with the Germans and not come over to us." Although continually on the move, each little family carried along its household effects, often including fowls. The crowing of cocks threatened more than once to give away a position, but, as Lettow-Vorbeck noted, "An order issued in one force that the crowing of cocks before 9 A.M. was forbidden brought no relief."

Lettow-Vorbeck, the great improviser, learned to make bread without wheat and how to fashion boots from hides. ("It is convenient if a man can kill an antelope and make a boot," he said.) He insisted on every European learning to be his own artisan and he trained his troops to live off the land.

It was in February 1917 that a curious aberration in the *Schutztruppe* occurred. Captain Max Wintgens, a professional officer of great ability, broke away from the force under Kraut and, without orders, struck off on his own, waging his own little campaign. He took with him about 700 askaris, several hundred carriers, three small field guns, and thirteen machine guns. Both Lettow-Vorbeck and Hoskins were taken by surprise.

No one knows what caused Wintgens to do this (there are conflicting stories) nor does anyone know what he intended to accomplish. He moved at a rapid pace, clearing the country of all supplies as he moved, thus ensuring that his British pursuers would have to be supplied from their rear; in fact, supply problems brought them to a standstill, for they were forced to follow wherever he led and through areas he had devasted. It seemed at first that he was headed for Rhodesia, but he turned north and west through territories the Allies had thought were safely under their control.

Murray's Column was the first to take up the pursuit, but Murray was 200 miles behind. Some units that did catch up with Wintgens were roughly handled. A KAR detachment that got in the way was badly cut up, losing 19 killed and 26 seriously wounded. Northey called for help and Hoskins sent Major H. G. Montgomerie with 300 men, mostly former German askaris, from Morogoro to Tabora. These turncoat troops were so new to the British service that words of command had to be given in German. Montgomerie marched out of Tabora in search of Wintgens, but his force was too small to do more than try to keep track of his movements.

By 1 May Wintgens was seen as such a menace that a special command was established to deal with him. It was called EDFORCE after its commander, Brigadier General W. F. S. Edwards, and it consisted of a KAR battalion (Major Montgomerie's unit), the 130th Baluchis, 400 men of the Cape Corps (a coloured, i.e., mixed race, unit from South Africa), some ruga-ruga, and fifty mounted askaris—in all, 1,700 rifles and 14 machine guns. Edwards established his headquarters at Tabora, towards which Wintgens seemed to be heading.

The Belgians, having obtained most of the territory they coveted in East Africa and regarding their conquered provinces as secure, had returned most of their troops to the Congo, but they too felt threatened by Wintgens's approach and agreed to cooperate. On 23 May the 6th Belgian Battalion captured Wintgens himself—or rather, Wintgens allowed himself to be captured, for he had contracted typhus and surrendered to get treatment. He did not, however, surrender his troops. *The Times* reported that the Belgians, as a tribute to the "valor and courtesy" which distinguished him "from all the German leaders whom the Belgians had encountered on the battlefields of Europe and Africa" permitted him to retain his sword. Lieutenant Heinrich Naumann now took command of the far-ranging German column, and he proved himself as capable and as resourceful as Wintgens.

When van Deventer replaced Hoskins as commander-in-chief, he asked the South African government for a force of mounted men to chase Naumann, and the 10th South Afri-

can Horse was raised and sent to East Africa for that purpose. The Nigerians also joined the hunt and soon there
was the equivalent of a brigade each of Belgians and British troops, nearly 4,000 men, in pursuit of fewer than 500
askaris led by a German lieutenant.

On 26 May a Nigerian regiment, moving west from Morogoro on the Central Railway, stopped to take on water
and wood fuel about sixty miles south southeast of Tabora.
At just this time Naumann, having cut telephone and telegraph lines, was crossing the railway through a culvert in
thick bush less than two miles away. He had sent out patrols
down the tracks on both sides of his crossing point, and one
of these collided with a Nigerian patrol, which lost two dead
and five wounded before withdrawing. When a strong
Nigerian force came up, it encountered not the German
patrol, which had now rejoined the rear guard of Naumann's column, but a British railway repair crew coming
out from Tabora. The two British units fought a sharp little
skirmish with each other while Naumann skipped away
north in the direction of Mwanza.

Two weeks later a British airplane, mistaking the 4th
Nigerians for the German column, dropped darts on them
while Naumann was crossing a river nine miles away. As
Naumann's intentions were a mystery, British troops were
sent helter skelter, for, as one British officer said in a succinct understatement, "the situation was extremely confused."

Fear spread in circles from the rampaging column; a
rumour circulated that Naumann actually intended to
invade British East Africa. Stories of the savagery of the
German askaris and their masters grew ever more horrify-
ing. Captain Walter Downes wrote:

> Pilage and rape seemed to be the order to the day with Nau-
> mann's troops, while several cases of murder were also reported.
> The Germans in East Africa were not far behind their brothers
> in Europe for frightfulness.

At the end of August Naumann carried out a daring raid on
Kahe, burning stores, looting trains, and wrecking the sta-

tion there. His intrusion into the area north of the Central Railway was an embarrassment to the British in more ways than one. The Hague Convention of 1907 had laid down that the government of the occupying power must be a military government established by the commander-in-chief of the occupying army. The British, never imagining that a German force would ever again be seen north of the Central Railway, had ignored the Convention and on 1 January 1917 had installed a Colonial Office administrator for the occupied area. He was in an anomalous position: legally under the commander-in-chief, but actually under the Colonial Office. The result when Naumann came on the scene and German, British, and Belgian troops were again tramping through villages and corn fields, was a greater than usual administrative muddle. In an attempt at a solution, civilian employees were given military ranks and kept at their jobs.

The Belgians found and attacked Naumann at Ikoma, halfway between Lake Natron and Lake Victoria, but they came to grief and were only saved by the arrival of Major Drought and his "Skin Corps." Not until 30 September was Naumann finally surrounded close to the British East African border near Kilimanjaro by 4 KAR, the South African Horse, and the Cape Corps. On 2 October he surrendered. He still had with him 14 Europeans, 165 askaris, and 250 carriers. Wintgens and Naumann had been on the loose for eight months and had cut a twisting, turning swath through nearly 2,000 miles of territory. Naumann was charged with murder and was for some time kept in close confinement. However, there was scant evidence and he was never brought to trial.

Lettow-Vorbeck disapproved of the Wintgens–Naumann adventure. "It is to be regretted," he wrote after the war, "that this operation, carried out with so much initiative and determination, became separated so far from the main theatre of war as to be of little use." This was myopic of him for they did for him what he did for the Germans fighting on the Western Front: they drew off forces the Allies would rather have used elsewhere. In this case, as *The Times* said, "The chase of Naumann deprived General van Deventer of troops whose services would have been very useful in the principal theatre of operations." Van Deventer also spoke of this "remarkable raid" and remarked that "the force which carried it out was composed of first-class askaris, well led."

In the south, where van Deventer's men now faced Lettow-Vorbeck and the main German force, living conditions improved somewhat when the country began to dry out in June. An officer of the 129th Baluchis wrote, "Yesterday we got some potatoes, the first I have had in this country, and they might have been the choicest fruit from the way we fell on them."

The principal engagement of the mid-year dry season for the British was at Narungombe, forty miles west of Kilwa in the southeast, where Captain Eberhard von Lieberman had retreated with eight companies, two small field guns, and 48 Maxims. He controlled several waterholes and occupied an extremely strong position. On 19 July the British launched an attack upon him, but their right flank became mired in a papyrus swamp and was swept away by machine gun bullets. Many of the men in 3 KAR were recruits enduring their first battle. A frontal assault was to have been covered by the fire of newly arrived Stokes mortars, but the crews were new and ill trained and some of their shells fell among the Gold Coast Regiment. (Nevertheless, German askaris complained that the mortars were unfair as they did not make enough noise to give warning.)

By noon nearly all the British officers had been shot away; platoons and companies were commanded by African NCOs. The Germans launched a furious bayonet attack, but the Gold Coast Regiment stood firm, and even counterattacked. The Germans threw themselves into another attack at dusk and were beaten back by 3 KAR, which then counterattacked, capturing a machine gun.* Lieberman's force

---

* This machine gun stood for many years just outside the main barracks of the King's African Rifles, and it stands today outside the gate of the 3rd Kenya Rifles.

then melted away. Van Deventer noted that "the enemy's capacity for resistance has not been weakened by the rainy season, and the moral and training of his troops remains high."

There were many frustrating small battles for the British in the southeastern corner of the colony. On 2 August they attacked the German outposts and the following day put in a three-pronged attack on Lettow-Vorbeck's main positions, but these had not been properly reconnoitred and they were surprised by a serious and determined resistance. The British were repulsed; Punjabis, left unsupported in the centre, lost seven out of eight of their British officers, three Indian officers, and 255 other ranks. It was a disaster. A counterattack failed. When a general retirement was ordered, it was discovered that the Germans had slipped behind their lines and attacked their supply column, and that the carriers had thrown down their loads and bolted. A KAR officer with impressive restraint called it "an exhausting and disheartening day."

A few days later Lettow-Vorbeck and his troops had further cause for celebration when they heard by wireless the Kaiser's speech on the occasion of the third anniversary of the war. "[It] delighted us all," said Lettow-Vorbeck. He had further cause to celebrate when it was announced that he had been promoted to the rank of major general (then equivalent to the rank of brigadier general in the British and American armies).

In September 1917 van Deventer announced that "the situation is ripe for the main advance. . . . Sufficient motor transport is at this time available for the whole force." It had taken van Deventer three and a half months to reach this happy state, even after the strenuous efforts of Hoskins. On 10 September he moved his headquarters down the coast to Kilwa, and nine days later his major offensive began. A force from Lindi advanced southwest while another force from Kilwa pushed south, threatening the Germans on their flank and rear. With overwhelmingly superior manpower and adequate supplies and transport, both forces made satisfactory progress, moving slowly but almost without pause until December. There was, however, one important setback.

In October the last big battle and the bloodiest of the entire campaign was fought in the bush about forty-five miles up the Lukuledi River from Lindi at a place called Mahiwa, which gave its name to the battle, and at the tiny village of Nyangao (no longer to be found on maps). The German position was on a ridge behind the dry bed of a small stream. The British began their attack at daybreak on 17 October and the fighting was continuous through the day, attack and counterattack succeeded each other without respite under a scorching sun. It was a battle of trenches and dugouts, grenades and machine guns, of bayonet charges, of blood, mud and all the classic features of World War I as practiced on the Western Front in Europe.

The British forces were commanded by Brigadier General Gordon Beves, a fifty-three-year-old South African. Lettow-Vorbeck remembered Beves, and he remembered how at the Battle of Reata (11 March 1916) he had recklessly thrown his men up a hill to destruction in a frontal attack. He now shrewdly gambled on Beves repeating that manoeuvre. He strengthened his centre and placed it under Wahle, who had recently joined him. As he said later: "I thought it expedient to increase the disadvantage that the enemy was bringing on himself by his costly frontal attack and used all my available strength in such a way that the enemy by increasing the fierceness of his frontal attack was bleeding himself to death."

The Nigerians had had only a half pound of rice per man for three days and they were badly shaken by German shellfire. One of their shallow trenches received three direct hits in succession. According to Walter Downes, "the trees above this trench were dripping blood for two days afterwards from limbs and trunks of men that had been blown up and been wedged between the branches."

It was in the course of this battle that Brigadier General Henry deC. O'Grady, an Indian Army officer who had come

The wounded ready to be moved from Myango, after the battle of Mahiwa

out as a staff officer with the ill-fated Indian Expeditionary Force 'B' and had risen to become a general and a commander, impressed his soldiers with his coolness under fire by strolling along the line accompanied only by his orderly, asking everyone if they had seen his dog, O'Meara.

The night of 17 / 18 October was comparatively quiet, but the battle was renewed in all it fury at first light. The Germans concentrated on a gap between two columns, and the last remnant of the 25th Royal Fusiliers was nearly annihilated trying to stem it. Of the nearly 2,000 men sent out with the original units and in drafts, only 200 had been left to go into battle and only 50 were still on their feet with rifles in their hands after the battle. By nightfall of the second day both sides fell back exhausted. The casualties had been heavy.

The British lost more than half of their men—2,700 out

of a total of 4,900. German losses were 95 killed and 422 wounded out of 1,500 engaged. Lettow-Vorbeck called this battle a "splendid victory" and the most serious defeat the British had suffered since Tanga. True, the British had failed to carry his positions, but he was forced to withdraw and he knew that he could not afford another such "splendid victory"; the losses were far more serious for him than the greater losses were to van Deventer.

After the battle there were charges of atrocities committed by German askaris. Captain Downes claimed that search parties "brought back the most terrible reports of German brutality. Indian and Nigerian soldiers, who had obviously been wounded in the various actions, had been bayoneted later, in the most indecent manner, as they were crawling to places of safety. Any number of men were in this way obscenely murdered by the enemy." Downes also told how Captain A. L. deC. Stretton's "small Nigerian 'boy,' aged ten years, was found with his body a mass of bayonet wounds—a victim of foul murder. Close to the boy's corpse lay the 1st Battalion's pet monkey, which had been shot at close quarters and then had a bayonet driven through its body."* The War Diary of the 129th Baluchis, who six weeks after the battle passed through the area, noted: "Bodies must still by lying about in the bush. Smell very bad."

The character of the British forces had changed dramatically since Smuts had arrived with his South Africans. In November 1917 nearly a third of the British forces in East Africa were Indian, but in that month it was decided that all Indian troops should be withdrawn before the beginning of the rainy season. With the additional KAR battalions and the arrival of the Nigerian Brigade, the Gold Coast Regiment, the West India Regiment (blacks from the West Indies), the Rhodesia Native Infantry, and a battalion of Cape Coloureds from South Africa, the colour of British combatants was primarily black. By February 1918 more than 90 percent of the combatants on both sides were black

---

* Atrocity stories are usually hard to prove. During the war Lord Northcliffe offered a prize for undoctored photographic evidence of a German atrocity, but it was unclaimed even by the armistice.

Africans. Only 4 percent of British infantry came from Britain.

Hampered by serious supply problems and with the British still trying to catch him in a pincer movement, Lettow-Vorbeck decided after Mahiwa to take a new tack. He had supplies for six weeks; he still had one *Königsberg* gun and a Portuguese mountain gun he had captured, but he had only 400,000 rounds of small arms ammunition, and most of this was for the old 1871 pattern rifles that used black powder—"Smokies" they were called. He decided to reduce his forces and invade Portuguese Africa (Mozambique).

Leaving behind all his sick and wounded (98 Germans and 425 askaris) at a place called Chiwata, he took his remaining force to the Rovuma River, the boundary between German and Portuguese territories in East Africa. When the British entered Chiwata they found and released 121 prisoners of war, some of whom were dressed in bark cloth and skins. These were known as the "old men," for they had been captured at Tanga in November 1914.

In the hard marching of the days ahead Lettow-Vorbeck continued to shed those unable to keep up. Batches of sick, wounded, and battle-weary men—about 50 Europeans and 600 Africans—were left behind at various camps. At one, an excited British officer, apparently under the illusion that Lettow-Vorbeck had at last been cornered, dashed about with his revolver drawn demanding to know his whereabouts.

Many of the sick and wounded laughed, and one raised his head and called out cheerily, "The general? He's gone to hell!"

Among those ordered to remain behind and surrender was Max Loof, whom Lettow-Vorbeck had never learned to like. The ex-captain of the *Königsberg* was bitter at being dumped and complained that he was being thrown to the wolves to allow Lettow-Vorbeck to escape. Doubtless the *Schutztruppe* commander would have like to have left Schnee behind as well, but the governor proved durable and stayed the course.

Lettow-Vorbeck's fighting force now consisted of only

about 200 Europeans and 2,000 askaris, but they were the fittest and best. To these he intended to join a sizeable German force under Captain Theodor Tafel, which was fighting its way southeast from the Mahenge district. Tafel had managed to defeat several of Northey's units and in November 1917 he anticipated joining forces with Lettow-Vorbeck.

Pretorius the elephant hunter was in hospital, but his African spies continued to bring him intelligence, and one day he was brought a note taken from a captured German messenger. It was from Tafel to Lettow-Vorbeck:

> Yesterday I had to fight with the enemy. I vanquished them and managed to capture their food, but their supplies together with mine can only last three days. I am trekking to the top of the Bangala River and will follow it down [to the Rovuma].

Pretorius, although still ill, left the hospital and arranged for all food supplies on Tafel's line of march to be destroyed and for every tribe in his path to be threatened with swift retribution if any aid was given him. Tracking down the column, he noted how "weary and dispirited" his troops were. From an observation post on a ridge he saw that in spite of all his efforts Tafel's and Lettow-Vorbeck's columns were only about a mile apart and were about to converge. Then, as he watched, Tafel's column halted and he saw the officers confer. Soon after he watched the column turn off in a new direction. He did not know why, but he was delighted.

The day after Lettow-Vorbeck crossed the Rovuma, Tafe had successfully ambushed a detachment of the 129th Bal· uchis and the 25th Indian Cavalry and inflicted heavy casualties, the Indians losing 40 percent of their strength. Next day, as the Indians were trying to recover from their disaster, they were utterly astonished to witness the surrender of a portion of Tafel's column—30 Europeans, 180 askaris, 640 carriers, and 220 African women. Early the following morning Tafel destroyed all his weapons and surrendered the remainder of his column. A total of 95 Europeans and 1,200 askaris with all their carriers surrendered to some 100 exhausted Indian soldiers they had just routed. "It was an amazing sight when his column was marched past the forward troops with all its attendants and impedimenta," wrote Arthur Martin. "It was said that the column was seven miles long, made up of soldiers, porters and innumerable camp followers in the way of wives and children."

Tafel had apparently concluded that Lettow-Vorbeck had abandoned him when, in fact, as Pretorius had seen, he was less than a day's march away. A handful of Tafel's men who refused to surrender did manage to find Lettow-Vorbeck and their news of the surrender came as a "severe and unexpected blow" to him. It was an act he himself never considered.

Early in the morning on 25 November 1917 Lettow-Vorbeck's advance guard waded across the Rovuma a little above its confluence with the Ludjenda and entered Portuguese territory, the rest of the *Schutztruppe* following. Even before all were across they engaged a Portuguese force of about a thousand men who had just come up with orders to prevent the crossing. The Germans and their askaris made mincemeat of them and not more than two or three hundred survived.

Thousands of pounds of supplies fell into Lettow-Vorbeck's hands—six British machine guns, thirty horses, medical supplies, European food, and many long-unseen delicacies. There was, he admitted, "a fearful mêlée" as askaries and carriers fell to looting, and it was some time before the officers could restore order. Enough new Portuguese rifles were collected to equip nearly half of his force, plus a quarter of a million rounds of small arms ammunition. With one blow he had solved a great part of his problems. "It was a perfect miracle," he crowed, "that these troops should have arrived so opportunely as to make the capture of the place so profitable to us."

The Portuguese askaris taken prisoner were converted into carriers and loaded with the newly captured supplies. As the advance continued, other Portuguese posts were knocked over with equal ease. The leading company had orders not to pause when a Portuguese post was encountered, but to attack at once and capture it. The Portuguese proved to be inept at war. One unwary supply column simply marched into the German camp. "It was a welcome capture," chortled Lettow-Vorbeck, who felt, with reason, that he had come into a land of milk and honey. The natives greeted them with friendship, for their Portuguese rulers had not endeared themselves.

It did indeed seem miraculous. Just as his future had looked most grim, his fortunes blossomed. There was even an added bonus for crossing the Rovuma: As they were no longer in German East Africa, Schnee could no longer pretend to have jurisdiction over him. He had indeed been obstructive and obtuse. At one point he had refused to permit officers to sign chits for needed food and supplies and he had ordered administrators to demand payment for everything commandeered by the *Schutztruppe*. Lettow-Vorbeck had once put a pistol to the head of a district commissioner to obtain a ferry he needed, an action Schnee called "buccaneering" in a report he was preparing to send to Berlin.

Schnee had stayed with the *Schutztruppe*, perhaps without at first realizing how the crossing of the river changed his status. He had, said Lettow-Vorbeck, previously used his authority "in such a way as to interfere most seriously with that of the commander-in-chief, and had often encroached upon my sphere of activity. I had been powerless to prevent this, but now that we were outside the Protectorate I attached the greatest importance to the fact that now, at any rate, I had a free hand." Understandably, he relished the task of informing Schnee of his changed station in life. The British stayed any protest Schnee might have made by dispatching an officer of the 3rd Nigerians under a flag of truce to inform him that his colony had been formally declared an Allied protectorate. Schnee stayed on to the end, but all pretense of authority was gone.

King George V sent General van Deventer a congratulatory message on his ejection of the *Schutztruppe* from German East Africa, but when the message was read to the troops, many who heard it were well aware that the campaign was not finished simply because the Germans had crossed the Rovuma. Lieutenant Arnold Wienholt, remembering Smuts's claim to have won the war nearly a year earlier, said, "The sale of the bear's skin has twice been concluded, though the animal himself, in the shape of von Lettow and his little army of picked men is very much alive."

25

War Comes to Portuguese East Africa

C aptain Walter Downes of the 4th Nigerians recorded that "On 5th November [1917] a startling rumour got about that a German airship had left Europe for German East Africa." When Max Loof was taken prisoner he was asked about it, but he replied quite honestly that he knew nothing. For once, rumour proved to be true; there was indeed a German zepplin so bound, and, most astonishing if Captain Downes's date is correct, news of its flight was circulating sixteen days before its departure.

The Germans had soon discovered that zepplins were too vulnerable to be used for bombing or reconnaissance missions, but their ability to stay aloft for long periods and to fly nonstop for thousands of miles could not be matched. These were the features which led the German Admiralty, though it had no direct responsibility for the fate of Lettow-Vorbeck, to the notion that a zepplin loaded with useful stores could be sent to East Africa.

The first zeppelin selected to make the 3,600-mile trip was the L–57, but on a trial run on 8 October 1917 it was

Portuguese East Africa

struck by lightning and destroyed. It was replaced at once by the L–59, an airship 78 feet 5 inches in diameter and lengthened by 100 feet to 743 feet. Built at Friedrichshafen in the autumn of 1917, it encompassed 2,418,700 cubic feet when completed. It was powered by five M HSLu engines with a total of 1,200 horsepower and had a useful lift of 114,400 pounds. Its estimated range was 10,000 miles.

It was stocked with fifteen tons of medical supplies, machine guns, ammunition, bush knives, binoculars, and other useful things—even sewing machines. As it was not expected to return, all its parts were designed for other uses after landing. The balloon envelope could be used to make shelter tents; its muslin lining, bandages; its gas bags, sleeping bags; huts and a wireless tower could be built from the Duralumin frame; the catwalks had leather treads which could be used to make boots. The only nonessential on board was a case of wine to celebrate the L–59's safe arrival.

Dr. Hugo Eckener, its designer, flew it with Captain Ernest Lehman (who in 1937 died in the crash of the *Hindenburg*) from Friedrichshaven to Jamboli (Yambol), Bulgaria, where

Zeppelin L59

it was turned over to Lieutenant Commander Ludwig Bockholt. Although not the most experienced airship commander, Bockholt had distinguished himself by a remarkable exploit. While commanding the L–23 he had captured the Norwegian schooner *Royal,* carrying mining timbers to England. A prize crew lowered from the zeppelin sailed the ship into a German port. It was the first and only time a zeppelin ever captured a ship at sea.

On 21 September, after a couple false starts, Bockholt and an all-volunteer crew of twenty-one left Jamboli in the L–59. Travelling first over friendly Turkey, they headed out over the Mediterranean, flying between Crete and Rhodes, and then the length of British-controlled Egypt and on into the Sudan.

The most precarious part of the journey was encountered over the desert, where the sun's glare caused severe headaches and even hallucinations among the crew, and the ship rolled so violently that many crewmen were made airsick.

Overbuoyant during the day in the rising hot air, it became dangerously heavy at night, once dropping from 3,100 feet to 1,300 feet and nearly colliding with a mountain. Buckholt steered by celestial navigation.

At dusk on 22 November the ship reached a latitude on a level with the Second Cataract of the Nile above Aswan. At forty-five minutes past midnight, about 125 miles west of Khartoum, a faint radio message was received, ordering the L–59 to turn back. There was some debate among the crew as to whether or not the message was authentic, a debate which has been continued by historians for seventy years. Did the Admiralty learn that Lettow-Vorbeck had left German East Africa and assume that he would soon surrender? Or did British intelligence officers send the message as a ruse?

The British certainly knew that the Germans intended to send the airship; British air crews in Africa had been alerted. But had the British known the time and the date of the actual flight, they would surely have sent pursuit planes stationed in Egypt and the Sudan to intercept it. Yet the L–59 encountered no British aircraft and a week after its return to Bulgaria, British intelligence officers in East Africa were still trying to determine where it was to land.

Whatever the source of the message, Bockholt decided it was genuine and the great airship turned back. The crew, keyed up for the adventure, now drooped. Gripped by lassitude, they went through the motions of their duties. At 3 P.M. on 25 November the L–59 returned to Jamboli, ending the longest sustained flight in history. The airship had been airborne for 95 hours and had travelled 4,220 miles—and it still carried eleven tons of fuel, enough for another sixty-four hours of flight, a further 3,700 miles.*

No further attempt was made by land, sea, or air to succor Lettow-Vorbeck, but at this time he hardly needed out-

---

* Bockholt perished in a fiery crash of another zeppelin while on a mission to bomb Malta in April 1918, the result, it would seem of an accident rather than enemy action. The L–59 was turned over to the British at the end of the war and her fate is unknown.

side help. Portuguese East Africa with its friendly natives and well-supplied, badly defended supply depots was a guerrilla leader's dream. December 1917 found his troops in the centre of a group of Portuguese plantations, amid vegetable gardens, orchards, fields of corn, berry bushes, and provisions of all sorts. One officer wrote in his diary: "Never have we fared so well during the past four years." On Christmas Eve the officers prepared a surprise for their general: a real bed with clean sheets and a bug-proof mosquito net. On Christmas Day they ate roast pork and drank Portuguese wines, ending the feast with real coffee and cigars. What soldier on campaign could ask for more?

Everywhere the Africans welcomed them as "nothing less than heaven-sent deliverers from their cruel and cowardly oppressors." Arnold Wienholt, back scouting for the British, complained that he and other intelligence officers "never got the slightest voluntary help or information from any native. . . . We English, as the friends of the Portuguese, naturally found the inhabitants against us." In fact, the British were often led astray by false information.

Consequently, Lettow-Vorbeck seemed like a phantom; no one knew when or where he would appear. He appreciated the situation and exploited it. "We Germans enjoyed a good reputation among the intelligent natives of Portuguese Africa," he said. Every fort they blew up was to them "a little Bastille going up in flames."

The *Schutztruppe*, now pared down to the fittest, bravest and best, must have constituted one of the most efficient fighting units in the world. Certainly it was the best for bush fighting in East Africa. On the march they routinely marched two hours and rested for a half hour. In this fashion a marching column could cover fifteen, even twenty miles in six hours. At the mid-day halt the Europeans smeared hippopotomus fat on chunks of bread; lunch was a foreign notion to the Africans, but many of the *schutztruppen* adopted it. Lettow-Vorbeck, reminiscing after the war, looked back fondly on these moments: "It was very jolly when the whole force bivouacked in this way in the forest, in the best spirits, and refreshed ourselves for fresh exertions, fresh marches, and fresh fighting."

His force was now divided into units, each consisting of three companies, a field hospital, and a supply train. Sound tactical judgement, exceptional energy and initiative were required of subordinate commanders, particularly those commanding the advanced companies or detached columns, and they were usually given wide discretionary powers. The advance unit was commonly a day's march ahead of the main column and the rear column a day behind. The fighting companies in the lead carried little more than their rifles, machine guns, and ammunition. "The askaris marched gaily forward, straight as lances, and with their rifles reversed over their shoulders, as has always been the custom in rifle regiments," said Lettow-Vorbeck. "Lively conversation was kept up, and after the plundering of an enemy's camp . . . cigarette smoke rose on all sides."

The carriers, women, children, and "boys" had to learn march discipline, to keep to the proper pace and distance. Intelligent boys were taught to be signalers, and they marched along with their worldly goods on their heads. One confided his dream of one day travelling to Berlin and visiting the Kaiser:

> The Kaiser will say to me, "Good-day, my son," and I will give him an exhibition of my signaling. He will then give me roast meat and present me to the Empress. The Empress will say, "Good-day, my child" and will give me cakes and show me the shop windows.

The carriers' loads weighed twenty-five kilograms and were shifted from head to shoulder and back again. Many marched barefoot; if a thorn stuck in their foot, they took a knife and calmly cut out flesh and thorn. The askaris still carried along their wives and children, each woman weighted with her own and her husband's possessions, and frequently a baby, for babies were born on the march; fighting did not stop for birthing. "The women were kept in order and protected by a European or a trustworthy old non-commissioned officer, assisted by a few askaris," wrote Lettow-Vorbeck. "They all liked gay colours, and after an important capture, the convoy, stretching for miles, would look like a carnival procession."

Among the most extraordinary phenomena of the East Africa campaign must be counted the remarkably high morale maintained by the *Schutztruppe*, Europeans and Africans, particularly in the last year of the war. Major J. R. Sibley, a modern writer, has said that this "must rank as one of the major command achievements in the First World War." Marching through strange lands far from home, often living under the most primitive conditions, without letters or news of any sort, constantly fighting and constantly retreating, with only a faint hope of final victory, they all—officers, askaris, carriers, and followers—soldiered on.

The British tried their best to destroy the morale of the askaris by offering inducements for them to desert. In January 1918 British aircraft located the *Schutztruppe* and showered them with leaflets in Swahili, which few could read:

> You all roam around in the bush like monkeys. What do you expect to gain from these Germans? Here there is sheer comfort waiting for you. . . . As for food, you'll be given flour meal, rice, sugar, dates, meat, fish and seasoning of every kind. . . . Return to us. This is where you belong, where you can rest from your troubles. You've gone through a lot. . . . Why do you accept German paper money which is totally worthless? . . . English askaris are paid with silver money. . . . The whole world is fighting the Germans, and the Germans will be totally defeated both in Europe and out here. . . . Friends, the Germans are lying to you. . . . The English . . . came to save you from German brutality.

Such crude propaganda persuaded some to desert. "Many were war weary," said Lettow-Vorbeck. "Added to this, there was in many cases the feeling of uncertainty as to where the campaign was going to lead them. . . . The English propaganda . . . fell in many cases on fruitful ground, and, as a result, a number of good askaris and even older non-commissioned officers deserted. Small annoyances, such as are bound to arise—the persuasion of the women and so on—all contributed to their decision to desert. . . . The impulsiveness of the black makes him very sensitive to insinuations." But this was a temporary situation and "the old lust of battle and the old loyalty returned, even among those who had begun to hang their heads." Some even returned and were welcomed back into the *Schutztruppe* fold.

Captured German askaris often tried to escape and some succeeded. One small group, captured while out foraging by a British patrol, escaped when their captors "fought quite a deadly action with another British detachment in thick bush."

A number of British and Portuguese officers who had been taken prisoner were carried along with the main column. Lettow-Vorbeck spoke admiringly of the British officers, who "accepted as a matter of course the hardships of long marches. . . . They bore everything with a certain humour and it was obviously interesting to them to see the war from the German point of view." He thought the Portuguese officers contemptible: "For the most part they were infested with syphilis and were carefully avoided by the English prisoners." They were certainly not up to his standard of campaigning. They consumed their rations too quickly, their boots wore out from lack of proper care, and they did not learn to make the best of their situation; their senior officer worried him with his constant complaints. He would have freed them all had they been willing to give their parole.

The Portuguese in Africa emerged from the war with a poor reputation as soldiers. Dr. Ludwig Deppe, formerly chief of the hospital at Tanga and now with Lettow-Vorbeck, watched as a *Schutztruppe* African corporal who had captured a Portuguese sergeant tried to sooth his weeping, terrified prisoner. He "caressed the white man and tried to comfort him . . . as a mother comforts her child."

Early in 1918 van Deventer sent Lettow-Vorbeck a demand

for his surrender. This, said Lettow-Vorbeck, "strengthened me in my belief that our escape had taken him by surprise, and that our invasion of Portuguese East Africa had put him at a loss."

No area in Portuguese territory offered the German forces the resources needed for a long occupation, so Wahle was sent off with a sizeable force westward and Captain Franz Koehl led another detached force toward the east coast, while Lettow-Vorbeck continued with the main body south, up the valley of the Lujenda River and on into country almost unknown to Europeans. He found elevated, fertile land with a healthy climate—an ideal theatre for a compact and mobile force accustomed to living off the land.

Van Deventer, presented with a new set of problems, most of which revolved around Portuguese officials (who were obstructive) and conditions within the Portuguese colony (which were primitive), could now look forward to an arduous campaign, for, as he said in a dispatch (21 January 1918), "the country is vast and communications are difficult." His first problem was to obtain the cooperation of the Portuguese and their assent to British troops tramping about in their territory. When this was finally given, British forces landed at Porto Amelia (Pemba) and two columns were sent inland: One under Lieutenant Colonel George Gifford, a young and able officer, and the other under Lieutenant Colonel R. A. de B. Rose, who had served in the Cameroons campaign.

On 12 April Gifford's column, composed entirely of KAR battalions, collided with Koehl's column near a place called Medo. There was considerable confusion and Medo has been aptly called a soldiers' battle. The fighting took place in exceedingly difficult country: thick jungle where roads were mere tunnels through bamboo thicket and elephant grass. At this season, long stretches of the road were more suitable for boats. Lieutenant Colonel H. Moyse-Bartlett in his history of the KAR described the battle:

> Medo was a hard-fought action in which both sides maintained for many hours a considerable volume of fire, the Germans

exploiting to the full the accurate shooting of their well-trained askaris and changing the position of their machine guns with a skill that struck some recently joined officers . . . as uncanny. When daylight came on the 13th . . . [the British] set about clearing the battlefield and evacuating the wounded. Every tree and bush within the sight was scarred with bullet marks; blood, dirt and flies abounded. The dead were laid in rows and the equipment was stripped from their stiffening bodies. The field hospital was packed with men, white bandages gleaming upon naked black limbs. It was late afternoon before the dead were buried.

The first six months of the last year of the war saw many small fights, but, Medo aside, only one battle of major importance. Near Korewa, amidst rocky hills and thick bush, on 22 May, the British almost accomplished what they had often tried to do: surround a major portion of the *Schutztruppe*. German casualties were not high—11 Germans and 49 askaris killed or taken prisoner—but Koehl's column, which was the unit attacked, had not yet recovered from the indecisive battle at Medo and it lost all its transport, 100,000 rounds of small arms ammunition, the last 67 rounds for the Portuguese mountain gun, and large quantities of medical supplies, food, and baggage. Schnee, who was with Koehl, lost all his baggage. Lettow-Vorbeck, by way of recompense, presented him with a pair of blue socks, which, he said, "his wife had made for me at the beginning of the war, but which unfortunately had faded."

Korewa ended the first phase of the campaign in Portuguese East Africa. A Boer scout with Lettow-Vorbeck summed it up: "This is a queer war. We chase the Portuguese, and the English chase us."

chapter 26

The End of the
Schutztruppe

On 1 June Lettow-Vorbeck crossed the broad Lurio River near Vatiua. From the crossing point he pushed south through extremely rugged country where steep hills rise in every direction out of a sea of near impenetrable bush. Pursued by a heavy Portuguese column and six British columns, the smallest of which was at battalion strength, he fought numerous rearguard actions. The KAR's historian summed up the pursuit as "a monotonous series of seemingly endless marches, interspersed with minor actions against a rearguard that never stood for long."

Desperately in need of food and supplies, the *Schutztruppe* attacked and captured Alto Molocue, a Portuguese administrative and supply centre, where they acquired a herd of pigs (soon turned into sausages), and 75,000 pounds of foodstuffs. Not long after, on 1–3 July, they captured the town of Nhamacurra, where they picked up two field guns and a few shells. When a steamer on the river innocently landed, they found on board a British doctor with a much-needed load of medical supplies, including quinine.

At the nearby railway station, defended by British and Portuguese troops, they fought a swift, bloody battle, driving off the defenders. The Allied force left behind 209 dead and 540 prisoners. Many of the dead had attempted to swim the Nhamacurra River and had been drowned or taken by crocodiles. Here Lettow-Vorbeck made the biggest haul of the campaign. His supply officer, he said, was "in despair" trying to find enough carriers for all the loot. There were 350 Portuguese and British rifles, ten machine guns, 300,000 kilograms of food, and enough clothing for everyone, askaris and carriers. There was also more wine and schnapps than could possibly be carried. The troops were allowed to drink their fill, but, said Lettow-Vorbeck, "with the best will in the world it was impossible to drink it all." Morale soared; many carriers asked to be promoted to askaris.

In the *Schutztruppe*'s path and not far distant lay Quelimane, a major port, and Lettow-Vorbeck reasoned that the British and Portuguese, in an effort to get between him and such an attractive objective, must be racing down a road parallel to his own. They were. He therefore allowed them to dash past him while he gave his troops a rest; then he changed direction and headed north, leaving the British to sit in their hastily thrown up defences well behind him.

Some British columns were still marching south when he was marching north. One of these, the 3/3rd KAR, slower than others, was pounced upon and scuppered; its commanding officer, Lieutenant Colonel Hugh Carey Dickinson, was taken prisoner—along with his adjutant, his medical officer, and his dog. Lettow-Vorbeck's reputation as a soldier was such that Dickinson asked to be taken to him so that he might shake his hand. Some former German askaris who had enlisted in the KAR now rejoined the *Schutztruppe*. It was in this fight that the Germans captured a trench mortar, the first they had seen, and they wasted no time in turning it upon its former owners.

On 24 August there was a sharp fight at Namarroe when a German column under Captain Erich Müller encountered a detachment of the 2/4th KAR. A week later, at a place called Lioma, Lettow-Vorbeck had what he described as his narrowest escape. He lost 29 Europeans, 17 of whom were killed, and about 200 askaris, as well as a large quantity of stores and 48,000 rounds of ammunition. The three battalions of the KAR who took part in this fight also lost heavily.

The way back to Rovuma was now clear, but quite suddenly Europeans and Africans alike were stricken by the second of the three waves of the influenza pandemic which struck down soldiers and civilians all over the world. Although they had by this time entered a fertile country, the columns were burdened by men too sick to stand. There were not enough stretchers and not enough fit men to carry those they had. Men fell behind to die or be captured. Schnee sent Lettow-Vorbeck a demand that he give up or he would hold him personally responsible for the deaths of the sick. Still, Lettow-Vorbeck would not halt. He and his men staggered on until on 28 September they once more reached the Rovuma and splashed across it with all their followers and impedimenta, back into their former homeland.

Eight hippopotamuses were shot that evening and the *Schutztruppen* feasted to celebrate their return. It was with dismay that van Deventer, his soldiers, and his superiors in England learned that German forces were again back in the colony and were marching towards Tabora. No one knew whether they would continue northward or turn in some new direction.

The *Schutztruppe* snapped up a few supply depots and their health began to improve, but as the askaris and carriers came into familiar country they began to desert. "The nigger's love of home is too strong," grumbled Lettow-Vorbeck. At Songea his advance guard ran into strong opposition and he realized that he would encounter stronger and stronger forces the further north he marched. In mid-October, therefore, he veered westward, passed around the north end of Lake Nyasa, and invaded Northern Rhodesia. He left behind, of course, his sick and wounded, this time including Kurt Wahle, the retired general who had fought for four years in a war he had fallen into by accident. He was now so ill that he had to be carried in a litter.

Although Lettow-Vorbeck lacked adequate maps, he marched off in the direction of Fife. Racing to beat him there was a strong column of KAR. Lettow-Vorbeck arrived first, but he found the place so stoutly defended by a detachment of Northern Rhodesia Police and civilian volunteers that he backed off, contenting himself with the capture of a nearby mission station, where he appropriated fourteen kilograms of quinine—enough, he reckoned, to last until June 1919. But events precluded the need for that much quinine. The adventures of the last German colonial army were drawing to a close.

Lettow-Vorbeck and his men trudged on, reaching Kajambi on 6 November. A circle of terror moved with his columns in Northern Rhodesia, where tales of German beastliness circulated swiftly. At the Catholic mission station at Kajambi he found that the missionaries had fled ("quite unnecessarily"), leaving behind a letter from a Westphalian nun who appealed to his humanity. He was annoyed: "She would certainly have spared herself many discomforts if both she herself and the other people attached to the mission had remained quietly at their posts."

Guided by a Rhodesian settler, a British force of about 750 KAR dogged the *Schutztruppe*. Too weak to attack, it contented itself with skirmishes with the German rearguard. Most of van Deventer's troops were concentrating at Tabora and along the Northern Railway hundreds of miles north. No one knew what Lettow-Vorbeck would do next. Indeed he scarcely knew himself as he marched unopposed to the south, towards Salisbury or perhaps Bulawayo, harassed by the constant problem of finding sufficient food and supplies.

On 9 November his advance guard captured Kasama, about a hundred miles from Fife, and here he acquired a little ammunition, some ox wagons, and a considerable supply of European food. Lettow-Vorbeck himself rode into Kasama on his bicycle on 11 November 1918, the day when, as yet unknown to him, the armistice took effect in Europe and elsewhere in the world. After conferring with the commander of his advance guard, he directed him to push on in the direction of the Chambezi River ferry, where it was expected that even more supplies could be captured. On 12 November, the first full day of peace in the rest of the world, Lettow-Vorbeck's troops fought a final skirmish with a British detachment under Major [later Major General] E.B.B. Hawkins on a river bank near Kasama. On 13 November Lettow-Vorbeck bicycled ahead of his main column to select a camp site. He was waiting for his column to come up when Captain Erich Müller pedalled up on a bicycle with news of the armistice. He had with him a message from van Deventer taken from a British motorcyclist captured at Kasama. Lettow-Vorbeck read:

> Send following to Colonel von Lettow Vorbeck under white flag:

> The Prime Minister of England has announced that an armistice was signed at 5 hours on Nov. 11th, and that hostilities on all fronts cease at 11 hours on Nov. 11th. I am ordering my troops to cease hostilities forthwith unless attacked, and of course I conclude that you will do the same. Conditions of armistice will be forwarded you immediately I receive them. Meanwhile I suggest that you should remain in your present vicinity in order to facilitate communication.

> —General van Deventer.

As the German line of march was along a British telephone line, Lettow-Vorbeck was able to confirm the message by tapping it, but he was puzzled. Although he knew nothing of the state of affairs in Europe, he was convinced that "the conclusion of hostilities must have been favourable, or at least not unfavourable to Germany." But about midnight that night he received a copy of another message from van Deventer:

> War Office London telegraphs that Clause Seventeen of the armistice signed by the German Govt. provides for uncondi-

tional surrender of all German forces operating in East Africa within one month from Nov. 11th.

My conditions are, First: that you hand over all Allied prisoners in your hands, Europeans and natives, to the nearest body of troops forthwith. Second: that you bring your forces to Abercorn without delay, as Abercorn is the nearest place at which I can supply you with food. Third: that you hand over all arms and ammunition to my representative at Abercorn. I will, however, allow you and your officers and European ranks to retain their personal weapons for the present in consideration of the gallant fight you have made, provided that you bring your force to Abercorn without delay. Arrangements will be made at Abercorn to send all Germans to Morogoro and to repatriate German askaris. Kindly send an early answer, giving probable date of arrival at Abercorn and numbers of German officers and men, askaris and followers.

When Lettow-Vorbeck learned that Article 17 of the Armistice required not his "unconditional surrender," as van Deventer had told him, but simply "evacuation of all German forces operating in East Africa," he protested vigorously. *Evacuation* was not at all the same as unconditional surrender. Angrily he sent off telegrams to Germany, and all the Allied governments, including the United States. He received no response.

The last of the *Schutztruppen* marched into Abercorn on 25 November and at noon, under the Union Jack on a parade ground surrounded by white wooden buildings, the brief ceremony took place. The troops were drawn up in a hollow square, still a proud military force. The *Schutztruppe* had suffered defeats; it had abandoned territory and retired in the face of superior numbers, but, as General C. P. Fendall correctly stated, "it had never been soundly beaten." Paul von Lettow-Vorbeck, its indomitable commander, saluted the Union Jack and then took out a pocket notebook, from which he read, first in German and then in English, his formal statement of surrender. He then called on his troops to lay down their arms. Brigadier General W.F.S. Edwards accepted the surrender in the name of King

George V. And so the German flag disappeared forever from Africa.

The Germans turned over a collection of captured weapons: a Portuguese field gun with forty rounds of ammunition, 37 machine guns (7 German and the rest British), and 1,071 rifles, all British or Portuguese. Now in British hands, in addition to Governor Schnee and General Lettow-Vorbeck, were 20 combatant officers, including one-legged Lieutenant Richard Wenig of the *Königsberg*, 6 medical officers, a veterinary officer, a senior chemist, a field telegraph officer, 125 European other ranks (including at least 15 ratings from the *Königsberg*), 1,156 askaris, 1,598 carriers, and uncounted women and children.

The *Schutztruppen* were now exposed to the unconcealed admiration of their former enemies. An officer with the Nigerian Brigade said: "To the very end they kept their tails up, and fought a one-sided contest with indomitable courage and exemplary dash, and they never failed to leave their mark on their opponents." Lettow-Vorbeck was particularly lionized, and one British officer went so far as to say: "We had more esteem and affection for him than [for] our own leaders." Lieutenant Colonel H. C. Dickinson, the highest ranking prisoner of the Germans, made a point of telling Lettow-Vorbeck how interesting he had found German methods and how much he admired the simplicity of their arrangements and the absence of friction. [Dickinson never left Africa. He died of influenza at Dar-es-Salaam.] General Northey, now governor of British East Africa, paid the German commander perhaps the highest compliment an Englishman in that era could give when he said that he "played the game all the way through."

The painful road back was eased by many courtesies. Lettow-Vorbeck and his officers were taken to the south end of Lake Tanganyika and then by ship to Kigoma. From there they went by rail to Tabora and finally on to Dar-es-Salaam, which they reached on 8 December. Lettow-Vorbeck found everyone "extraordinarily kind."

When they reached Dar-es-Salaam he, Schnee, Major

Kraut, and several other officers were taken, not to a prison, but to a "very pretty house," and van Deventer invited them to lunch. They were reunited with General Wahle, now completely recovered, and they formed a common mess. A car was placed at Lettow-Vorbeck's disposal and he was free to go about town as long as he was accompanied by a British officer.

Lettow-Vorbeck's only complaint was the length of time he was kept waiting for a ship at Dar-es-Salaam, but finally, on 17 January 1919—five years to the day since he first landed in German East Africa—he embarked with 114 German soldiers and sailors, 107 women, and 87 of their children for Cape Town and Rotterdam. A hero's welcome awaited the returning prisoners of war in Rotterdam, where they were feasted for two days before being put aboard a special train decorated with greenery, flags, and bunting. In Berlin the Brandenburg Gate was decorated in their honour and the mayor gave them a banquet.

Lettow-Vorbeck attributed his warm welcome in Germany to the feeling that "everyone seemed to think that we had preserved some part of Germany's soldierly traditions, had come back home unsullied, and that the Teutonic sense of loyalty peculiar to us Germans had kept its head high even under conditions of war in the tropics."

Paul von Lettow-Vorbeck was indeed a brilliant soldier who evoked universal admiration, for men admire bravery, endurance, persistence, courtesy in adversity and dignity in defeat. And these were qualities which he exemplified. He succeeded in what he set out to do, yet what he did was in the end worse than useless, for he could not prevent the victory of his country's enemies; he cost the lives of thousands and the health of tens of thousands more. He tore the social fabric of hundreds of communities and wrecked the economy of three countries. His splendid military virtues were devoted to an unworthy cause and his loyalty given to a bad monarch.

The discipline he was able to establish and maintain through four years of war must serve as an example for

General von Lettow-Vorbeck enters Berlin, 1919

officers in any army. He was, of course, often asked the secret of his success, and he gave this modest answer, which exemplifies but does not explain his leadership:

> I believe it was the transparency of our aims, the love of our Fatherland, the strong sense of duty and the spirit of self-sacrifice which animated each of our few Europeans and communicated themselves, consciously or unconsciously to our brave black soldiers and gave our operations that impetus which they possessed to the end. In addition, there was a soldierly pride, a feeling of firm mutual cooperation and a spirit of enterprise without which military success is impossible in the long run.

Lettow-Vorbeck remained in the army for only fourteen months after his return. During this time he suppressed a communist uprising in Hamburg and during the Kapp *Putsch* in March 1920 he put his troops at the disposal of right-wing reactionaries. As a result of the failed *Putsch* he was forced to resign in May. He then turned to politics and served ten years in the Reichstag. His name was a household word in the Weimar Republic, where undefeated German generals were thin on the ground. He was a vociferous nationalist who believed that "the healthy spirit of our German people will prevail again and once more tread the upward path." Unlike Schnee, who became an enthusiastic Nazi, he distrusted Hitler and his movement. Hitler once offered him the ambassadorship to the Court of St. James's, but he declined. He married shortly after his return and raised a family. Both sons were killed in World War II.

In 1929 he sat next to Smuts as a guest of honour at the anniversary dinner of the British East Africa Expeditionary Force. He and Smuts formed a lasting friendship; during the hard times in Germany immediately following World War II, Smuts sent food packages to him. When Smuts died in 1950, Lettow-Vorbeck sent his wife a moving letter of sympathy.

Isak Dinesen retained fond memories of the *Schutztruppe* colonel who had once brought her champagne on New Year's Eve, and in 1940, just one week before a German army invaded her homeland, she paid him a visit in Bremen. They reminisced about East Africa and spoke of the differences between the old Imperial Germany and the Nazi regime. They met once more in 1958 when he was eighty-seven and living in an apartment in Hamburg near his daughter Ruth, married to the wealthy count Christian von Rantzau. On his ninetieth birthday she sent him flowers. The old warrior died on 9 March 1964 at the age of ninety-four.

On his death the Bundestag made a fine, quixotic gesture of which he would have heartily approved: It voted to pay off his askaris. Few were left, and fewer still possessed the paper IOUs he had given them. A Hamburg banker was sent to Dar-es-Salaam to make the payments. Old men brought him bits of uniform as proof of their service, but tattered bits of cloth were not to be trusted. The canny banker, an old soldier himself, hit upon an infallible identification. He gave each applicant a broom and put him through the manual of arms. No askari ever forgot the German words of command or the drill.

Epilogue

The political fallout of the four German campaigns of the
Great War in Africa has not ceased—witness the concern of
the world for the political future of South-West Africa, now
often called Namibia. At Versailles in 1919 the Germans
were described as "cruel, brutal, arrogant and utterly
unsuited for intercourse with primitive people, lustful and
malicious in their attitude toward subject races." Under
Article 119 of the Treaty of Versailles Germany was forced
to renounce in favour of the "principal Allies and Associ-
ated Powers" all her rights and titles to her overseas possessions.

There was no serious discussion of political freedom for
the peoples in the former German colonies. It was agreed
that as these were "peoples not yet able to stand by themselves under the strenuous conditions of the modern world,
there should be applied the principle that the well being
and development of such peoples form a sacred trust of civilization." So the former German colonies were divided
among the conquerors of those colonies—the same countries who would undoubtedly have shared the spoils had
none of the Great War campaigns in Africa taken place,

although the divisions would undoubtedly have been quite different.

In what had been German East Africa, Belgium took the beautiful and populous highland cattle country in the northwest, now the independent nations of Rwanda and Burundi. Portugal was given a 400-square-mile tract on the coast known as the Kiongga Triangle, now part of Mozambique Britain took the rest and named it Tanganyika; in 1946 it became a United Nations Trust Territory and on 9 December 1961 it became a "republic" with a one-party political system and its own dictator; when the islands of Zanzibar and Pemba were added, the country's name was changed to Tanzania. All of South-West Africa was mandated to the Union of South Africa, and after World War II, when the League of Nations and its mandates were dissolved, South Africa refused to agree to the area becoming a United Nations Trust Territory.

France was given Neue Kamerun (that portion it had ceded to Germany in 1911) and four-fifths of the remainder of the Cameroons. The British took what remained, divided it into two provinces and attached them to Nigeria. On 11 February 1961 plebiscites were held in each. The northern province elected to remain a part of Nigeria; the southern province joined the new Federal Republic of Cameroon, which encompassed all of the former French portion. Togoland, now Togo, was split lengthwise, the western part to Britain and the eastern portion to France. The French were unhappy with this arrangement, however, because it gave the port of Lomé to Britain, so in 1920 the country was redivided and France was given the entire seaboard and Britain a larger chuck of the interior.

Under the Treaty of Versailles all German property, both public and private, in former German colonies was sold at auction and the proceeds set against the German reparation account. In Tanganyika 860 German estates were put on the block, and although Germans were forbidden to bid, some plantations were bought back through Indian or Greek dummies. At the beginning of World War II the largest plantation—45,000 acres of sisal—was owned by a former German officer.

The Great War seriously damaged the existing social structure throughout East Africa. In British East Africa 65 percent of the European population, mostly young men, had served in the army and more than two hundred thousand Africans had served as askaris or carriers. As a result of the protracted campaign, agriculture was neglected; cattle, horses, and other domestic animals died for want of veterinary care; the colony's transportation system crumbled. Drought and famine swept the country, as did the world-wide influenza epidemic. Many of the carriers and askaris came back to their tribes and villages with changed ideas: traditions were broken and innovations were demanded; many tribesmen were restless.

The Treaty of Peace contained some strange clauses, but perhaps none more bizarre than that under Section VIII, "Reparation and Restitution", concerning the return of a skull. The pertinent paragraph, which also deals with the return of a *Koran* to the King of Hedjaz, reads: "Germany is to restore within six months . . . the skull of Sultan Okwawa, formerly of German East Africa, to His Britannic Majesty's Government." Just what His Britannic Majesty wanted with it is unknown. In any case, no one seems to have been able to find it.

Select Bibliography

Adler, F. B., A. E. Lord, H. H. Curson. *The South African Artillery in German East Africa and Palestine, 1915–1919.* J. L. van Schalk, Pretoria (for the South African War Museum), 1958.

Abbot, Willis J. *The Nations at War.* Leslie-Judge, New York, 1917.

Alport, A. Cecil. *The Lighter Side of the War.* Hutchinson, London, n.d. (c. 1934).

Anon. *Belgian Congo.* Belgian Congo and Ruanda-Urangi Information Office, Brussels, 1959.

Anon. *The Belgian Congo.* Naval Intelligence Division (Geographical Handbook Series), BR 522. April 1944.

Anon. "Correspondence Relation to the Wishes of the Natives of the German Colonies as to their Future Government." H.M.S.O., London, 1918.

Anon. "Correspondence Relative to the Alleged Ill-Treatment of German Subjects captured in the Cameroons." H.M.S.O., London, 1915.

Anon. *French Equatorial Africa.* British Naval Intelligence Division. BR 515. December 1942.

Anon. *French West Africa*. 2 vols. BR 512 & BR 512A. Vol. 1—December 1943; Vol. 2—December 1944.

Anon. *Military Report on German South-West Africa*. Prepared by the General Staff, War Office, December 1906.

Anon. *Report on the Natives of South-West Africa and their Treatment by Germany*. H.M.S.O., London, 1918.

Anon. "The South African Forces and World War I." Compiled by the Documentation Service, South African Defence Force, n.d.

Anon. *Togoland*. Prepared under the direction of the Historical Section of the Foreign Office. H.M.S.O., London, January 1919.

Anon. *The Union of South Africa and the Great War, 1914–1918*. General Staff, Defence Headquarters, Pretoria, Government Printing and Stationery Office, 1924.

Barfield, Doreen. "The Battle of Trekkopies." *Military Historical Journal* (South Africa) December, 1971. Vol. 2, No. 2.

Botha, H. J., and J. Ploegar. "The German Contribution to the Military History of South-West Africa." *Militaria*, 2 / 4 of 1970.

Bouch, R. J. "The Action at Zantepansdrift, 31 October 1914." *Militaria*, 4 / 4 of 1974.

Bradley, Kenneth. "African Observer." Series of articles, 1937.

Brerelsford, W. V. (ed.) *The Story of the Northern Rhodesia Regiment*. Government Printer, Lusaka, Northern Rhodesia, 1954.

Bridgeman, Jon, and David E. Clarke. *German Africa: A Select Bibliography*. The Hoover Institution on War, Revolution, and Peace, Stanford University, 1965.

Bridgeman, Jon M. *The Revolt of the Hereros*. University of California Press, Los Angeles, 1981.

Buchman, Capt. Angus. *Three Years of War in East Africa*. John Murray, London, 1919.

Cagnolo, Fr. C. *The Aikikuyu, Their Customs, Traditions and Folklore*. Mission Printing School, Nyeri, Kenya, 1933.

Crankshaw, Edward. *Bismarck*. Viking, New York, 1981.

Charlewood, Commander C. J. "Naval Actions on the Tanganyika Coast, 1914–1917." *Tanganyika Notes and Records*, No. 54 March 1960 and No. 55 September 1960.

Chesterton, E. Keble. *The Königsberg Adventure*. Hurst & Blackett, London, 1932.

——. *Severn's Saga*. Hurst & Blackett, London, 1938.

Close, Percy. *A Prisoner of the Germans in South-West Africa*. T. Maskew Miller, Capetown, n.d. (c. 1919).

Corbett, Sir Julian S. *History of the Great War Based on Official Documents*. Vol. 1. By direction of the Historical Section of the Committee of Imperial Defence. Longmans, Green, London, 1920.

Crowe, Brig. Gen. J.H.V. *General Smuts' Campaign in East Africa*. John Murray, London, 1918.

Dane, Edmund. *British Campaigns in Africa and the Pacific, 1914–1918*.

Downes, Captain W. D. *With the Nigerians in German East Africa*. Methuen, London, 1919.

Eberlie, R. F. "The German Achievement in East Africa." *Tanganyika Notes and Records*, No. 55, September 1960.

Ewing, John. "South Africa in the World War." *Cambridge History of the British Empire*. Vol. 8, Cambridge University Press, 1936.

Fendall, Brigadier-General C. P. *The East African Force, 1915–1919*. H. F. & G. Witherby, London, 1921.

Ferrandi, Lt.-Col. Jean. *La Conquête du Cameroun-Nord, 1914–1916*. Charles Lavauzelle, Paris, 1928.

Fetter, Bruce. *The Creation of Elizabethville, 1910–1940*. Hoover Colonial Studies, Hoover Institution Press, Stanford California, 1976.

Flint, J. E. *Sir George Goldie and the Making of Nigeria*. Oxford University Press, Oxford, 1960.

Gann, L. H. *A History of Southern Rhodesia*. Chatto & Windus, London, 1965.

Gann, L. H. & Peter Duignan. *The Rulers of German East Africa, 1884–1914*. Stanford University Press, Stanford, California, 1977.

Garnham, P. *Malaria Parasites and Other Haemosporidia*. Blackwell Scientific Publications, Oxford, 1966.

Gardner, Brian. *German East: The Story of the First World War in East Africa*. Cassell, London, 1963.

Gordon-Brown, A. (ed.) *Yearbook and Guide to East Africa*. Robert Hale, London, various years.

Gorges, Brigadier General E. Howard. *The Great War in West Africa*. Hutchinson, London, 1930.

Hoedrich, Paul D. (ed.) *Infectious Diseases*. 2nd Ed., Harper & Row, New York, 1977.

Hamshere, C. E. "The Campaigns in German East Africa." *History Today*, April, 1965.

Hartcup, Gay. *The Achievement of the Airship*. David & Charles, London, 1974.

Haupt, Werner. *Deutschlands Schutzbebiete in Übersee, 1884–1918*. Podzun-Pallas-Verlag, Friedberg, 1984.

Holtom, Surgeon E. C. *Two Years Captivity in German East Africa*. Hutchinson, London, n.d.

Hordern, Lt Col. Charles. *History of the Great War: Military Operations, East Africa*. HMSO, London, 1941.

Hoyte, Edwin P. *The Germans Who Never Lost: The Story of the Königsberg*. Funk & Wagnalls, New York, 1968.

——. *Guerilla*. Macmillan, New York, and Collier Macmillan, London, 1981.

Hunter, Col. George W., J. Swartzwelder, David F. Clyde. *Tropical Medicine*. (5th edition) W. B. Saunders, Philadelphia, London, Toronto.1976.

Joelson, F. S. *Eastern Africa Today*. East Africa, London, 1928.

Johnson, Sir Harry. *The Story of My Life*. Bobbs-Merrill, Indianapolis, 1923.

July, Robert W. *A History of the African People*. Charles Scribner's Sons, New York, 1970.

Kaniki, M.H.Y. *Tanzania Under Colonial Rule*. Longmans, London, 1979.

Kaplan, Irving (ed.) *Zaïre, A Country Study*. Foreign Areas Studies, 3rd ed., The American University, Washington, D.C., 1979.

Kemp, Paul. "Monitors in W.W.I." *Military History* [U.K.] April 1984.

King-Hall, Admiral Sir Herbert. *Naval Memories and Traditions*. Hutchinson, London, n.d.

Langford, James. *30th Punjabis*. Osprey, Reading, 1972.

Lawford, Lt. Col. L. P., and Major W. E. Catto. *Solah Punjab: the History of the 16th Punjab Regiment*. Gale & Polden, Aldershot, 1967.

Lettow-Vorbeck, Gen. [Paul] von. *My Reminiscences of East Africa*. Hurst & Blackett, London, n.d. [c. 1920].

Lord, John. *Duty, Honor, Empire: The Life and Times of Colonel Meinertzhagen*. Random House, New York, 1970.

McLaughlin, Peter. *Ragtime Soldiers*. Books of Zimbabwe, Bulawayo, 1980.

Magee, Frank J. "Transporting a Navy Through the Jungles of Africa in Wartime." *National Geographic*, October 1922.

Martin, A. C. *The Durban Light Infantry*. Vol. 1, Privately printed. 1969.

Mason, Philip. *A Matter of Honour*. Holt, Rinehart & Winston, New York, 1974.

Meinertzhagen, Colonel R. *Army Diary, 1899–1926*. Oliver & Boyd, Edinburgh & London, 1960.

Meintjes, Johannes. *General Louis Botha*. Cassell, London, 1970.

Migel, Parmenia. *Titania*. Michael Joseph, London, 1967.

Miller, Charles. *Battle for the Bundu: The First World War in East Africa*. Purnell Book Services, London, 1974.

Millin, Sarah Gertrude. *General Smuts*. 2 vols. Faber & Faber, London, 1936.

Moore, Clark D. and Ann Dunbar (ed.). *Africa Yesterday and Today*. Praeger, New York, Washington & London, 1968.

Mosley, Leonard. *Duel for Kilimanjaro*. Ballantine Books, New York, 1963.

Moulaert, George. *La Campagne du Tanganyika, 1916–17.* L'Edition Universalle, Bruxelles, 1934.

Moyse-Bartlett, Lieutenant-Colonel H. *The King's African Rifles: A Study in the Military History of East and Central Africa, 1890–1945.* Gale and Polden, Aldershot, 1956.

Muller R. "Dracunculus and Dracunculiasis." *Advances in Parasistology,* Vol. IX, Academia Press, New York, 1971.

Neilsen, Thor. *The Zeppelin Story.* Allen Wingate, London, 1955.

O'Neil H. C. *The Royal Fusiliers in the Great War.* William Heineman, London, 1922.

———. *The War in Africa, 1914–1917, and in the Far East, 1914.* Longmans, London, 1919.

Orpen, Neil. *Gunners of the Cape: The Story of the Cape Field Artillery.* C.F.A. Regimental History Committee, Cape Town, 1965.

———. *The History of the Transvaal Horse Artillery, 1904–1974.* the Transvaal Horse Artillery Regimental Council, Johannesburg, 1975.

Osborne, Joyce M. "The Berlin Mission." *Tanganyika Notes and Records,* No. 54, March 1960.

Osuntokun, Akinjide. *Nigeria in the First World War.* Longmans (Ibadan History Series), London, 1979.

Ploeger, J. "The Action at Sanfontein (26 September 1914)" *Militaria* 4 / 1 of 1973.

Pretorius, Major P. J. *Jungle Man.* E. P. Dutton, New York, 1948.

Reitz, Deneys. *Trekking On.* Faber & Faber, London, 1933.

Russell, Major A. "The Landing at Tanga, 1914." *Tanganyika Notes and Records,* 1962.

Sayers, G. F. (ed.) *The Handbook of Tanganyika.* First issue. Macmillan, London, 1930.

Saward, Dudley. *Bomber Harris: The Story of Sir Arthur Harris* Doubleday, Garden City, N.Y., 1985.

Segal, Aaron. "Massacre in Rwanda." (booklet) Fabian Research Series 240. Fabian Society, 1964.

Shankland, Peter. *The Phantom Flotilla.* Collins, London, 1968.

Shelton, Richard N. "The First World War in German East Africa: August 5–November 5, 1914." Master's thesis, San Jose State University.

Sibley, Major J. R. *Tanganyika Guerrilla: East African Campaign 1914–18*. Pan / Ballantine, New York, 1971.

Silberbauer, Dick. "The Origins of South African Military Aviation: 1907–1919." *Cross and Cockade* (Great Britain) Vol. 7, No. 4, 1976.

Smithers, A. J. *The Man Who Disobeyed: Sir Horace Smith-Dorrien and His Enemies*. Leo Cooper, London, 1970.

Smuts, Jan Christiaan. "East Africa." *Century*, July 1918.

Smuts, J. C. *Jan Christiaan Smuts*. Cassell, London, 1952.

Steer, G. L. *Judgement on German Africa*. Hodder & Stoughton, London, 1939.

Stephenson, Lieut. Colonel A., et alia. *The Story of the Northern Rhodesia Regiment*. Government Printer, Lusaka, 1949. (First issued in 1945.)

Thatcher, W. S. *The Fourth Battalion, Duke of Connaught's Own 10th Baluch Regiment in the Great War (129th Baluchis)*. Cambridge University Press, Cambridge, 1932.

Thornhill, Christopher J. *Taking Tanganyika: Experiences of an Intelligence Officer, 1914–1918*. Stanley Poul, London, 1937.

Thurman, Judith. *Isak Dinesen. The Life of a Storyteller*. St. Martin's Press, New York, 1982.

Trevor, Tudor G. *Forty Years in Africa*. Hurst & Blackett, London, 1932.

Trew, Lt.-Col. H. F. *Botha Treks*. Blackie & Son, London, 1936.

Walker, H.F.B. *A Doctor's Diary in Damaraland*. Edward Arnold, London, 1917.

Whittall, W. *With Botha and Smuts in Africa*. Cassell, London, 1917.

Wiedner, Donald L. *A History of Africa South of the Sahara*. Random House, New York, 1962.

Wienholt, Arnold. *The Story of a Lion Hunt*. Andrew Melrose, London & New York, 1922.

Wilson, C.J., *The Story of the East African Mounted Rifles.* The East African Standard, Nairobi, 1938.

Wynn, Wynne E. *Ambush.* Hutchinson, London, 1937.

Young, Frances Brett. *Marching on Tanga.* W. Collins, London, 1917.

Index